Prizewinning
Political
Cartoons

Prizewinning
Political
Cartoons

2011 Edition

Edited by Dean P. Turnbloom
Foreword by Mark Fiore

PELICAN PUBLISHING COMPANY

The word "Pelican" and the depiction of a pelican
are trademarks of Pelican Publishing Company, Inc.,
and are registered in the U.S. Patent and Trademark Office.

Library of Congress Cataloging-in-Publication Data

Prizewinning political cartoons / edited by Dean P. Turnbloom ; foreword by Mark Fiore. — 2011 ed.
    p. cm.
  Includes index.
   ISBN 978-1-58980-888-1 (pbk. : alk. paper) 1. World politics—2005-2015—Caricatures and cartoons. 2. Political cartoons—Awards. 3. Editorial cartoons—Awards. I. Turnbloom, Dean P.
  D863.P75 2011
  909.83'1—dc22
                   2010046539

Original illustrations by Lucas P. Turnbloom appear on the following pages: 15, 41, 53, 57, 64, 79, 89, 92, 95, 101, and 107

Printed in Singapore
Published by Pelican Publishing Company, Inc.
1000 Burmaster Street, Gretna, Louisiana 70053

Contents

Foreword

By some divine confluence of spilled ink, jumping electrons, and scribbles in my sketchbook, the cartooning gods have seen to it that I am the one writing the foreword to the book you hold in your hands. I am honored to comply and lucky to be in this position. (Okay, there were also countless hours spent chained to a drawing table and computer that may have had something to do with this turn of events.)

Though my political cartoons happen to be animated, the core of political cartooning remains the same whether your work appears in newsprint, on Web sites, or affixed to telephone poles down by the docks: a political cartoon should *say* something. "Funny" is all well and good, but a true political cartoon should also have a definite point, opinion, or bone to pick. (Sorry, celebrity jokes don't count.) But I digress and am rapidly beginning to sound like a curmudgeon at too young of an age.

While this collection is made up of prizewinning political cartoons, there are many other great cartoons out there that, for a variety of reasons, have not yet been deemed prizeworthy. Those cartoons, however, are just as important as the prizewinning ones, for without a healthy political cartoon ecosystem, populated by cartoons of varying opinions and styles, there wouldn't be any prizewinning cartoons. The health of political cartooning as a whole is very important to fostering cartooning excellence.

This is where you come in.

If you see a political cartoon on the Web or in your local newspaper that you like, let the editor know it. Or if you see political cartoons running less frequently and miss that daily dose of satire, tell the editor you want your cartoons back. You'd be amazed at how responsive editors are to readers, particularly in this age of shrinking journalism. Just make a call, send an e-mail, or write a letter to the editor.

Then *you'll* be the real prizewinner!

Mark Fiore

Acknowledgments

First and always, I want to thank my wife, Nanette. More than anyone else, she has supported, encouraged, and made it possible for me to put this book together. She has spent endless nights watching as I obsessed over unanswered e-mails, late submissions, format errors, and lost files. Through it all, she has put up with a sometimes cantankerous and often sullen son of a gun, maintaining her own sanity and helping me maintain mine. She has my deepest gratitude and undying love. Thank you, Nanette.

I also want to thank each of the cartoonists who were so generous in allowing me to use their work for this book. Without their generosity, talent, and good grace I would have had nothing to celebrate with this book.

And once again, a special thanks to Ranan Lurie, whose early encouragement and kind words made me think this work might have some potential after all. His continued support and encouragement during the production of this third edition is sincerely appreciated. I count him as a friend.

Last, but certainly not least, I want to thank Pelican Publishing for giving me this opportunity. Thank you, Nina Kooij and especially Dr. Milburn Calhoun, for having faith in this small project.

Introduction

As I began the third entry in the *Prizewinning Political Cartoons Series,* I want to thank all the people who've bought the past volumes and will add this one to their collection. The format has changed once again, with fewer pages in this edition. This wasn't merely an editorial choice; it was forced upon us by the contests, which in a given year may or may not award runners up, second and/or third places for the varying awards. This year an unusual number have not deemed it necessary to do so. One change that occurred in the last volume is being carried forward in this one, with the Pulitzer winner writing the book's foreword.

One of the major criticisms of the 2008 edition of this book was that "many of the cartoons were repeated several times." In the 2010 edition, I capitulated, being a sycophant to public opinion (perhaps I should run for office), and, in an effort to answer this criticism, tried to signal where the repetitions were in that volume. This year, I believe, we have eliminated duplicates entirely due to the new format.

Also due to the changed format, we did away with the cartoonist interview.

Finally, I wanted to say what a great privilege it is to showcase the outstanding artwork in this volume, which entertains, informs, and sometimes even enrages. Regardless of your political point of view, you should agree that these cartoonists are worthy of their awards and this book is meant to record their achievements in a single volume for posterity.

Prizewinning Political Cartoons

Pulitzer Prize

The Columbia School of Journalism was founded in 1912, one year after the death of Joseph Pulitzer, and the first Pulitzer Prize was awarded in his memory in 1917. The Pulitzer was established to promote the highest standards of journalism for which Joseph Pulitzer stood. Each year more than 2,400 entries are submitted of which only about twenty-one receive the coveted award.

The Pulitzer Prize is primarily a "print media" award, and although online material is eligible for submission, it must be derived from print media. To quote the eligibility rules, "Since their creation in 1917, the Pulitzer Prizes have been awarded exclusively for newspaper journalism."

Pulitzer was quoted as saying, "Our Republic and its press will rise or fall together. An able, disinterested, public-spirited press, with trained intelligence to know the right and courage to do it, can preserve that public virtue without which popular government is a sham and a mockery. A cynical, mercenary, demagogic press will produce in time a people as base as itself. The power to mould the future of the Republic will be in the hands of the journalists of future generations." It would be interesting to know how Joseph Pulitzer would feel about the current decline of the newspaper industry as well as the state of the country and whether there was a connection between the two.

2010 Pulitzer Prize Winner
Mark Fiore, SFGate.com

Pulitzer Prize-winner Mark Fiore has been described by the *Wall Street Journal* as "the undisputed guru" of animated political cartoons. He has been featured on the *San Francisco Chronicle's* Web site, SFGate.com, for nearly ten years. His work also appears on Slate.com, CBSNews.com, MotherJones.com, and NPR's Web site. Fiore's political animations have appeared on CNN, *Frontline, Bill Moyers Journal,* and cable and broadcast outlets across the globe.

Fiore began his professional life drawing traditional political cartoons, with his work appearing in publications ranging from the *Washington Post* to the *Los Angeles Times.* In the late 1990s, he started experimenting with animation, and after a short stint at the *San Jose Mercury News,* he began devoting all his energies toward animation.

A 1991 graduate of Colorado College with a degree in political science, Fiore received the perfect send-off for a cartoonist. He accepted his diploma with commencement speaker Dick Cheney smiling approvingly.

Mark Fiore was awarded a Robert F. Kennedy Journalism Award in 2004 and has twice been honored with an Online Journalism Award for commentary from the Online News Association (2002, 2008). Fiore has received two awards for his work in new media from the National Cartoonists Society (2001, 2002), and in 2006, he was awarded the James Madison Freedom of Information Award from the Society of Professional Journalists.

To view Fiore's animations, visit his Web site at http://www.markfiore.com/blog/mark-fiore-pulitzer-prize-winning-entry-political-animation.

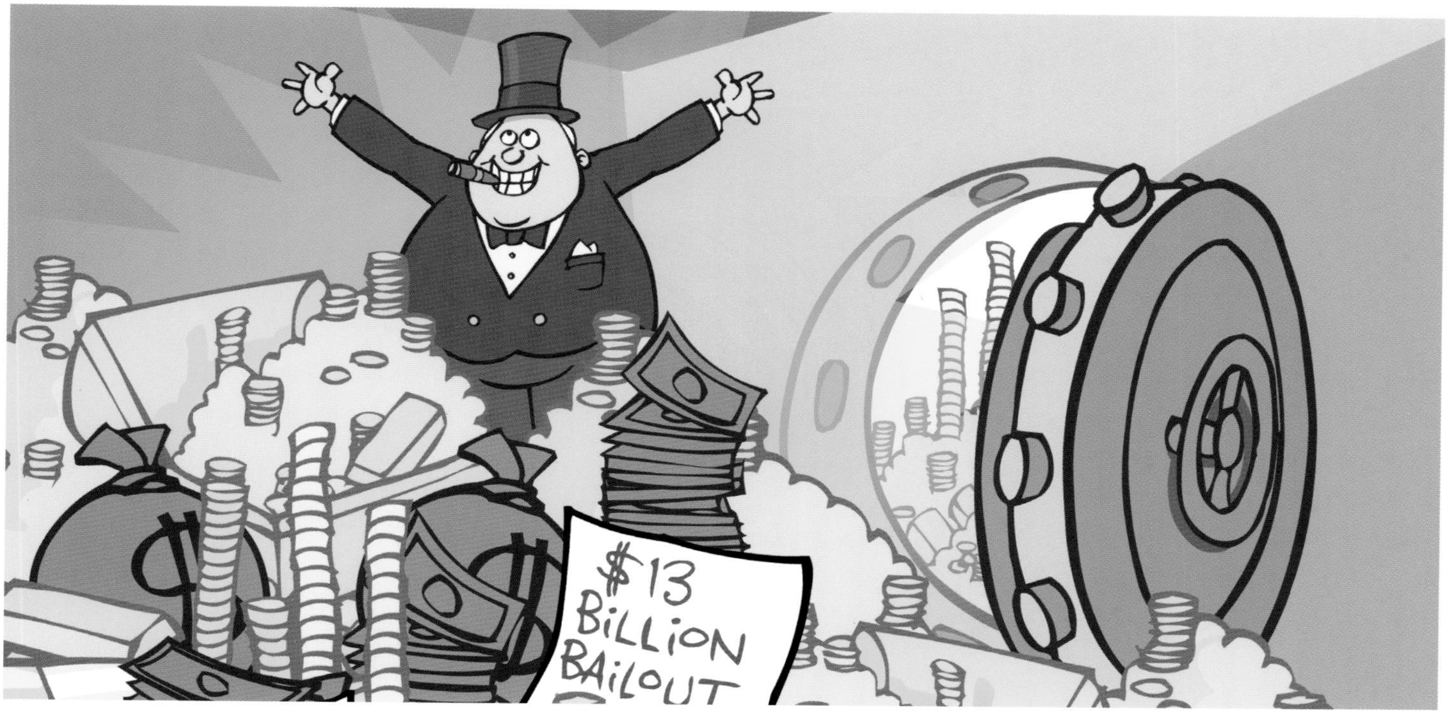
$13
BILLION
BAILOUT

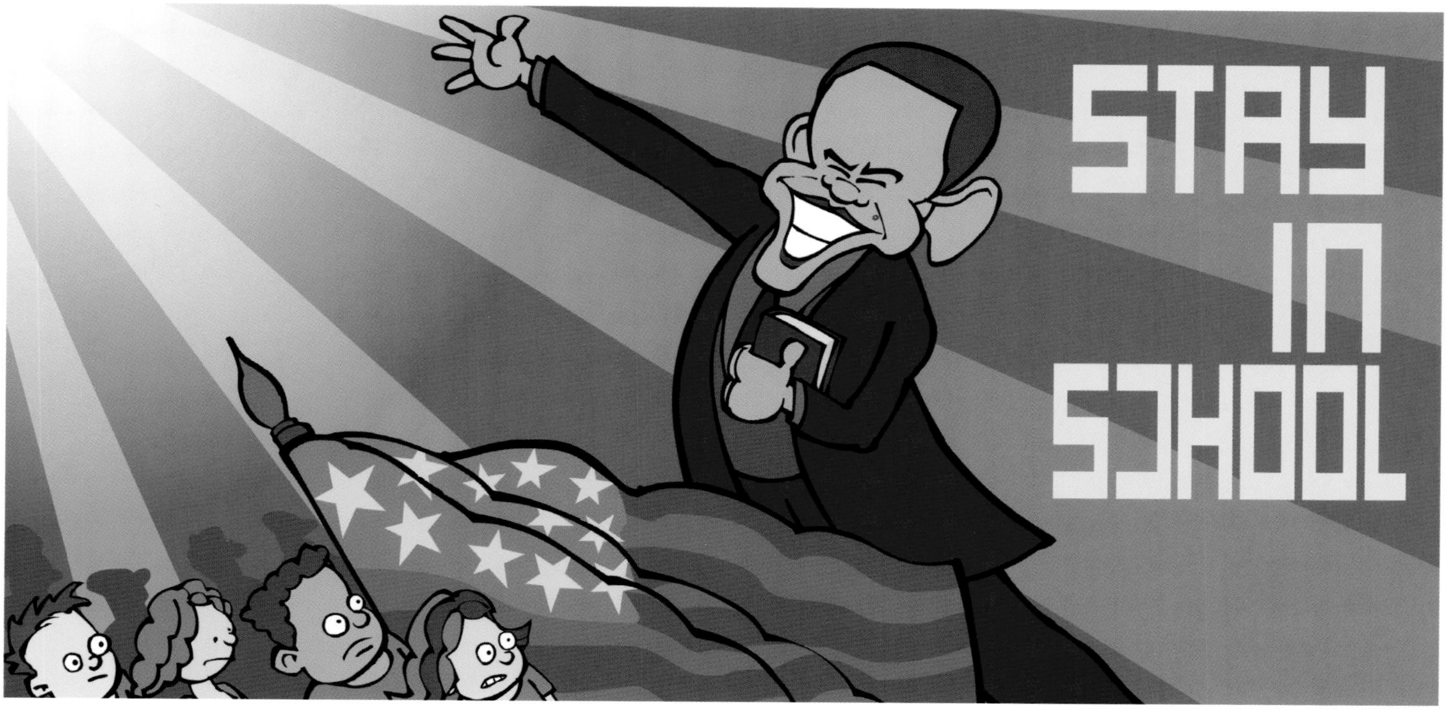
STAY
IN
SCHOOL

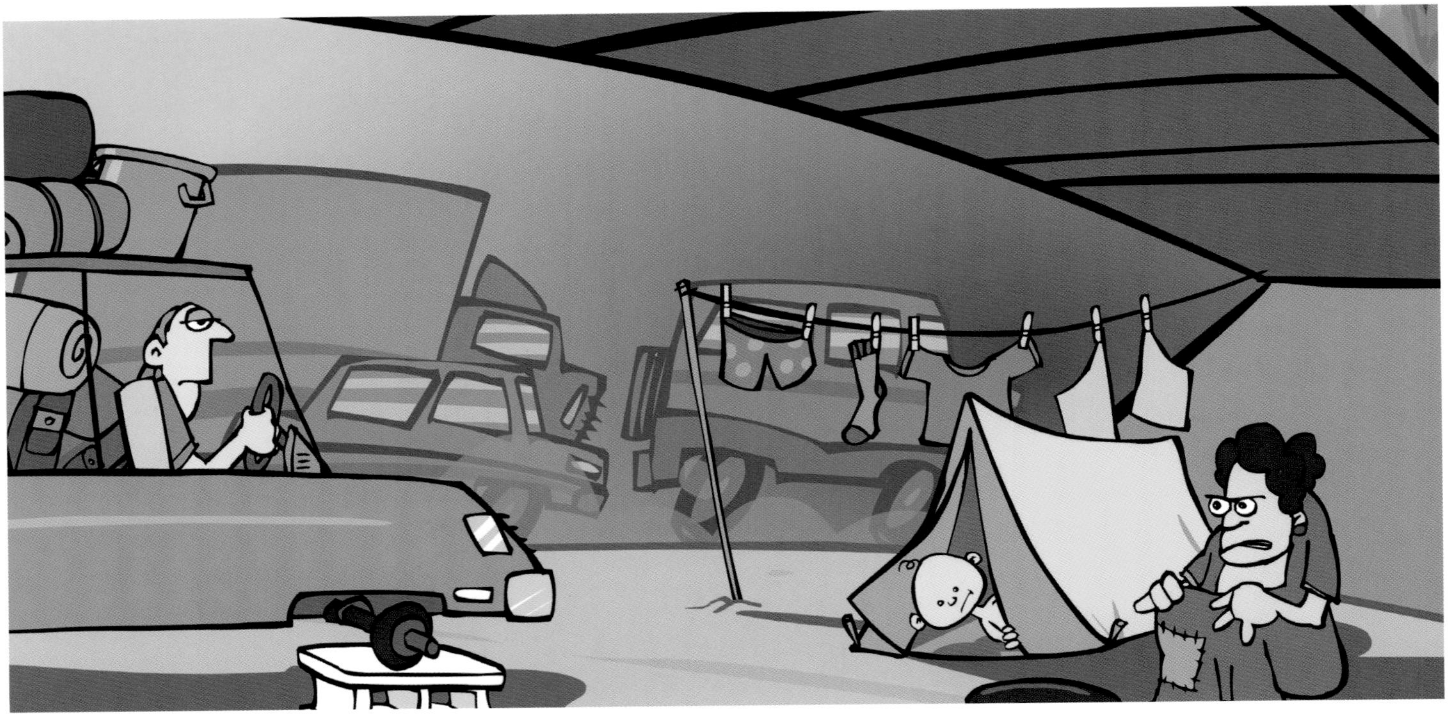

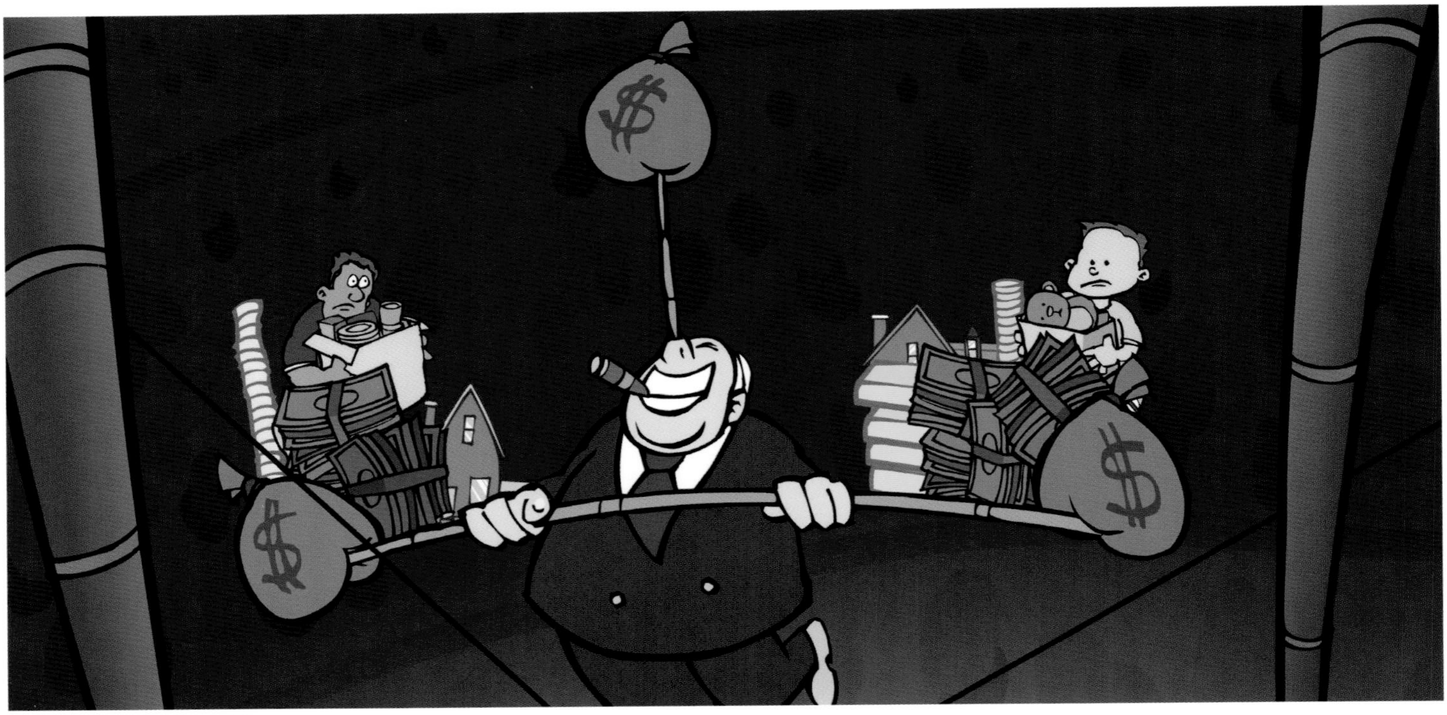

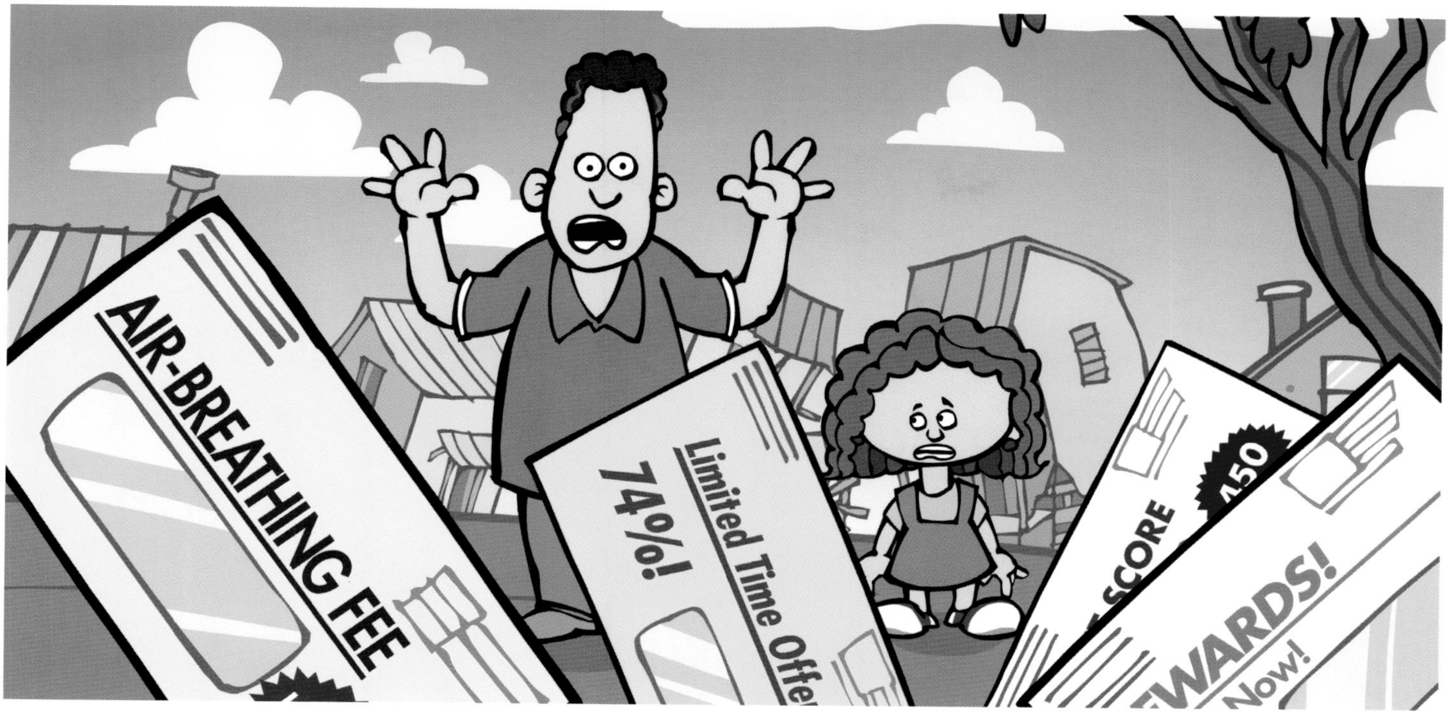
AIR-BREATHING FEE
Limited Time Offer
74%!
SCORE
450
EWARDS!
Now!

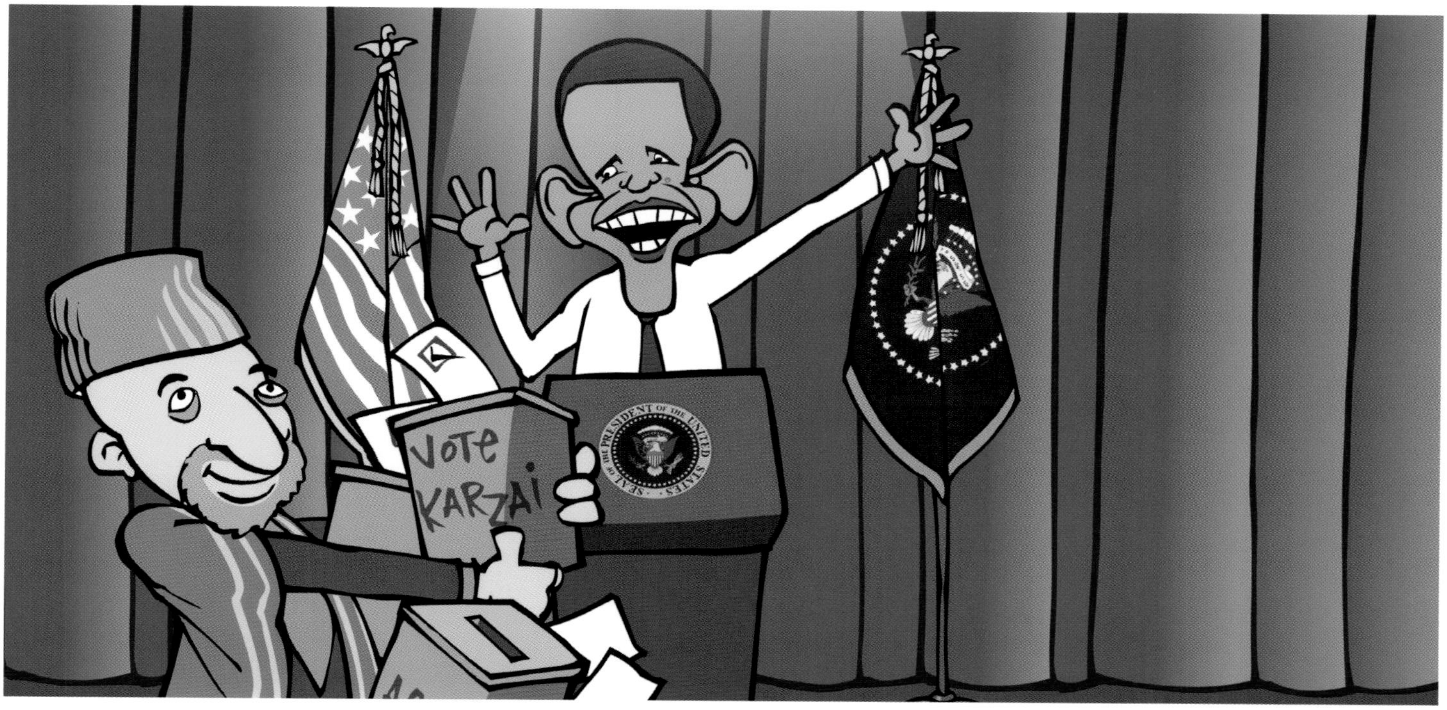
Vote
KARZAI
SEAL OF THE PRESIDENT OF THE UNITED STATES

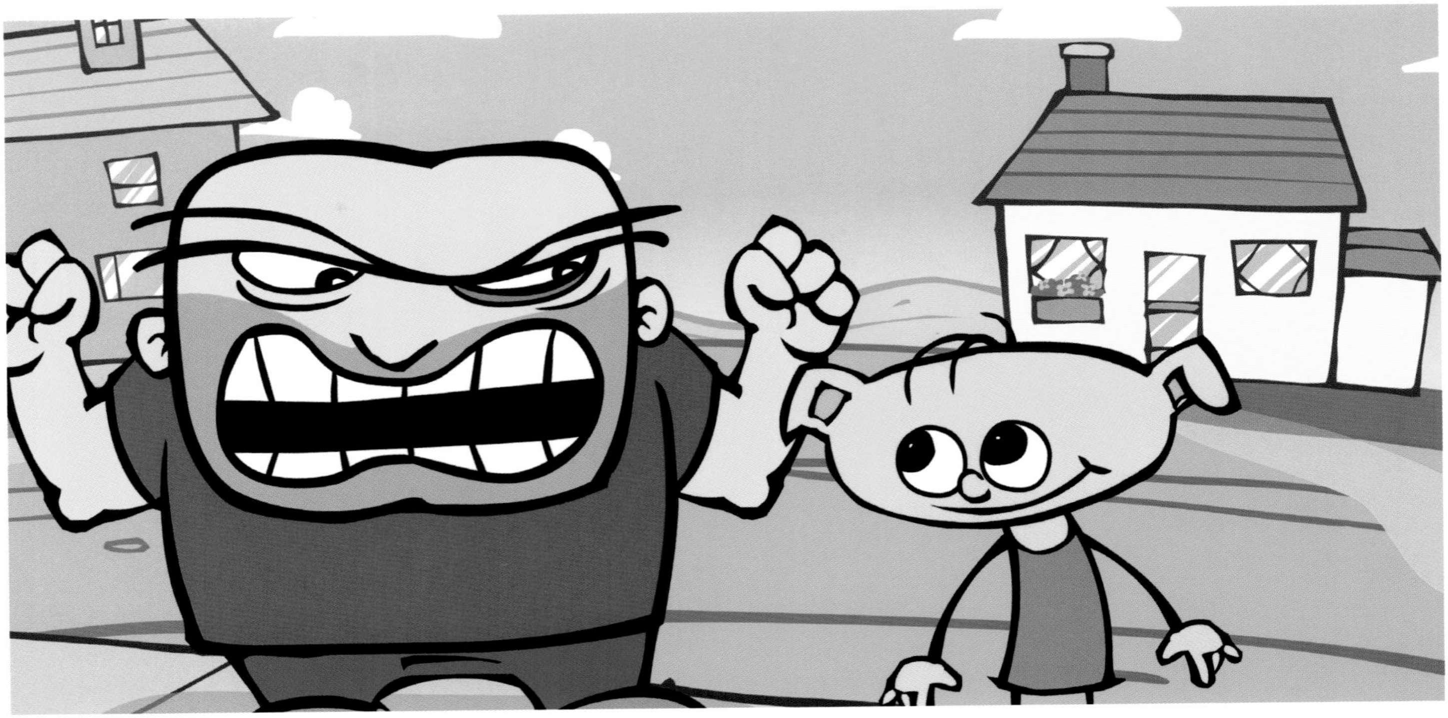

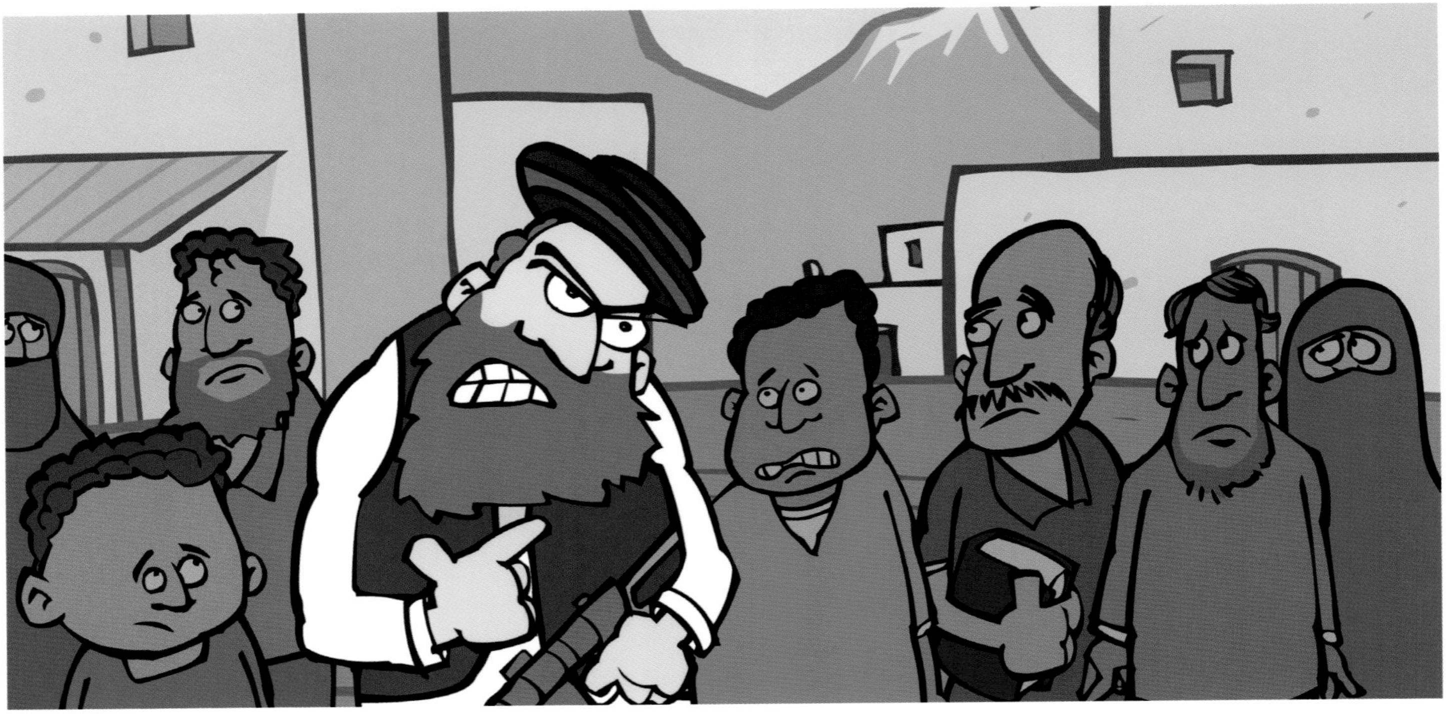

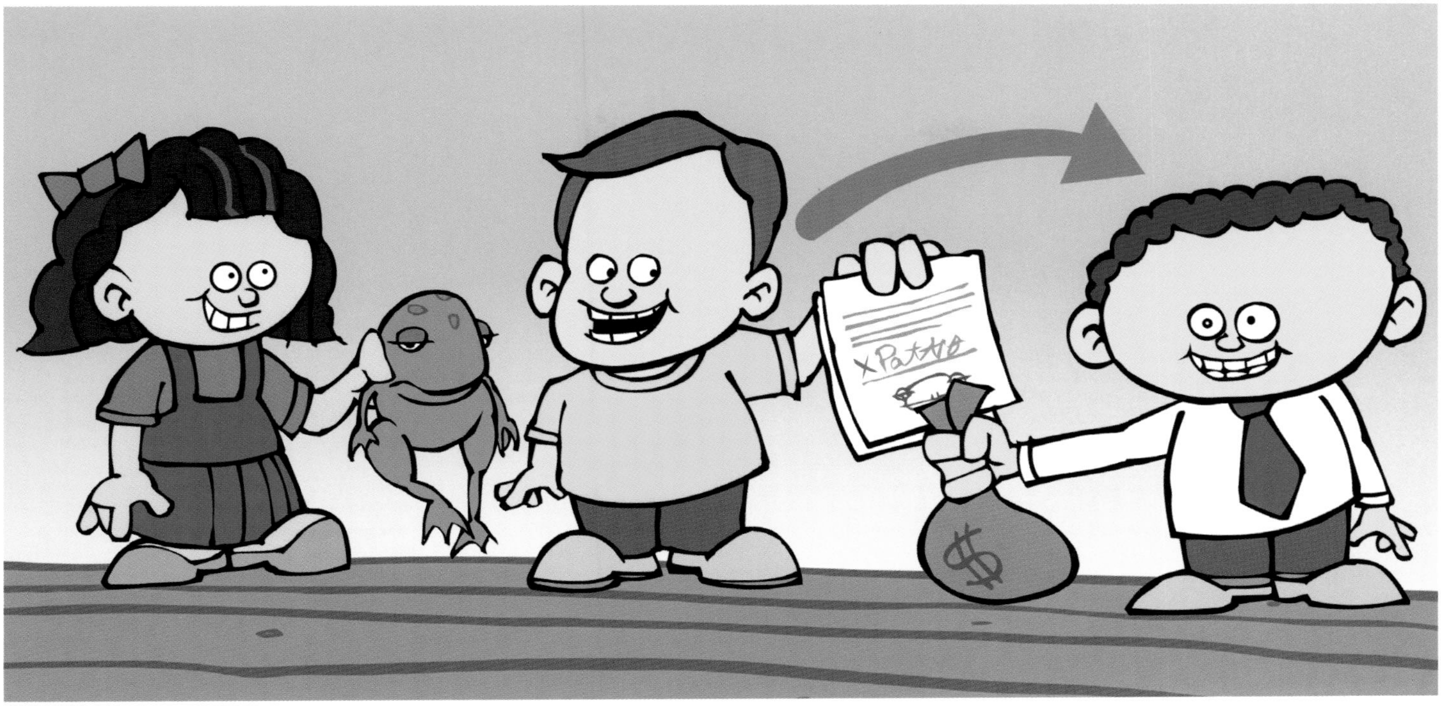

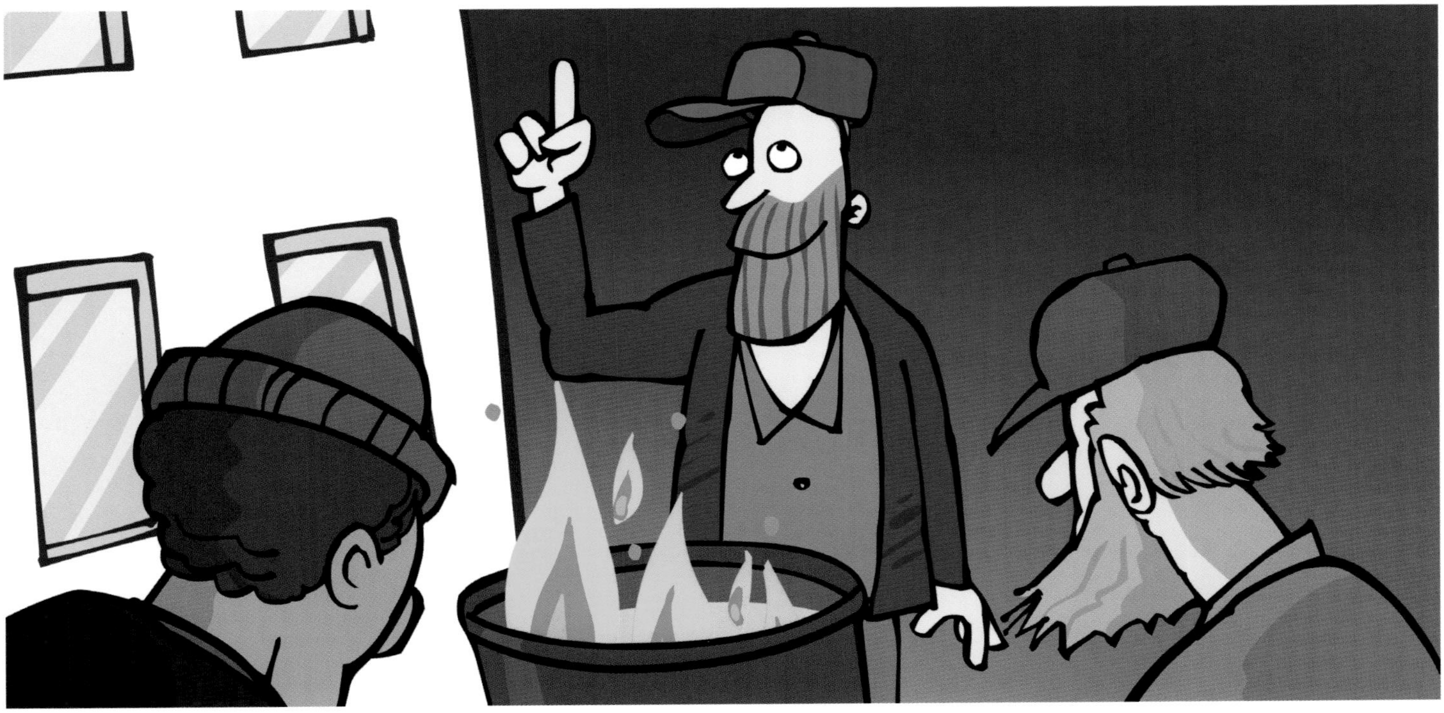

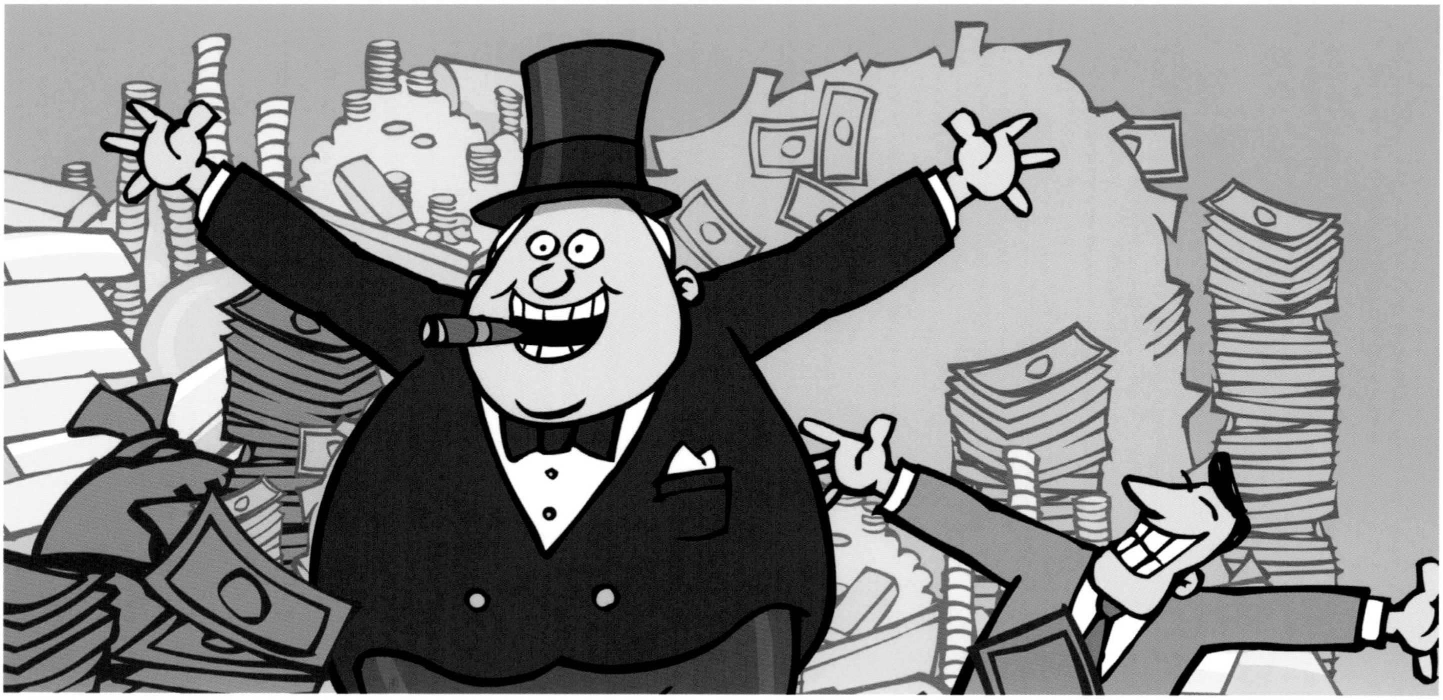

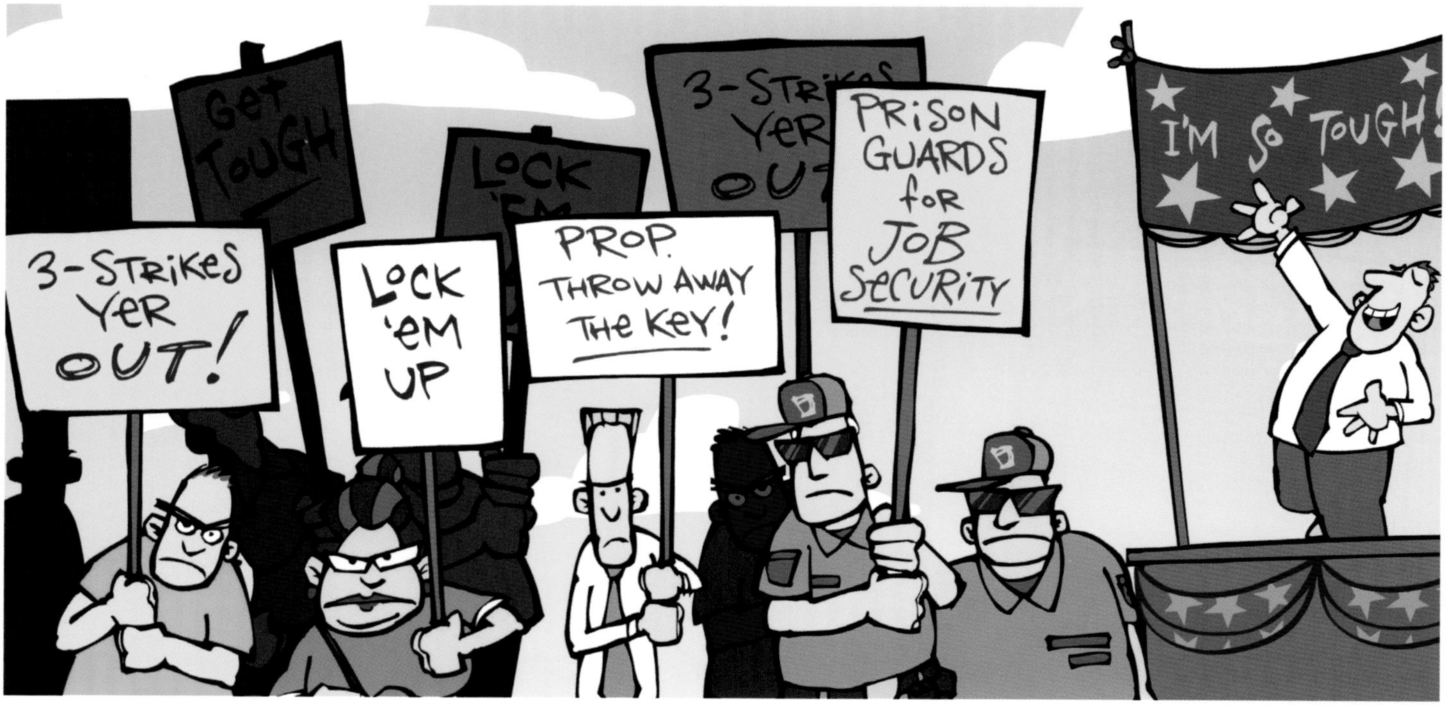

Get TOUGH
3-STRikes YeR OUT!
LOCK 'eM UP
PROP. THROW AWAY THE KEY!
PRISON GUARDS for JOB SECURITY
I'M SO TOUGH

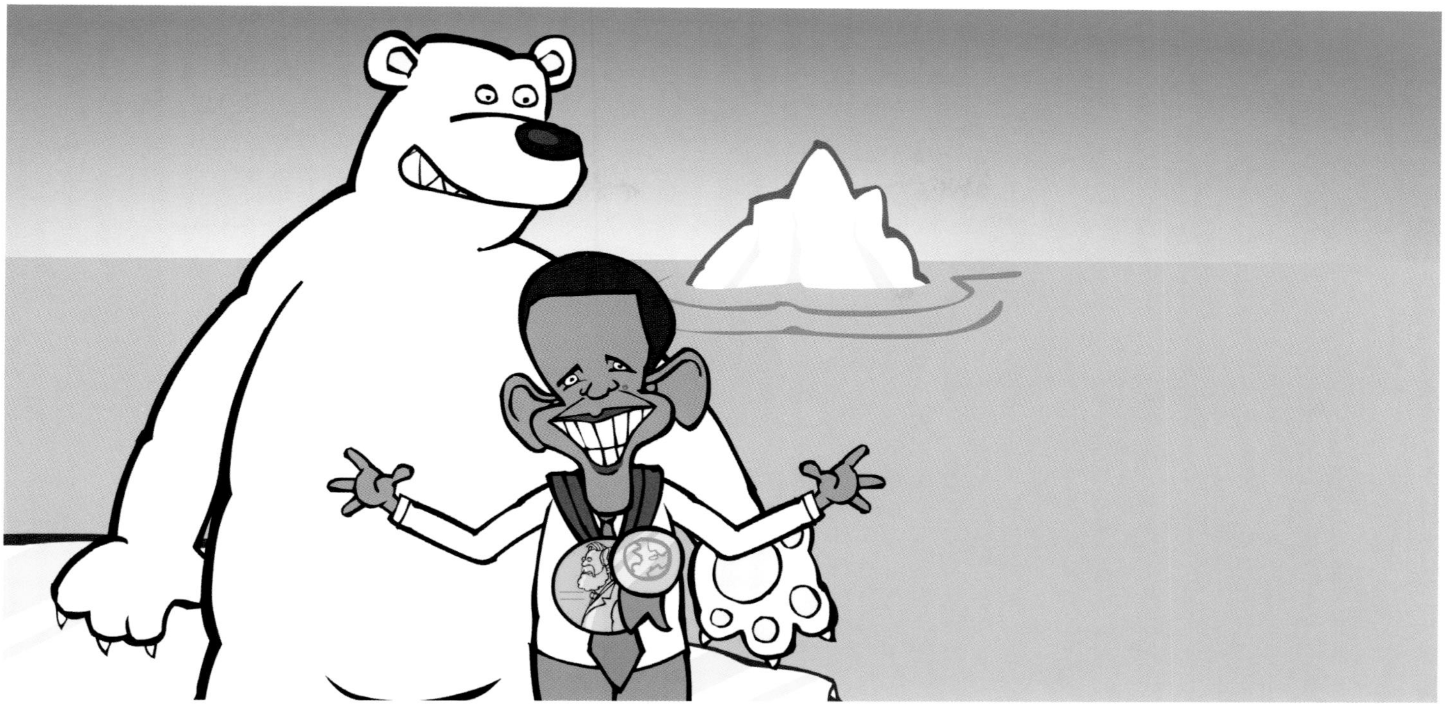

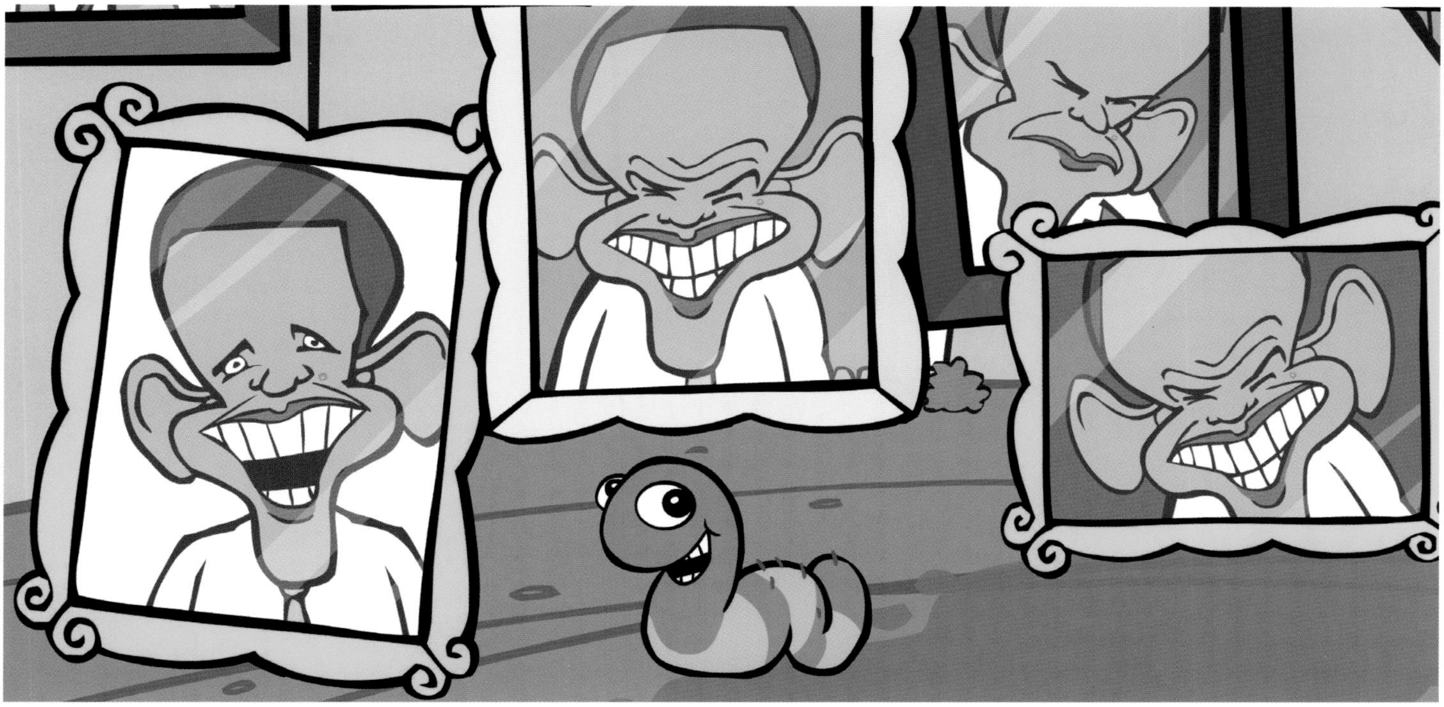

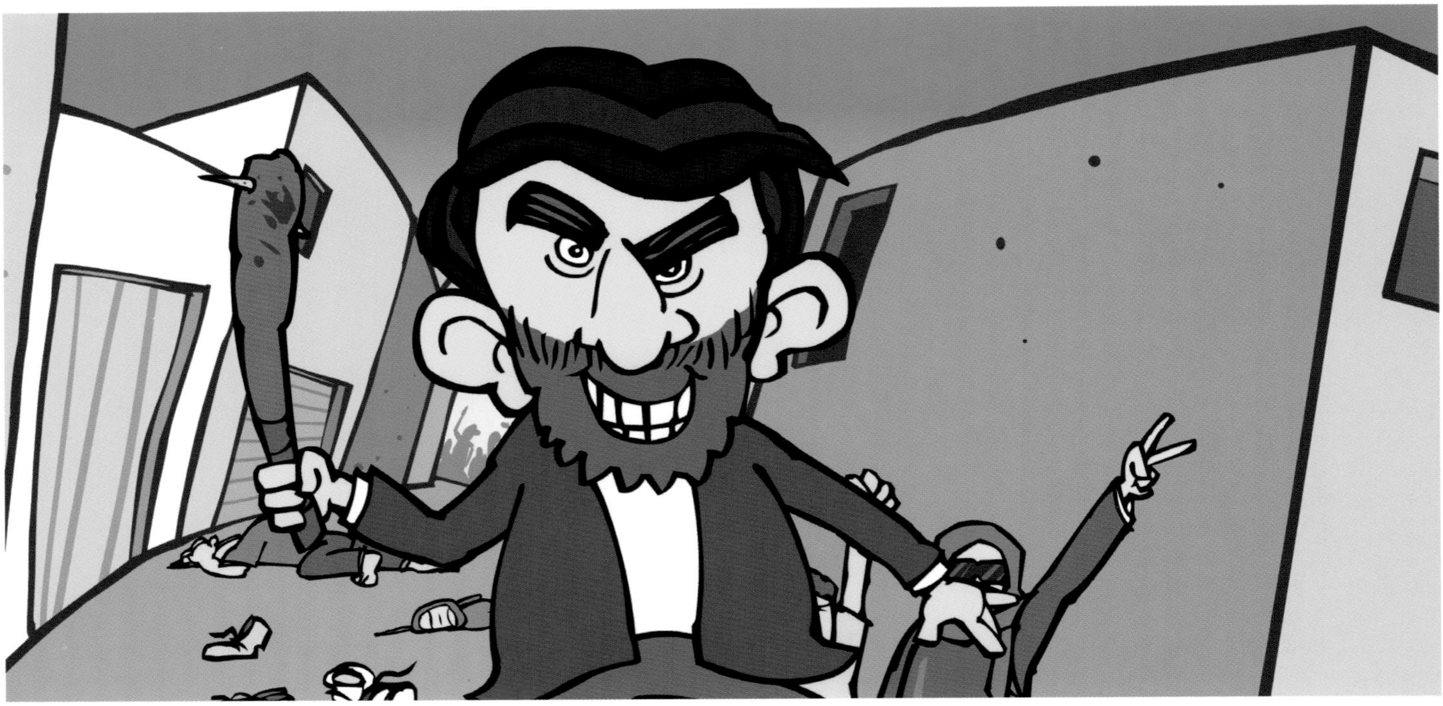

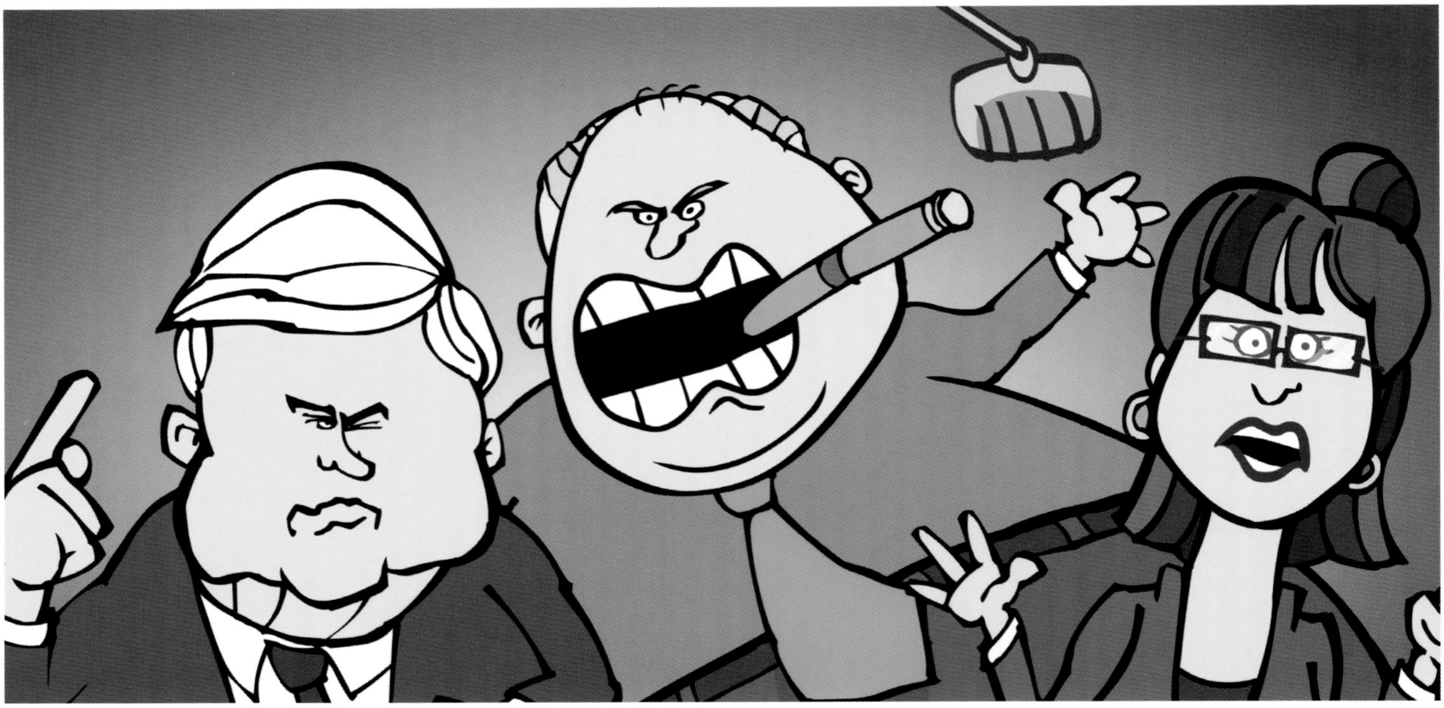

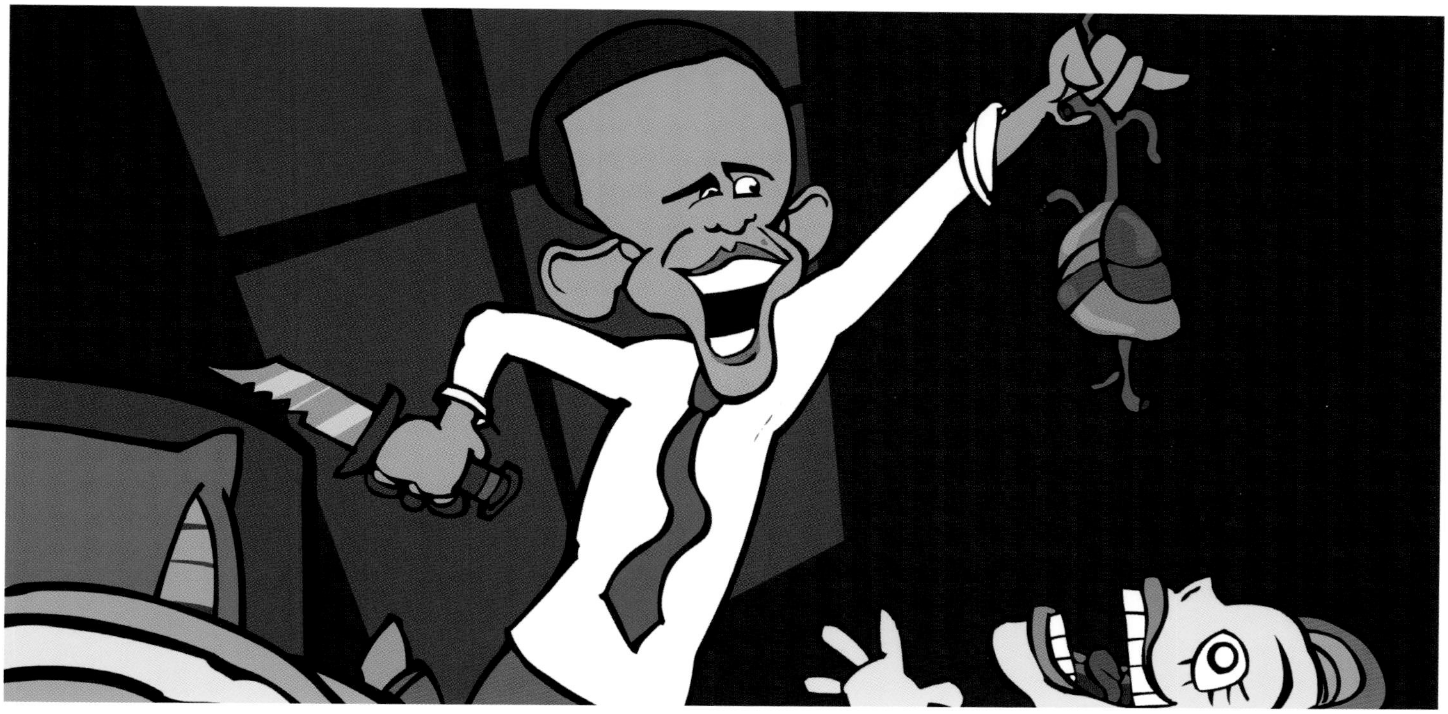

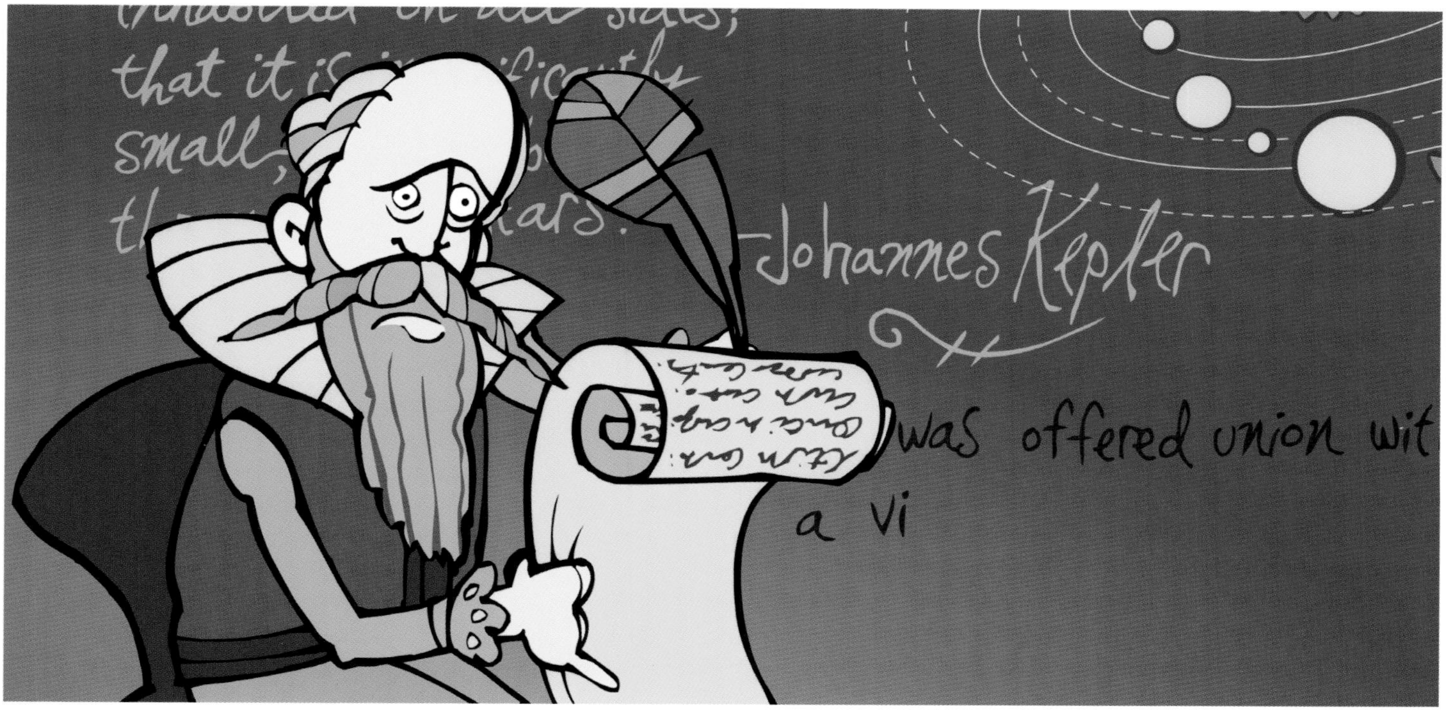
that it i
small,
Johannes Kepler
was offered union wit
a vi

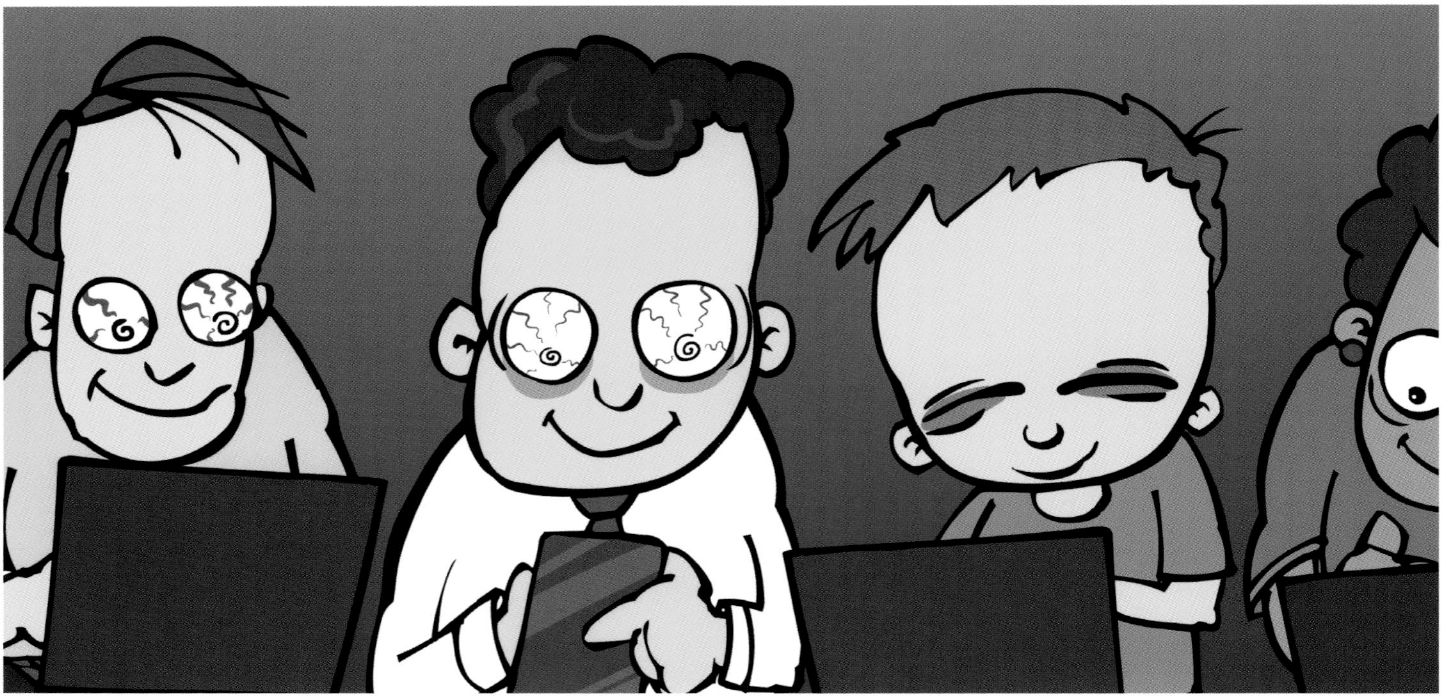

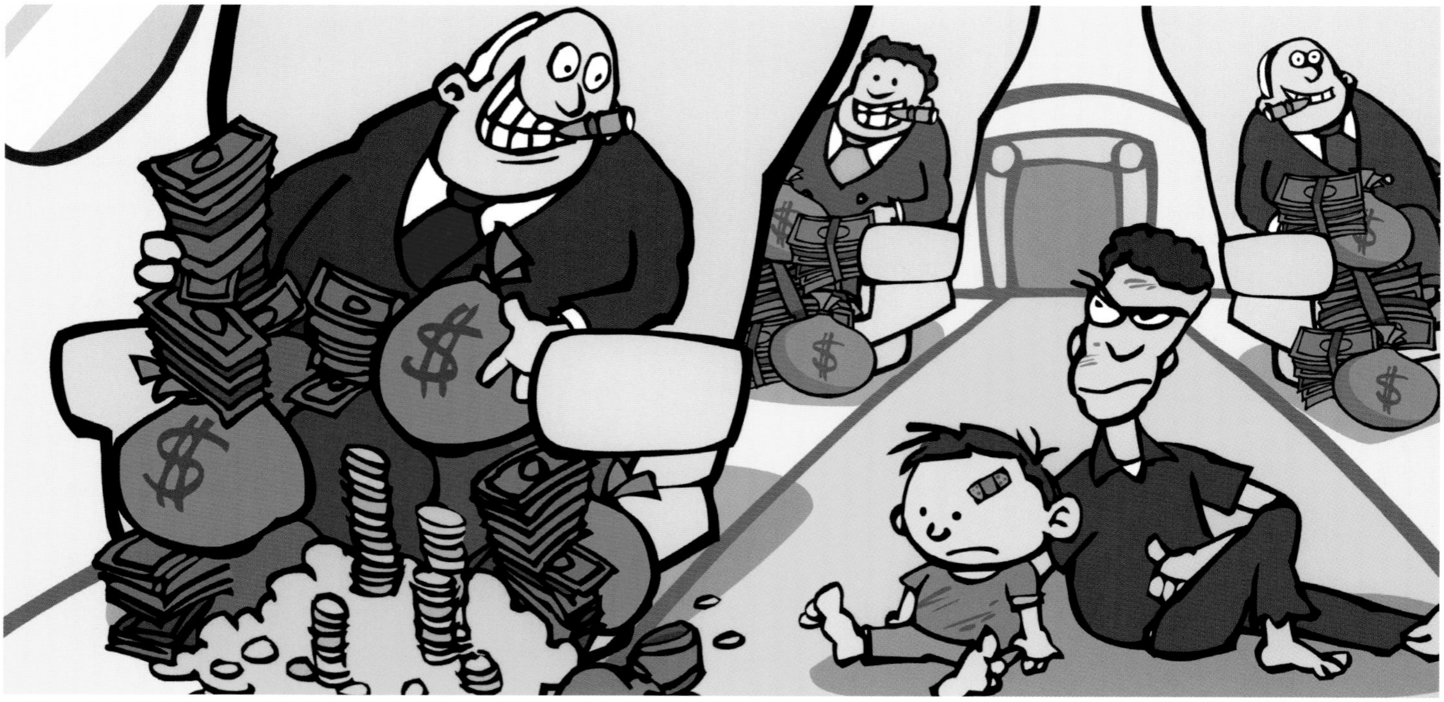

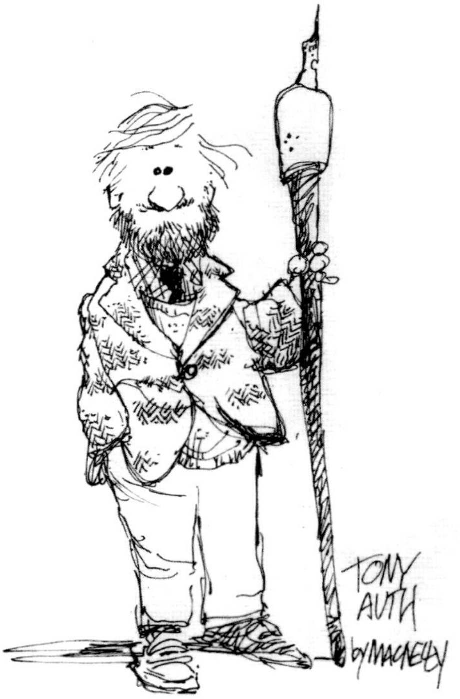
TONY
AUTH
by MACNELLY

2010 Pulitzer Prize Nominee

Tony Auth, *Philadelphia Inquirer*

Tony Auth graduated from the University of California, Los Angeles in 1965 with a degree in biological illustration. For the next six years, he served as chief medical illustrator at a large teaching hospital affiliated with the University of Southern California. During those six years, he did three political cartoons a week for a growing number of college newspapers.

Auth was hired as staff editorial cartoonist by the *Philadelphia Inquirer* in 1971, where he has happily been plying his trade ever since. Along the way, he has earned the two things Bill Mauldin once said were what you get when you do this for a living: awards and hate mail.

He has won, among many honors, the Pulitzer Prize, five Overseas Press Club Awards, the Sigma Delta Chi Award, the Thomas Nast Award, and the Herblock Prize.

Tony Auth lives with his wife, Eliza, and their two children in Wynnewood, Pennsylvania.

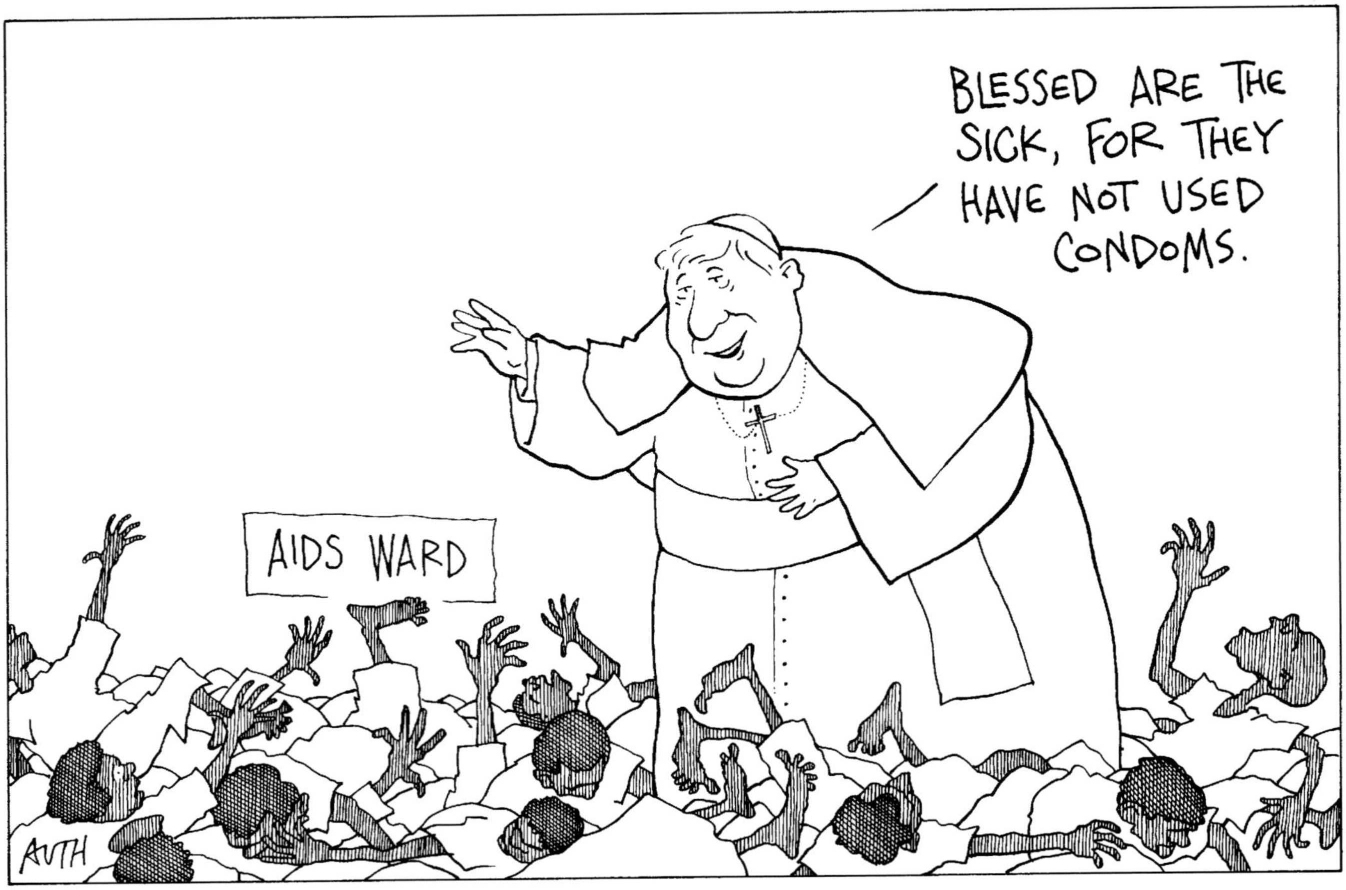
BLESSED ARE THE SICK, FOR THEY HAVE NOT USED CONDOMS.
AIDS WARD
AUTH

3.19.09 THE PHILADELPHIA INQUIRER. UNIVERSAL PRESS SYNDICATE.

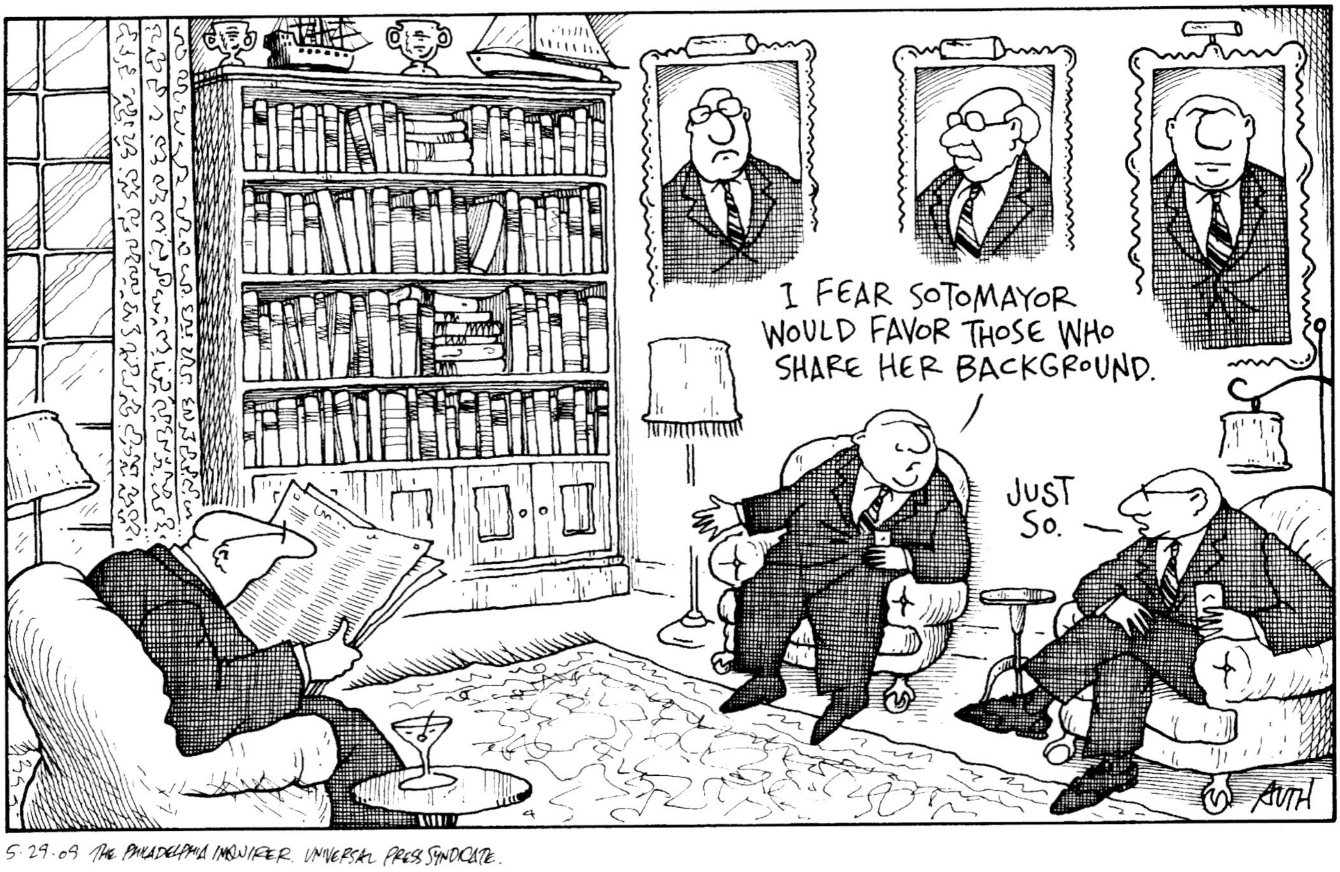
I FEAR SOTOMAYOR WOULD FAVOR THOSE WHO SHARE HER BACKGROUND.
JUST SO.
AUTH

5.29.09 THE PHILADELPHIA INQUIRER. UNIVERSAL PRESS SYNDICATE.

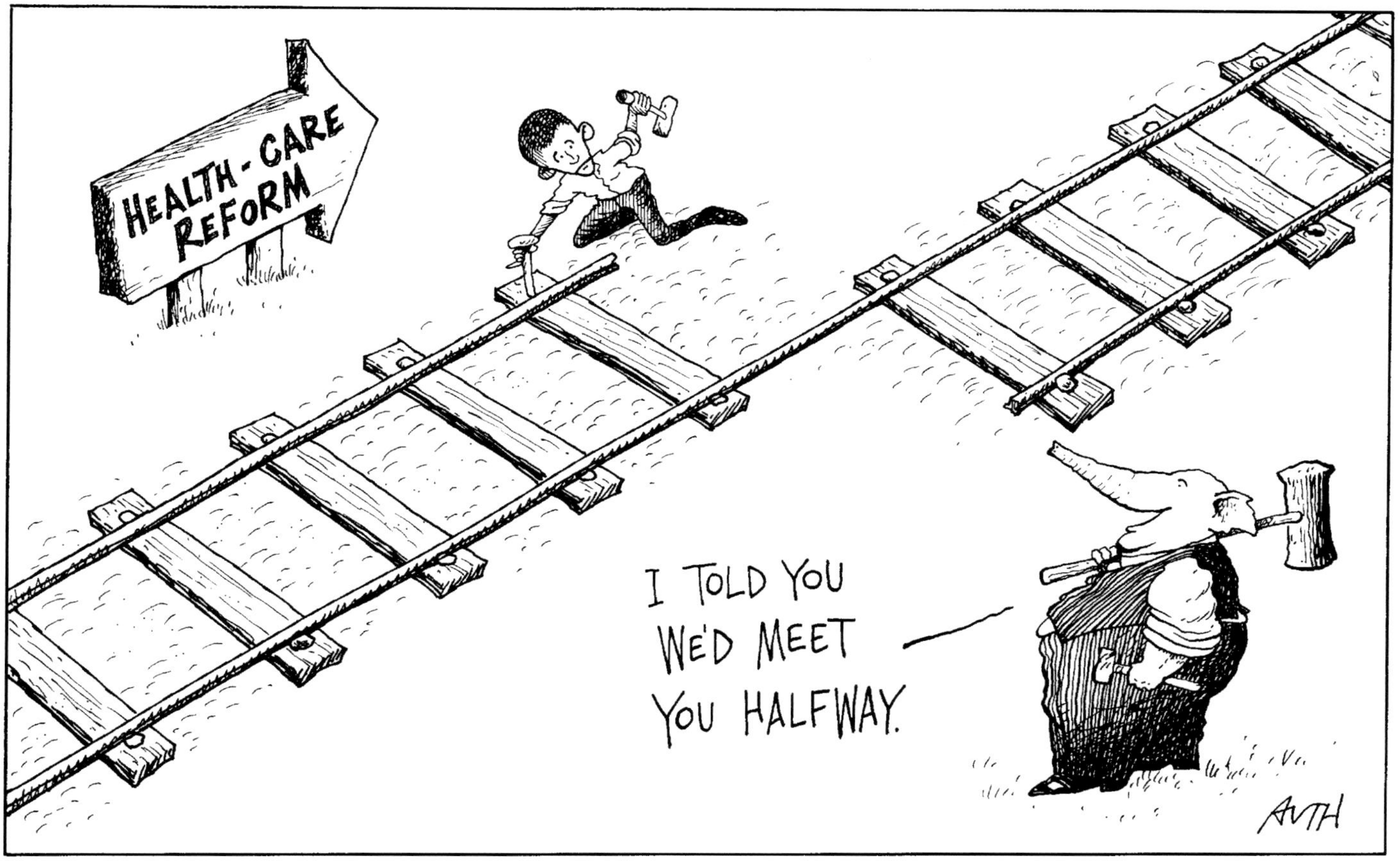
HEALTH-CARE REFORM
I TOLD YOU WE'D MEET YOU HALFWAY.
AUTH

9/1/09 THE PHILADELPHIA INQUIRER. UCLICK.

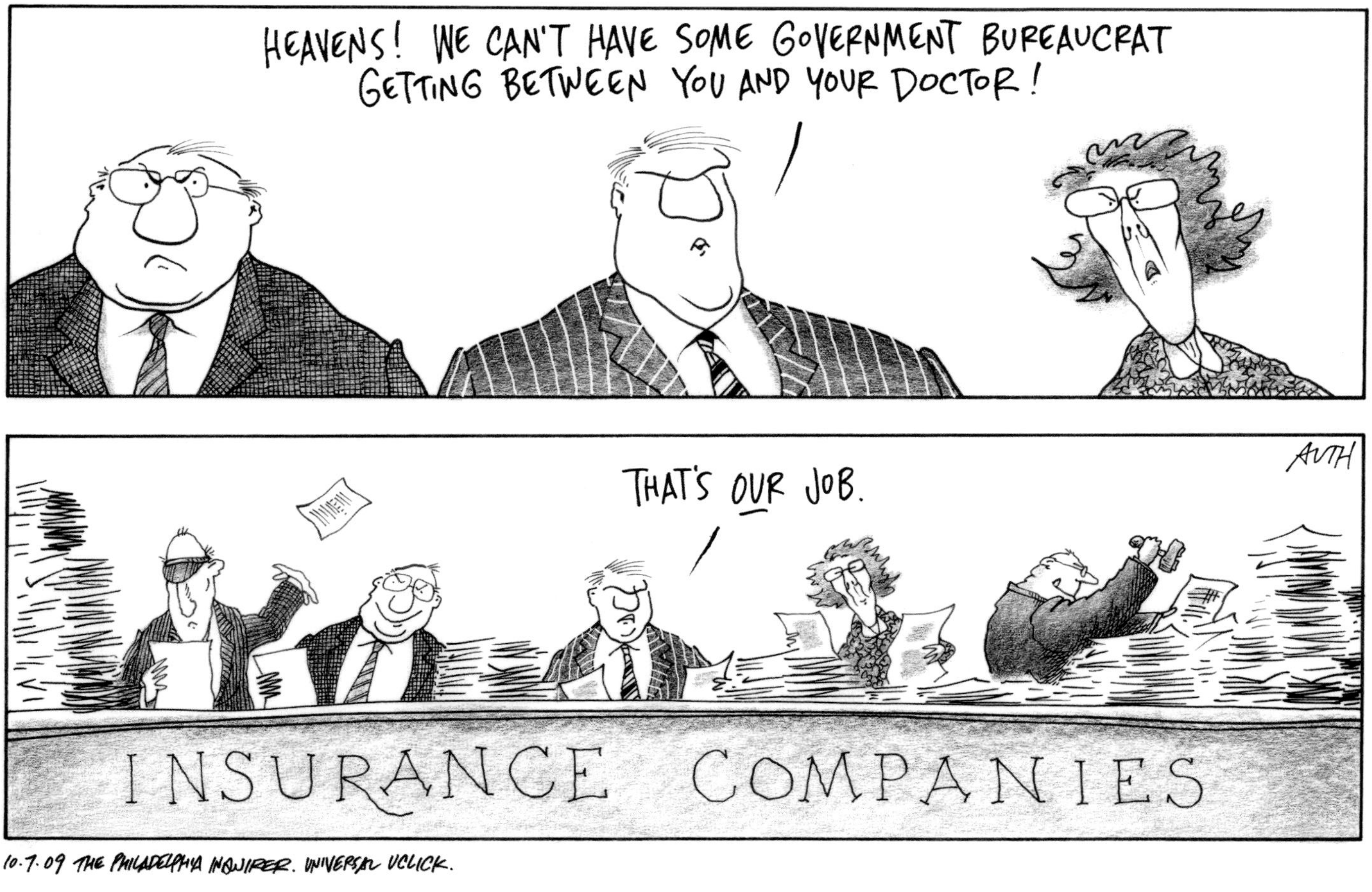
HEAVENS! WE CAN'T HAVE SOME GOVERNMENT BUREAUCRAT GETTING BETWEEN YOU AND YOUR DOCTOR!
AUTH
THAT'S OUR JOB.
INSURANCE COMPANIES

10.7.09 THE PHILADELPHIA INQUIRER. UNIVERSAL UCLICK.

11·6·09 THE PHILADELPHIA INQUIRER. UNIVERSAL UCLICK.

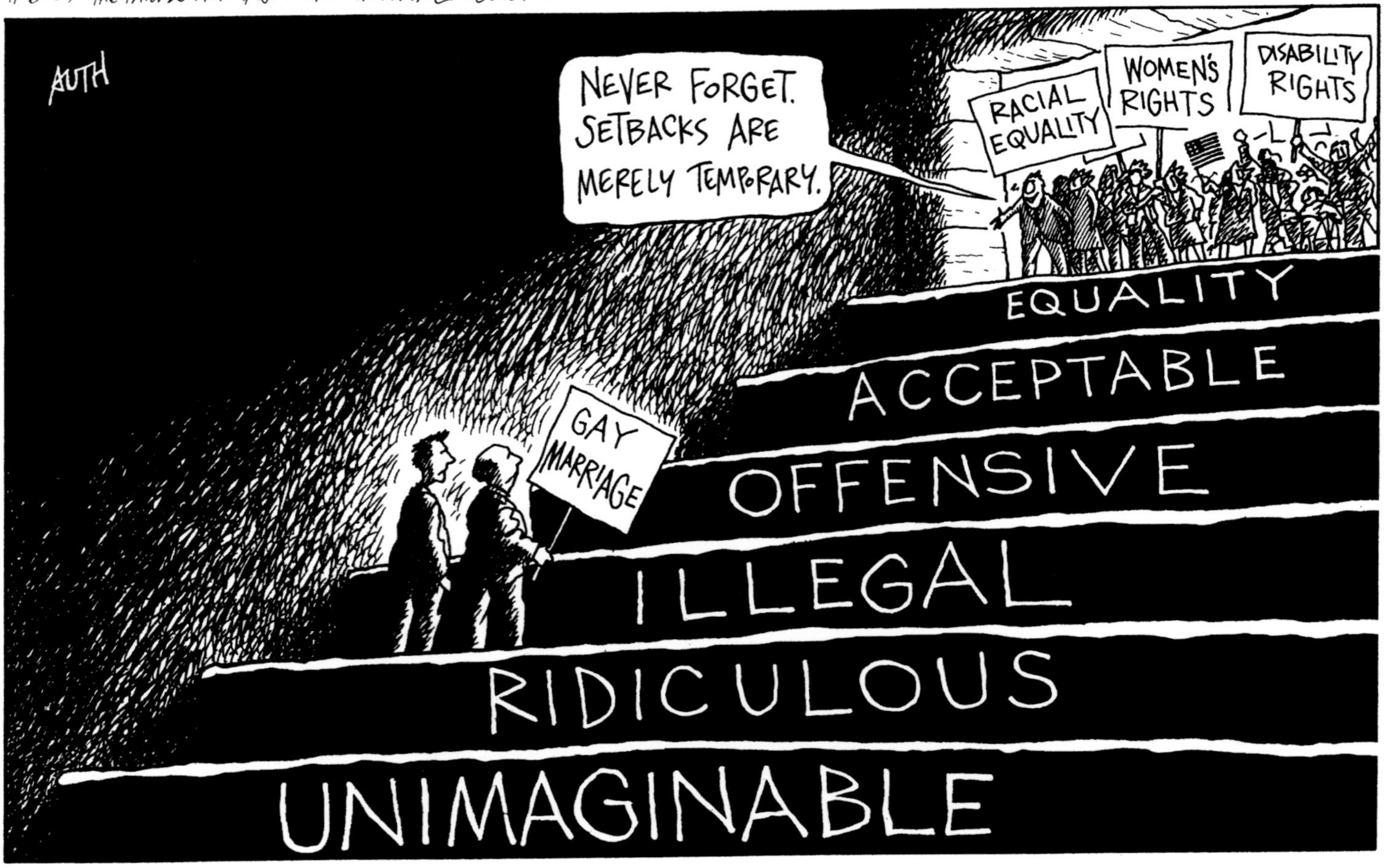
AUTH
NEVER FORGET. SETBACKS ARE MERELY TEMPORARY.
RACIAL EQUALITY
WOMEN'S RIGHTS
DISABILITY RIGHTS
GAY MARRIAGE
EQUALITY
ACCEPTABLE
OFFENSIVE
ILLEGAL
RIDICULOUS
UNIMAGINABLE

2010 Pulitzer Prize Nominee
Matt Wuerker, *Politico*

Matt Wuerker is a political cartoonist based in Washington, D.C. He is the staff cartoonist for the newspaper *Politico* and its Web site, Politico.com.

Prior to landing this full-time staff position, he worked as a successful freelance cartoonist. Over the past twenty-five years his cartoons have been published widely in publications ranging from dailies, including the *Los Angeles Times,* the *Washington Post,* and the *Christian Science Monitor,* to magazines, such as *George,* the *Nation,* and *Smithsonian,* to name a few. Both Tribune Media Service and NewsArt.com syndicate his caricature and illustration work internationally.

Two collections of his cartoons have been published, *Standing Tall in Deep Doo Doo: A Cartoon Chronicle of the Bush Quayle Years* and *Meanwhile, in Other News: A Graphic Look at Politics in the Empire of Money, Sex and Scandal.*

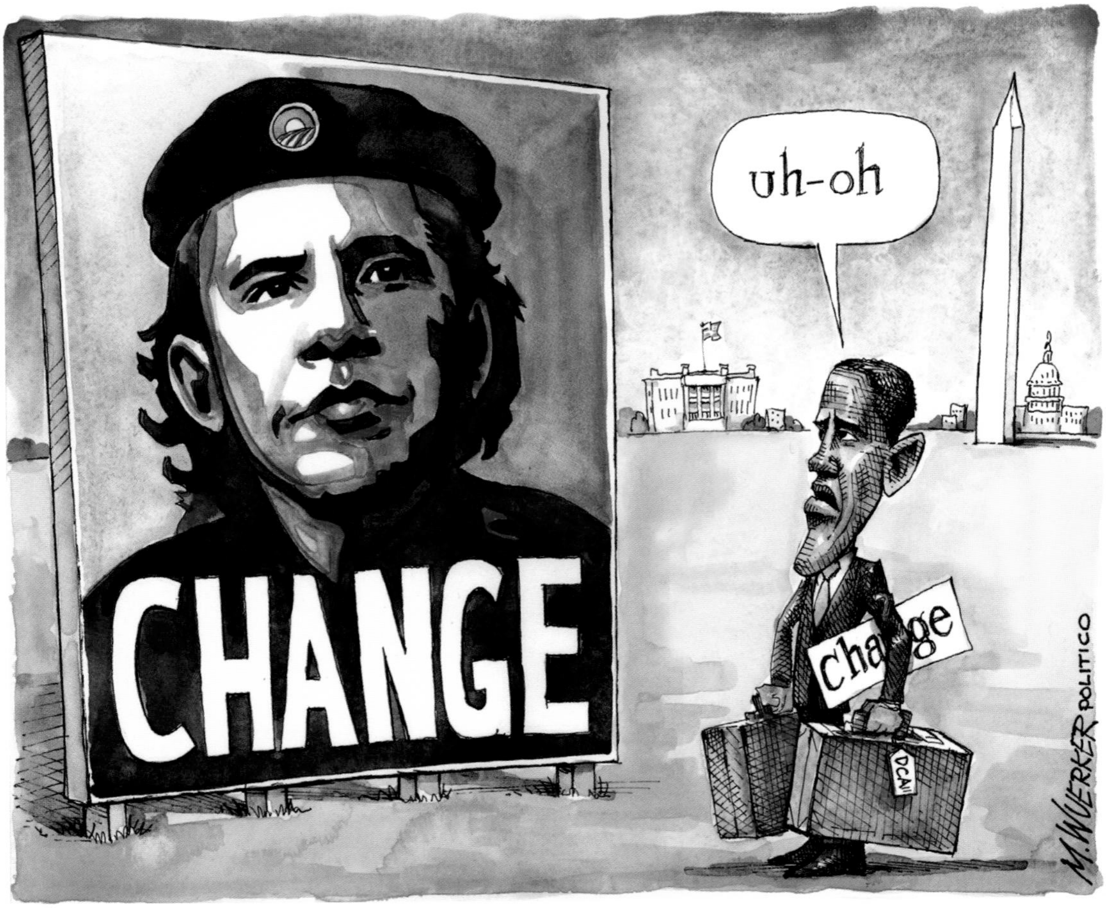
CHANGE
uh-oh
change
DCA
M. WUERKER POLITICO

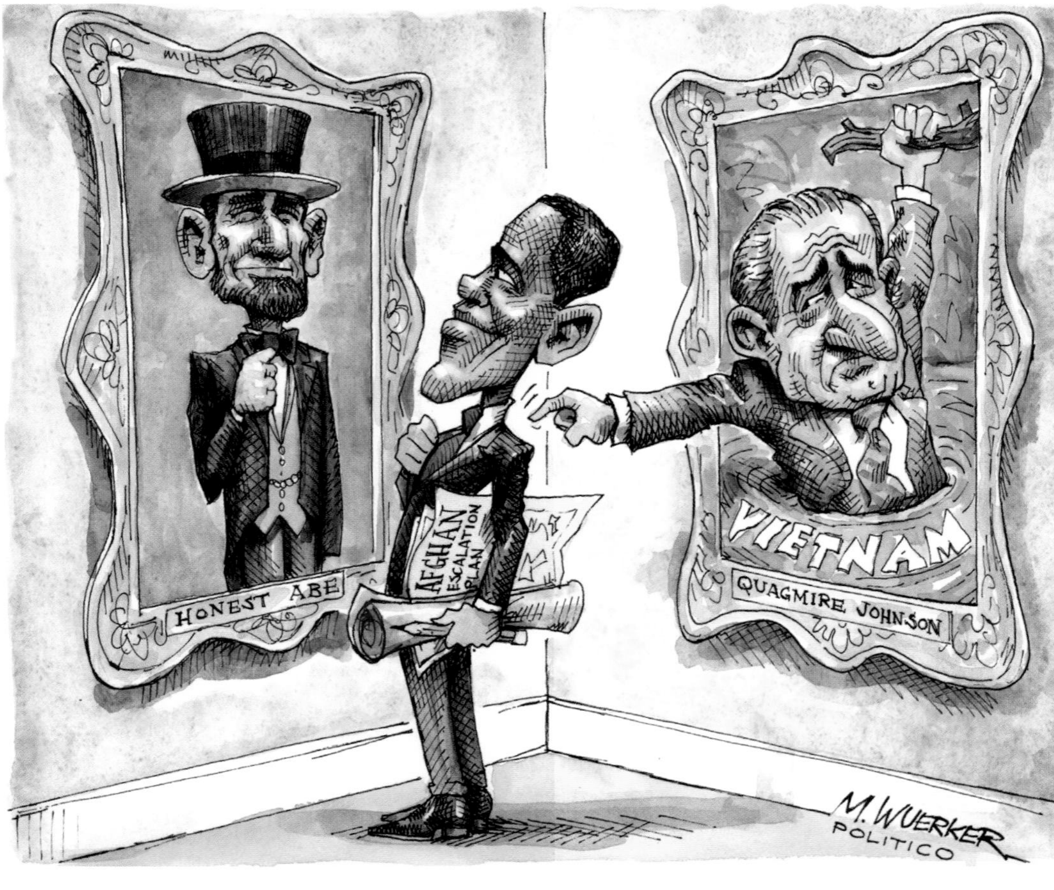
HONEST ABE
AFGHAN ESCALATION PLAN
VIETNAM
QUAGMIRE JOHNSON
M. WUERKER POLITICO

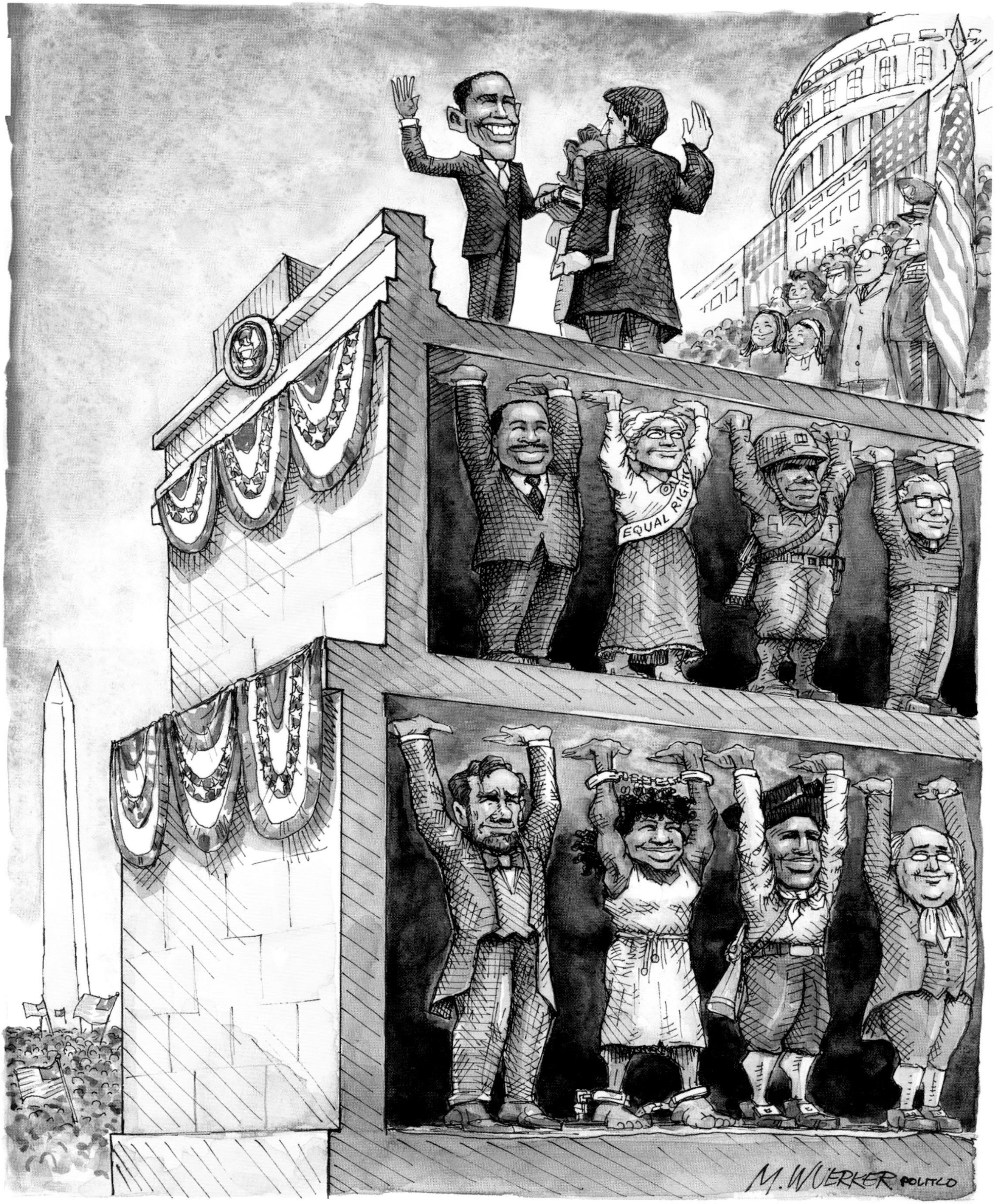
EQUAL RIGHT
M. WUERKER POLITICO

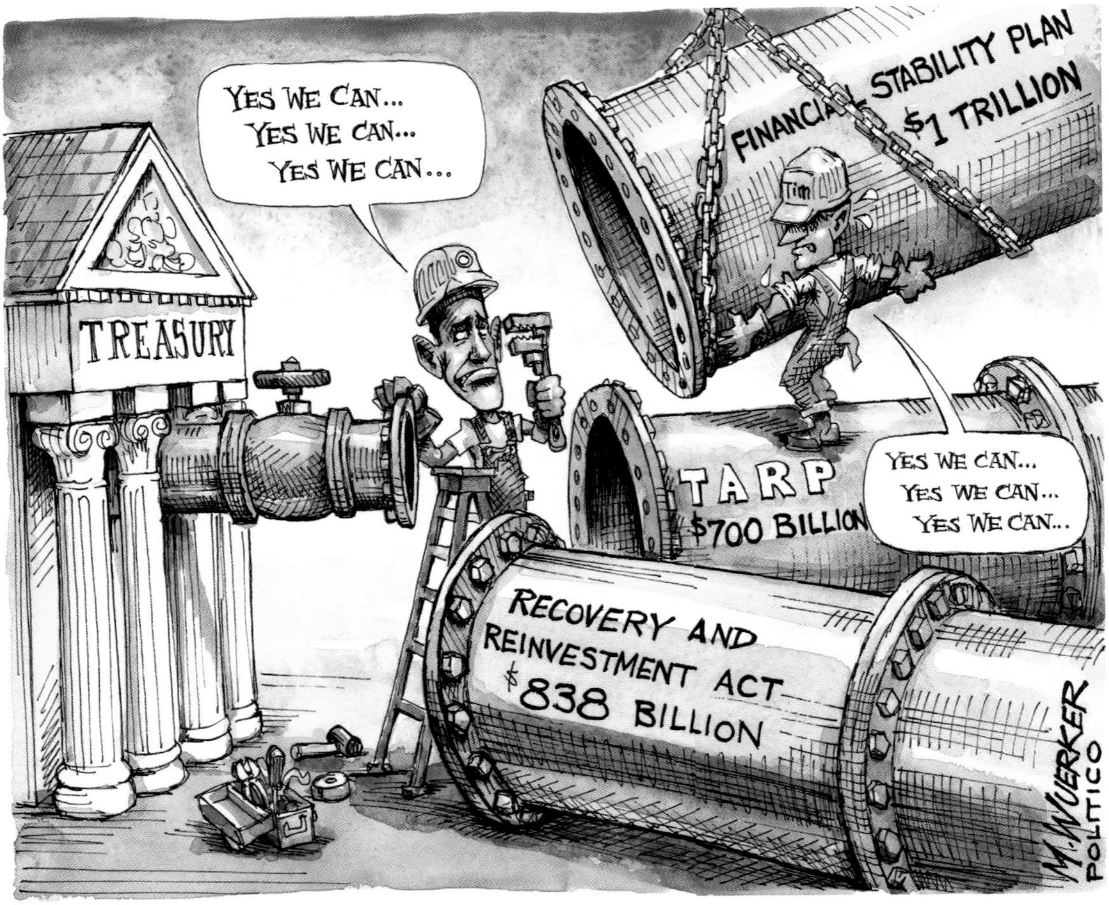
YES WE CAN...
YES WE CAN...
YES WE CAN...
FINANCIAL STABILITY PLAN
$1 TRILLION
TIM
TREASURY
YES WE CAN...
YES WE CAN...
YES WE CAN...
TARP
$700 BILLION
RECOVERY AND
REINVESTMENT ACT
$838 BILLION
M. WUERKER
POLITICO

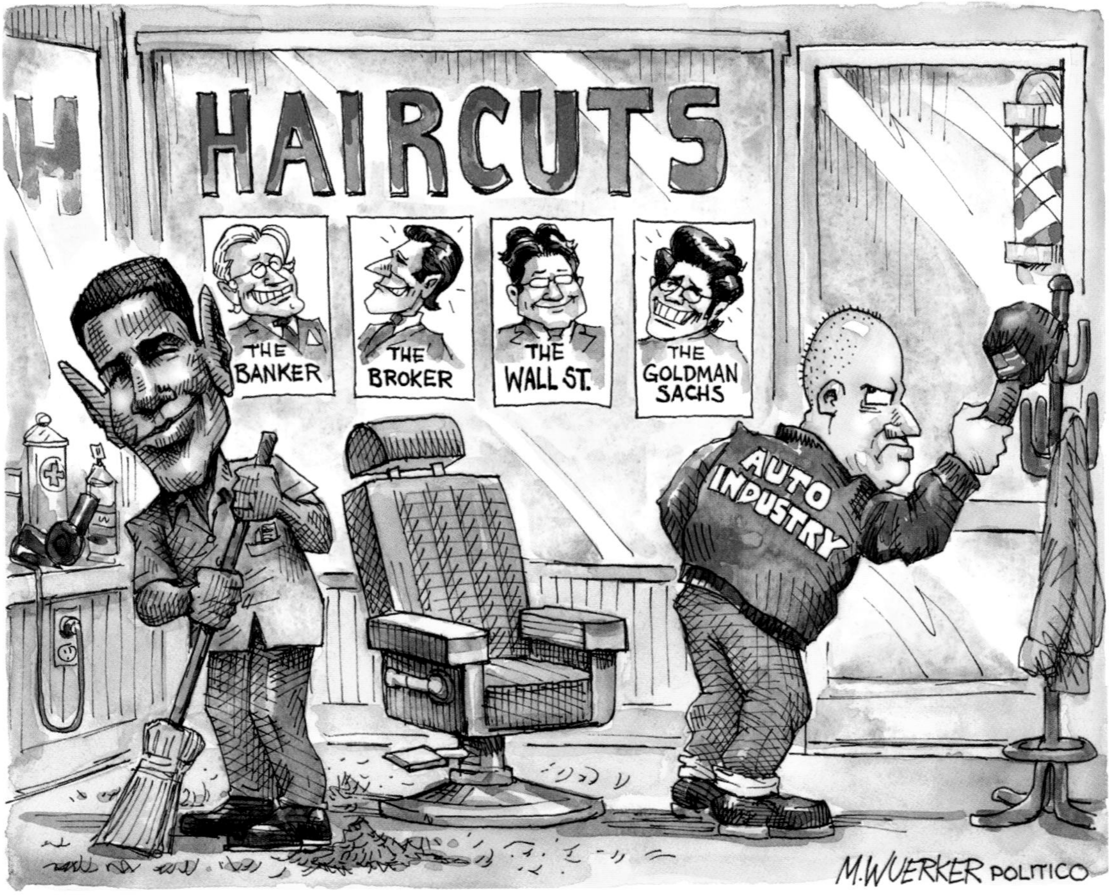
HAIRCUTS
THE BANKER
THE BROKER
THE WALL ST.
THE GOLDMAN SACHS
AUTO INDUSTRY
M. WUERKER POLITICO

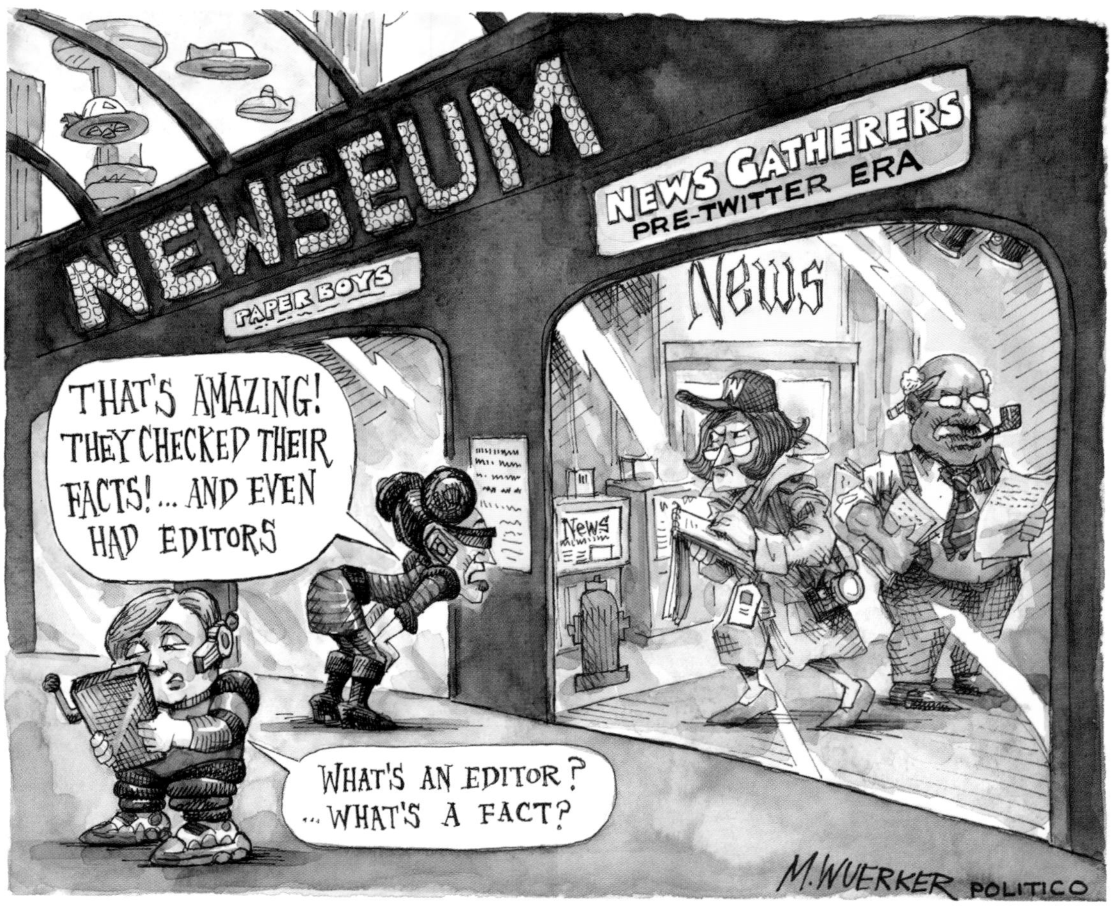
NEWSEUM
PAPER BOYS
NEWS GATHERERS
PRE-TWITTER ERA
News
THAT'S AMAZING! THEY CHECKED THEIR FACTS! ... AND EVEN HAD EDITORS
WHAT'S AN EDITOR? ... WHAT'S A FACT?
M.WUERKER POLITICO

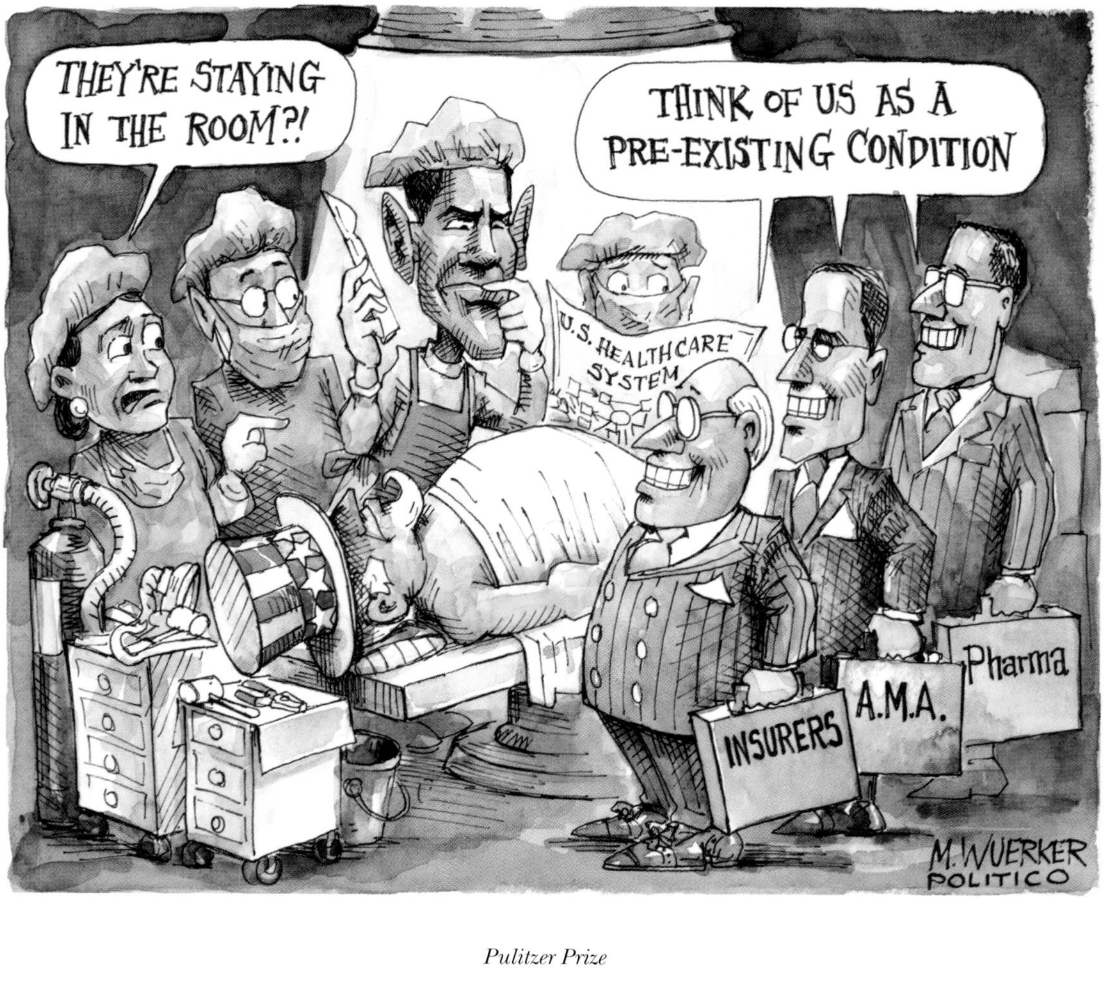
THEY'RE STAYING IN THE ROOM?!
THINK OF US AS A PRE-EXISTING CONDITION
U.S. HEALTHCARE SYSTEM
INSURERS
A.M.A.
Pharma
M.WUERKER POLITICO

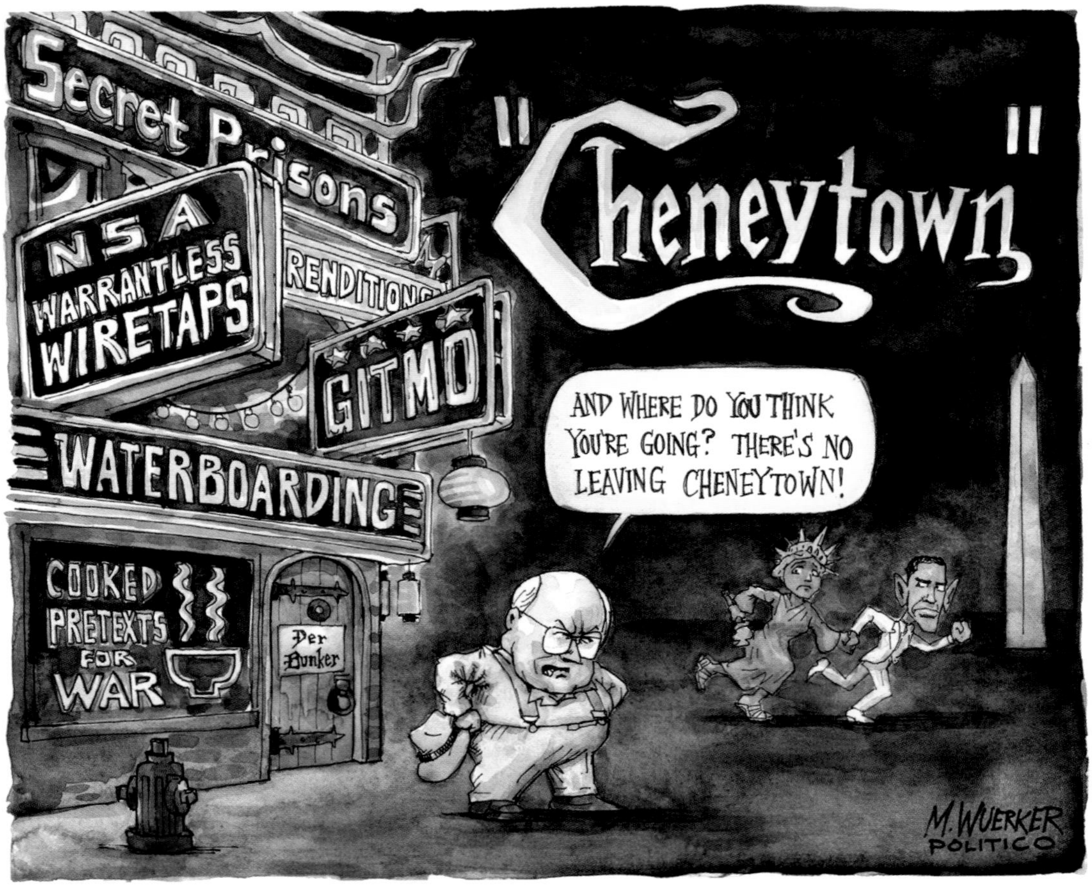
Secret Prisons
NSA
WARRANTLESS
WIRETAPS
RENDITIONS
GITMO
WATERBOARDING
COOKED PRETEXTS FOR WAR
Der Bunker
"Cheneytown"
AND WHERE DO YOU THINK YOU'RE GOING? THERE'S NO LEAVING CHENEYTOWN!
M. WUERKER POLITICO

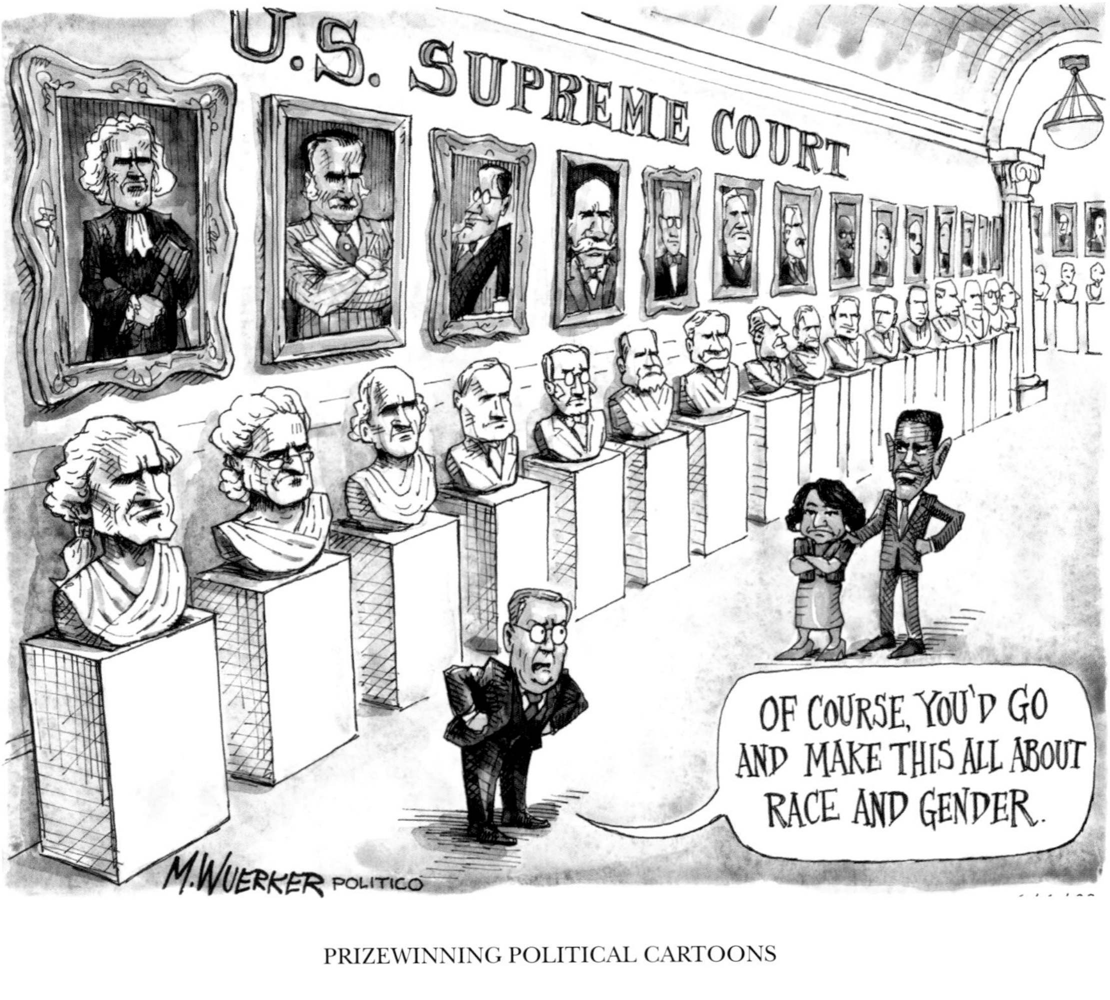
U.S. SUPREME COURT
OF COURSE, YOU'D GO AND MAKE THIS ALL ABOUT RACE AND GENDER.
M. WUERKER POLITICO

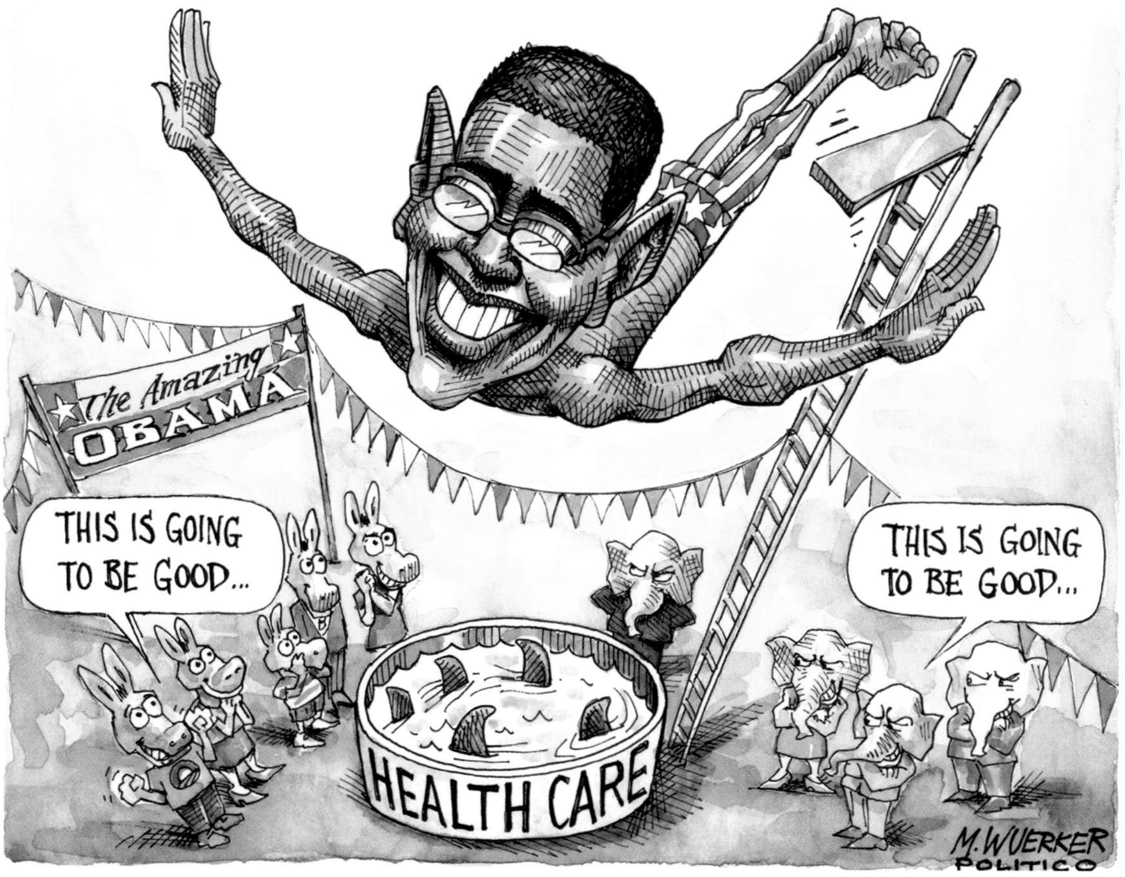
The Amazing
OBAMA
THIS IS GOING TO BE GOOD...
THIS IS GOING TO BE GOOD...
HEALTH CARE
M. WUERKER
POLITICO

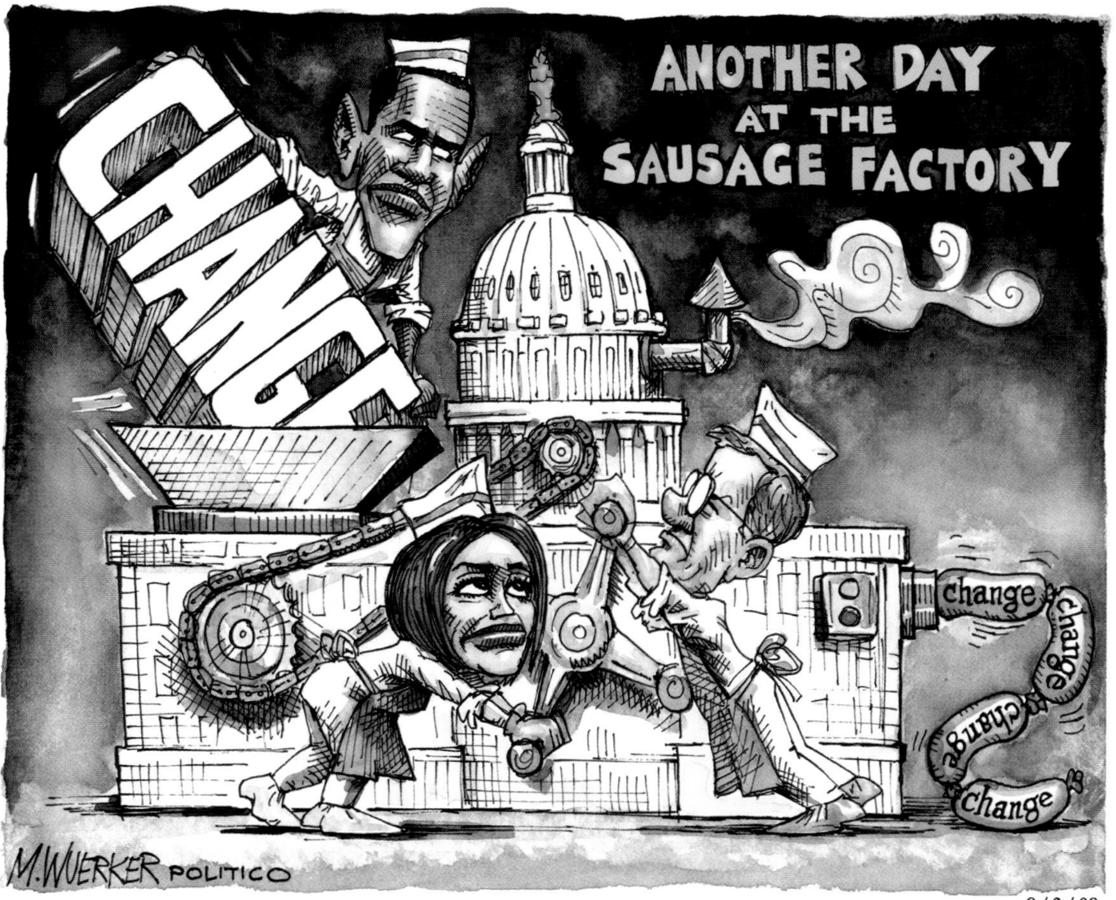
ANOTHER DAY AT THE SAUSAGE FACTORY
change
change
change
change
M. WUERKER POLITICO

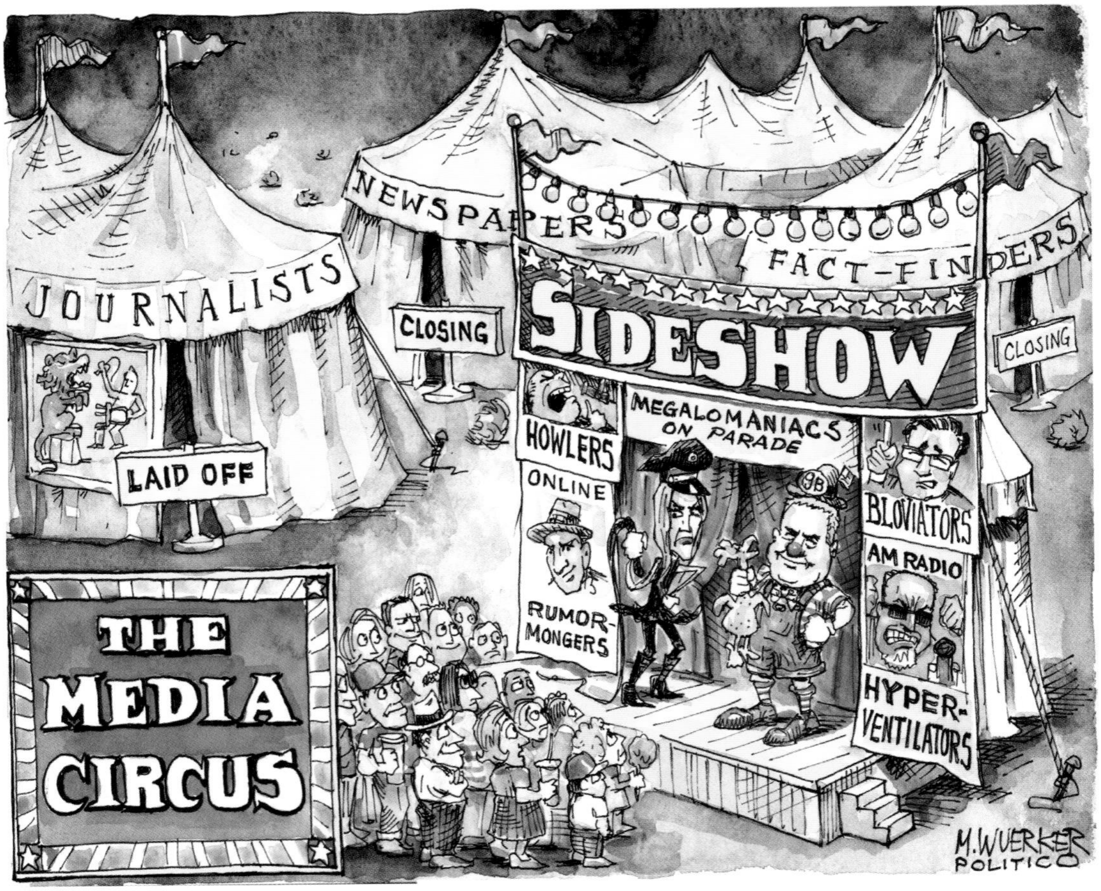
JOURNALISTS
NEWSPAPERS
FACT-FINDERS
CLOSING
CLOSING
SIDESHOW
LAID OFF
MEGALOMANIACS ON PARADE
HOWLERS
ONLINE
RUMOR-MONGERS
BLOVIATORS
AM RADIO
HYPER-VENTILATORS
THE MEDIA CIRCUS
M.WUERKER POLITICO

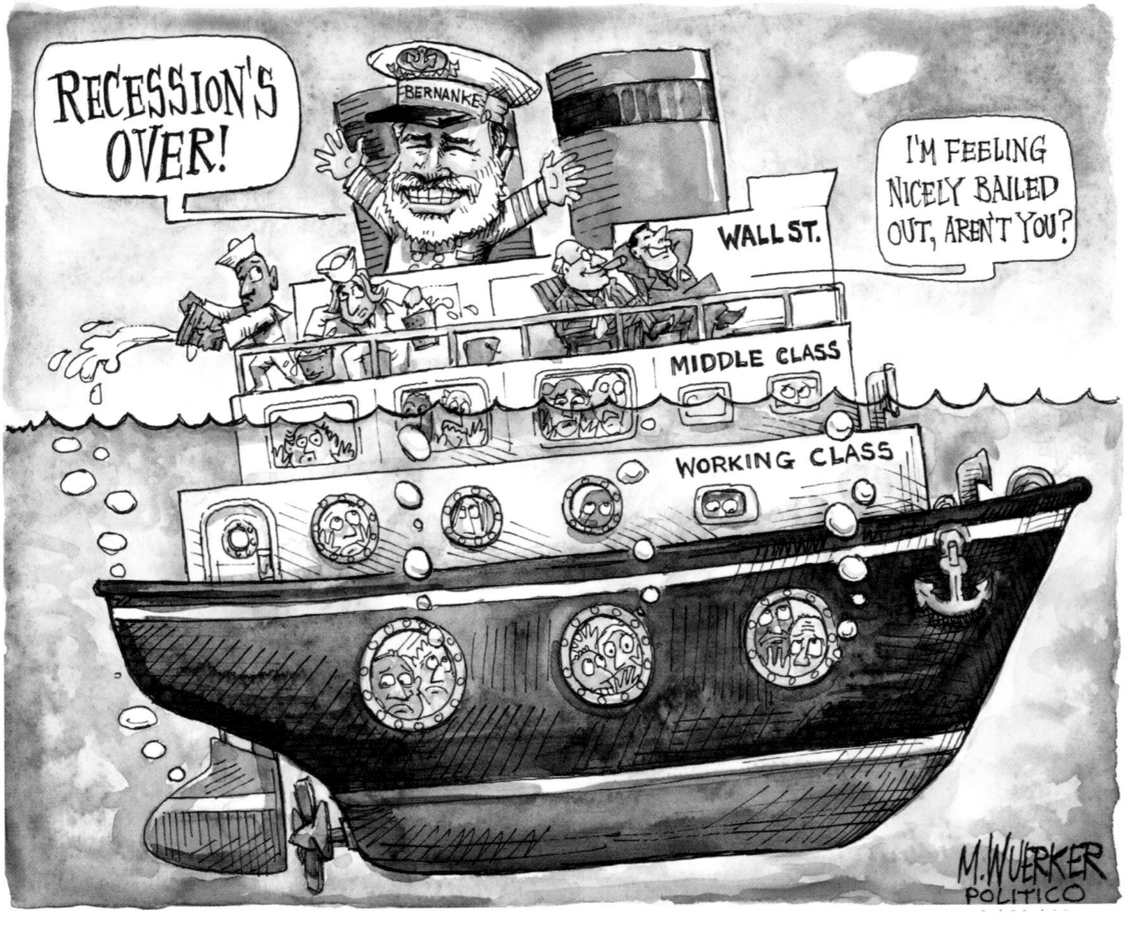
RECESSION'S OVER!
BERNANKE
I'M FEELING NICELY BAILED OUT, AREN'T YOU?
WALL ST.
MIDDLE CLASS
WORKING CLASS
M.WUERKER POLITICO

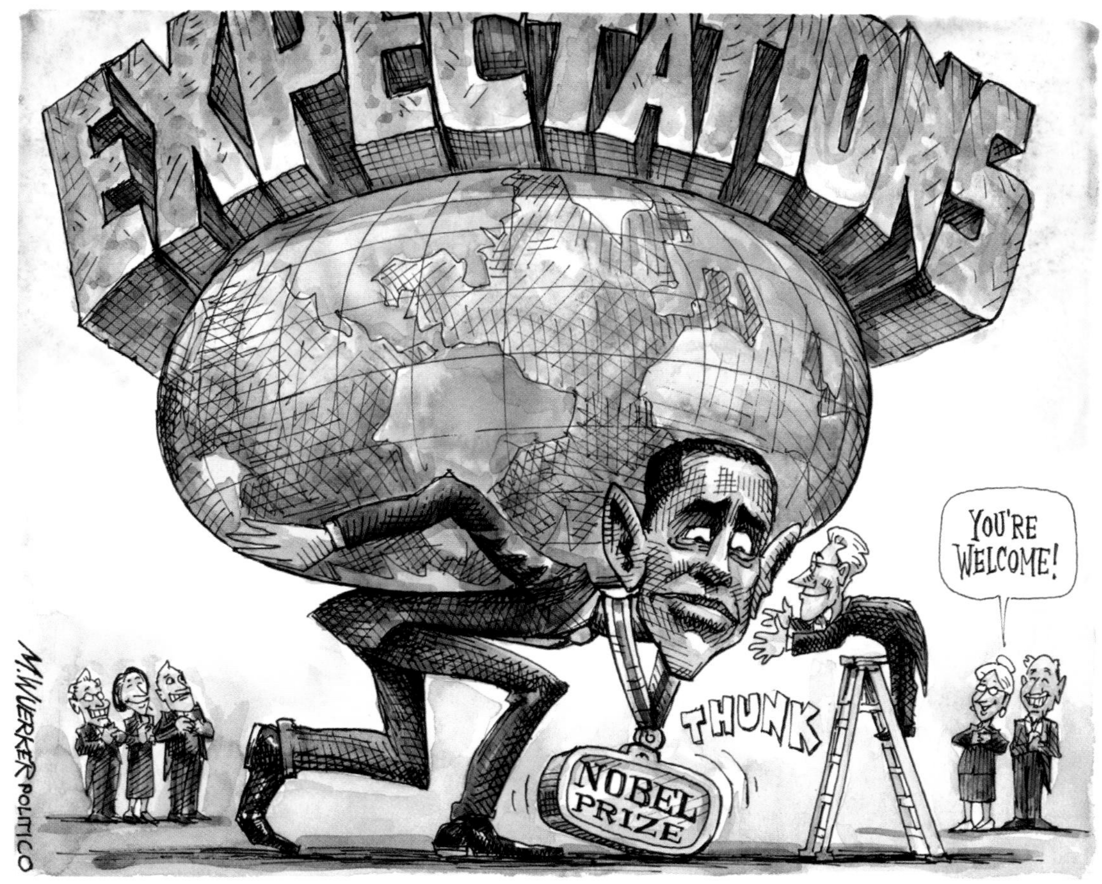
EXPECTATIONS
YOU'RE WELCOME!
THUNK
NOBEL PRIZE
M.WUERKER POLITICO

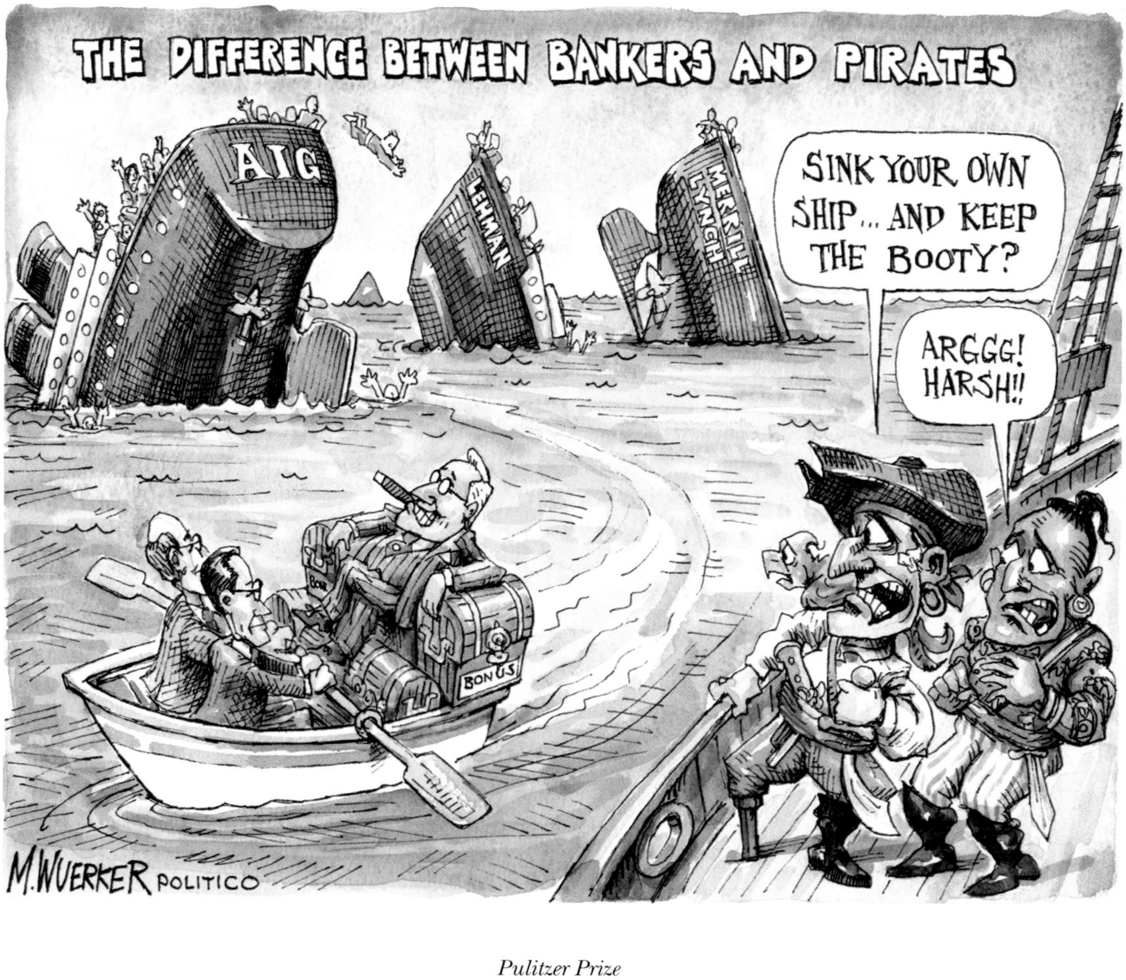
THE DIFFERENCE BETWEEN BANKERS AND PIRATES
AIG
LEHMAN
MERRILL LYNCH
SINK YOUR OWN SHIP... AND KEEP THE BOOTY?
ARGGG! HARSH!!
BONUS
M.WUERKER POLITICO

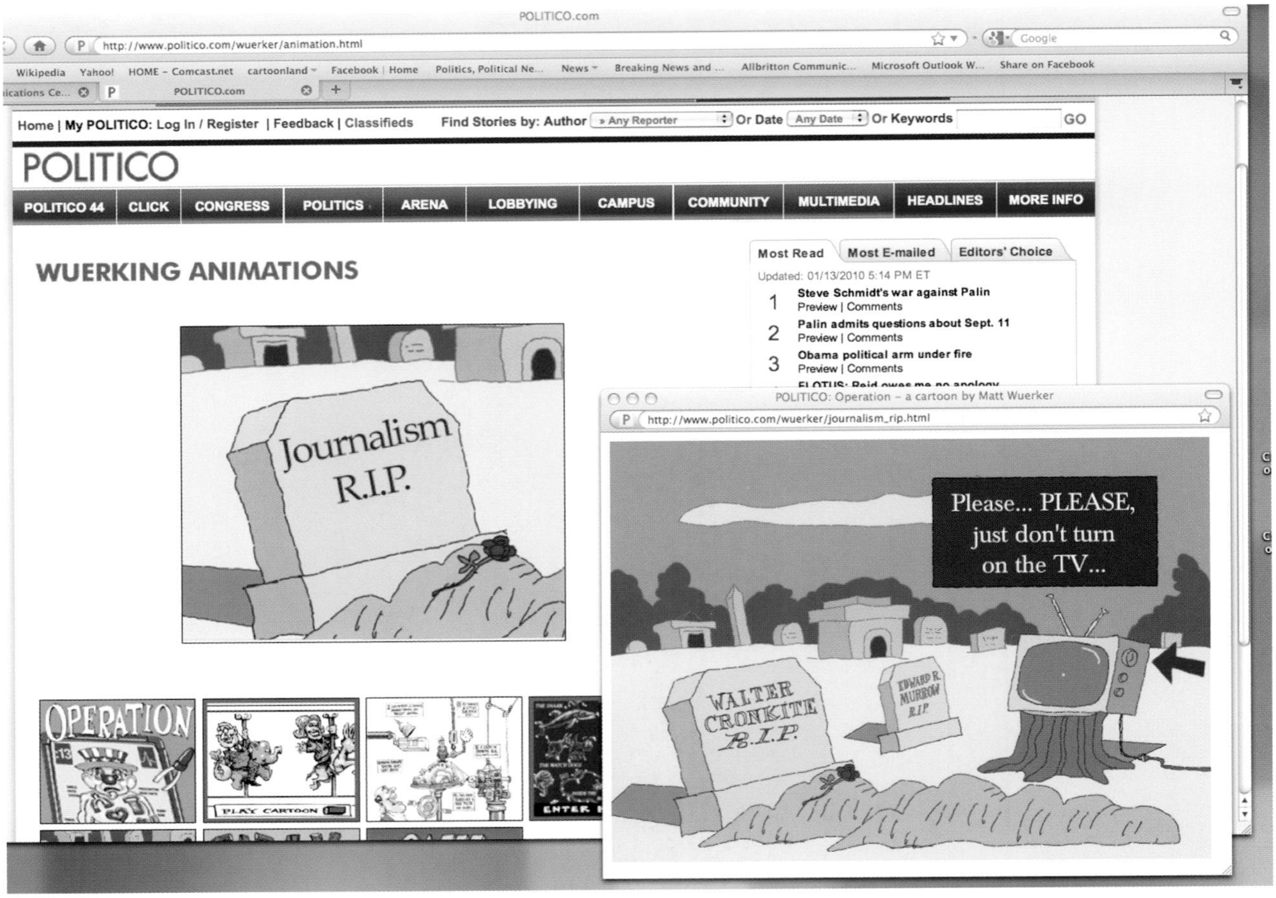
POLITICO.com
http://www.politico.com/wuerker/animation.html
Home | My POLITICO: Log In / Register | Feedback | Classifieds
Find Stories by: Author
Or Date
Or Keywords
GO
POLITICO
POLITICO 44
CLICK
CONGRESS
POLITICS
ARENA
LOBBYING
CAMPUS
COMMUNITY
MULTIMEDIA
HEADLINES
MORE INFO
WUERKING ANIMATIONS
Most Read
Most E-mailed
Editors' Choice
Updated: 01/13/2010 5:14 PM ET
1 Steve Schmidt's war against Palin
Preview | Comments
2 Palin admits questions about Sept. 11
Preview | Comments
3 Obama political arm under fire
Preview | Comments
Journalism R.I.P.
POLITICO: Operation - a cartoon by Matt Wuerker
http://www.politico.com/wuerker/journalism_rip.html
Please... PLEASE, just don't turn on the TV...
WALTER CRONKITE R.I.P.
EDWARD R. MURROW R.I.P.
OPERATION
PLAY CARTOON

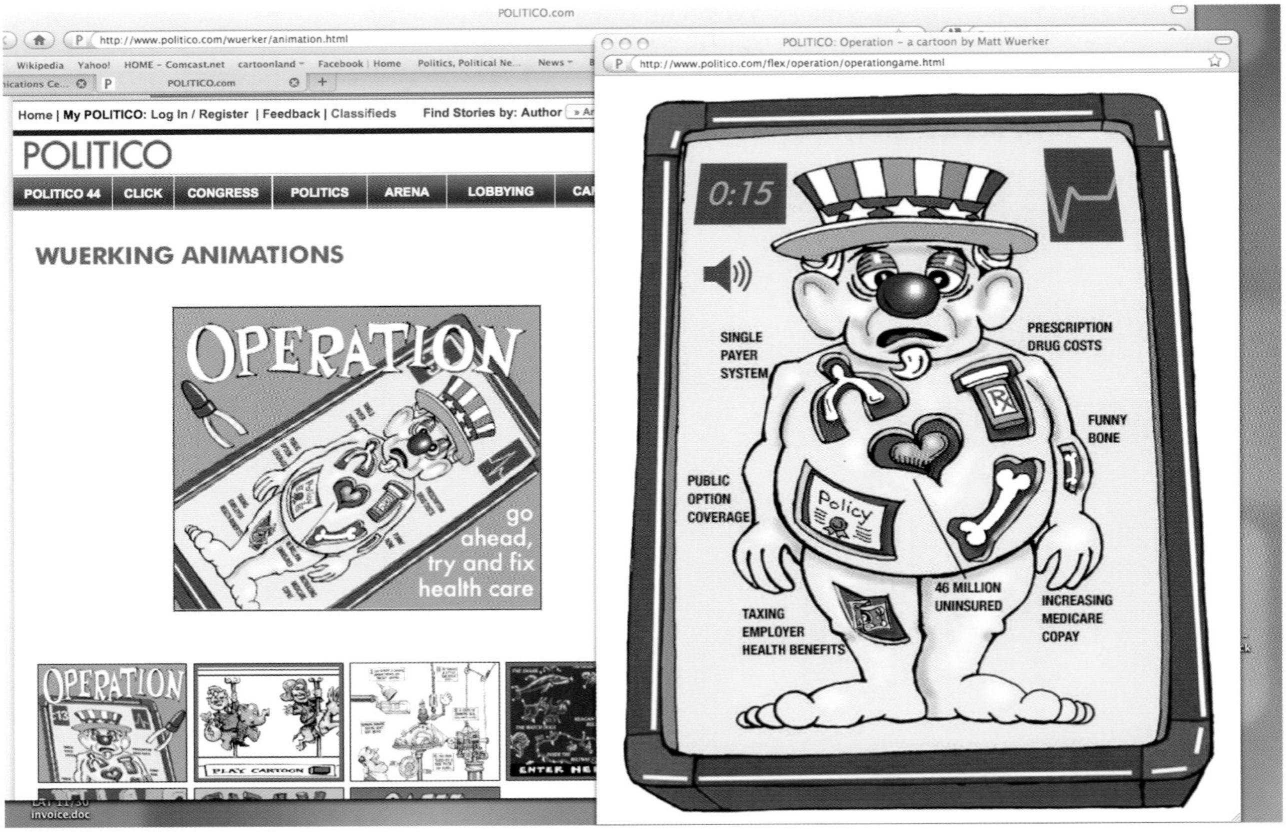
POLITICO.com
http://www.politico.com/wuerker/animation.html
Home | My POLITICO: Log In / Register | Feedback | Classifieds
Find Stories by: Author
POLITICO
POLITICO 44
CLICK
CONGRESS
POLITICS
ARENA
LOBBYING
WUERKING ANIMATIONS
OPERATION
go ahead, try and fix health care
PLAY CARTOON
POLITICO: Operation - a cartoon by Matt Wuerker
http://www.politico.com/flex/operation/operationgame.html
0:15
SINGLE PAYER SYSTEM
PRESCRIPTION DRUG COSTS
FUNNY BONE
PUBLIC OPTION COVERAGE
Policy
46 MILLION UNINSURED
TAXING EMPLOYER HEALTH BENEFITS
INCREASING MEDICARE COPAY

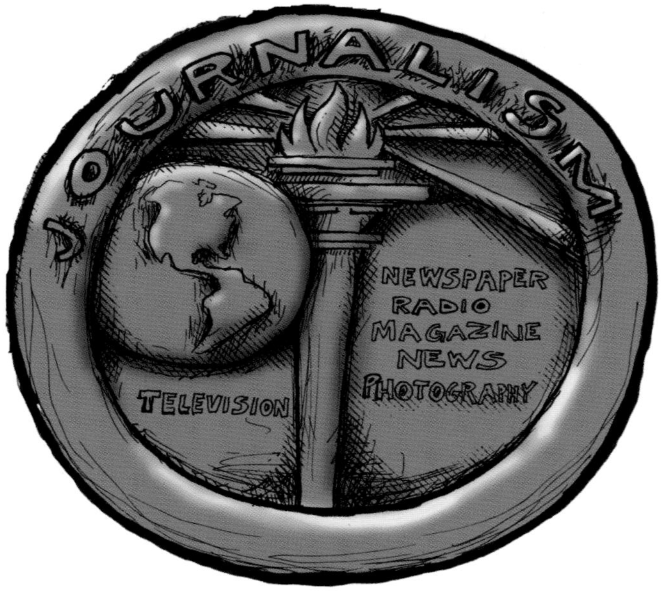
JOURNALISM
NEWSPAPER
RADIO
MAGAZINE
NEWS
PHOTOGRAPHY
TELEVISION

National Headliner Awards

The Press Club of Atlantic City founded the National Headliner Awards in 1934, and the awards are one of the oldest and largest national contests recognizing journalistic merit. First presented in 1935, National Headliner medallions have been presented to more than sixteen hundred outstanding writers, photographers, daily newspapers, editorial cartoonists, graphic artists, radio and television stations, and news syndicates. Membership in the National Headliner Club is exclusive to past recipients and the men and women who annually serve as consultants and judges for the program.

Unpaid volunteers do the majority of the work related to the National Headliner Awards, distinguishing it from those award programs supported by universities or foundations. These volunteers sift through hundreds of entries in three main categories and sixty-two subcategories. The three main categories are Print and Graphics, Online Journalism, and Radio and Television (Broadcast). Editorial cartooning is one of sixteen subcategories in the Daily Newspapers and News Syndicates Division of the Print and Graphics category. The entries are painstakingly catalogued and prepared for judging with each being prescreened before being sent to the final judging panel in order to distill the strongest entries.

2010 National Headliner Award Winner
Mike Peters, *Dayton Daily News*

Mike Peters was unavailable for this edition.

2010 National Headliner Award Second Place
Dana Summers, *Orlando Sentinel*

Dana Summers joined the *Orlando Sentinel* in May 1982 following two years in the same position with the *Dayton (OH) Journal Herald*. From 1977 to 1980, he was a staff artist at the *Fayetteville (NC) Times*.

Summers's cartoons are syndicated nationally by Tribune Media Services and appear regularly in such publications as the *New York Times*, the *Washington Post, Time, Newsweek*, and *USA Today*. He and *Sentinel* cartoonist Ralph Dunagin are co-creators of the popular strip "The Middletons." He is also the creator of "Bound and Gagged," a comic strip seen in one hundred papers nationally and internationally.

Born in Lawrence, Massachusetts, Summers is a graduate of the Art Institute of Boston and has attended Massachusetts College of Art. He started cartooning during the 1970s, freelancing for weekly and college newspapers in Massachusetts.

Among his many honors are the Citation of Excellence, twice awarded to him by the Overseas Press Club; the John Fischetti Editorial Cartoon Competition Award; and the Society of Professional Journalists' Sigma Delta Chi Southeast Award, which he has won three times.

Summers and his wife, Mary Jane, are parents of three and live in Orlando, Florida.

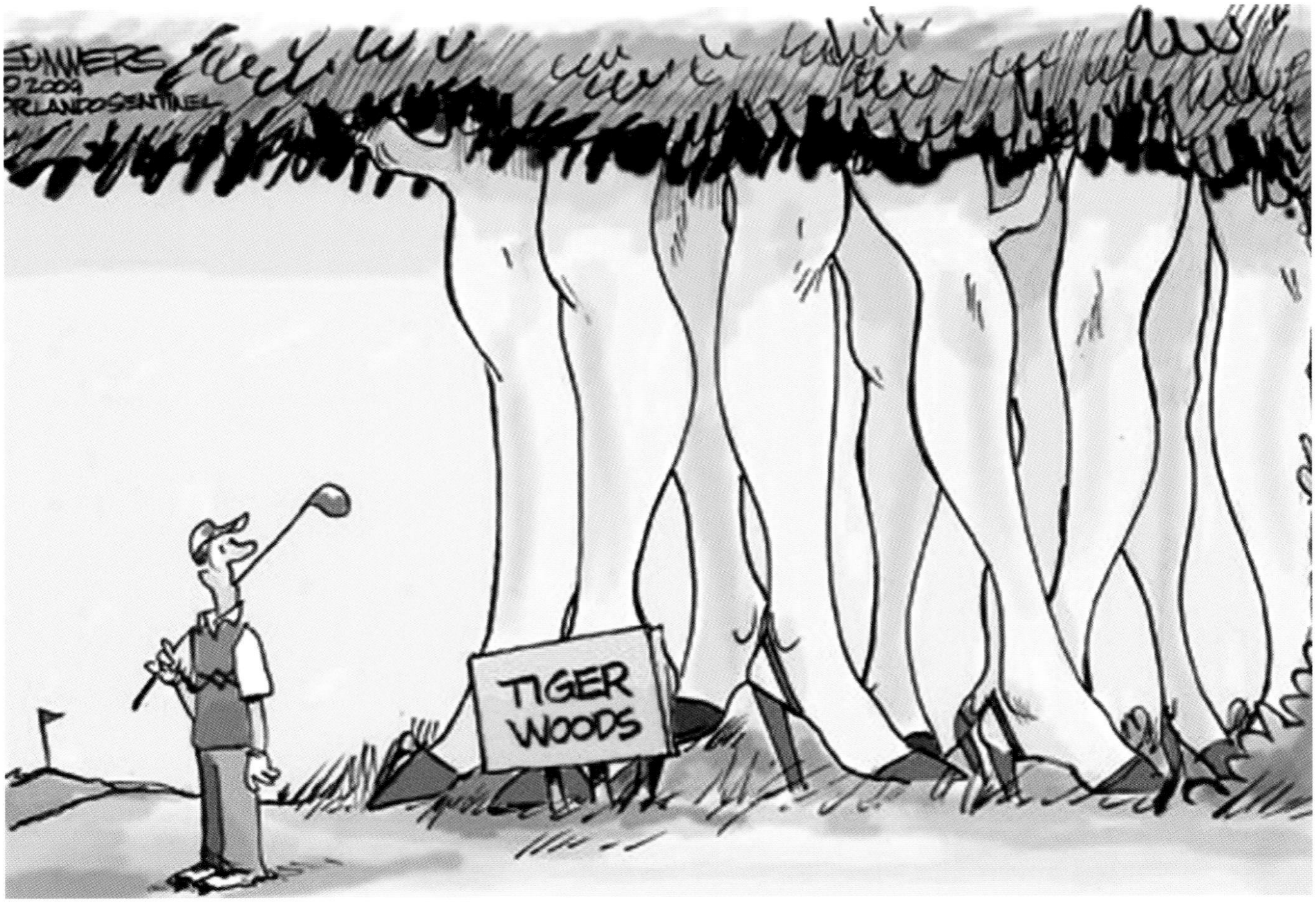
SUMMERS
©2009
ORLANDO SENTINEL
TIGER WOODS

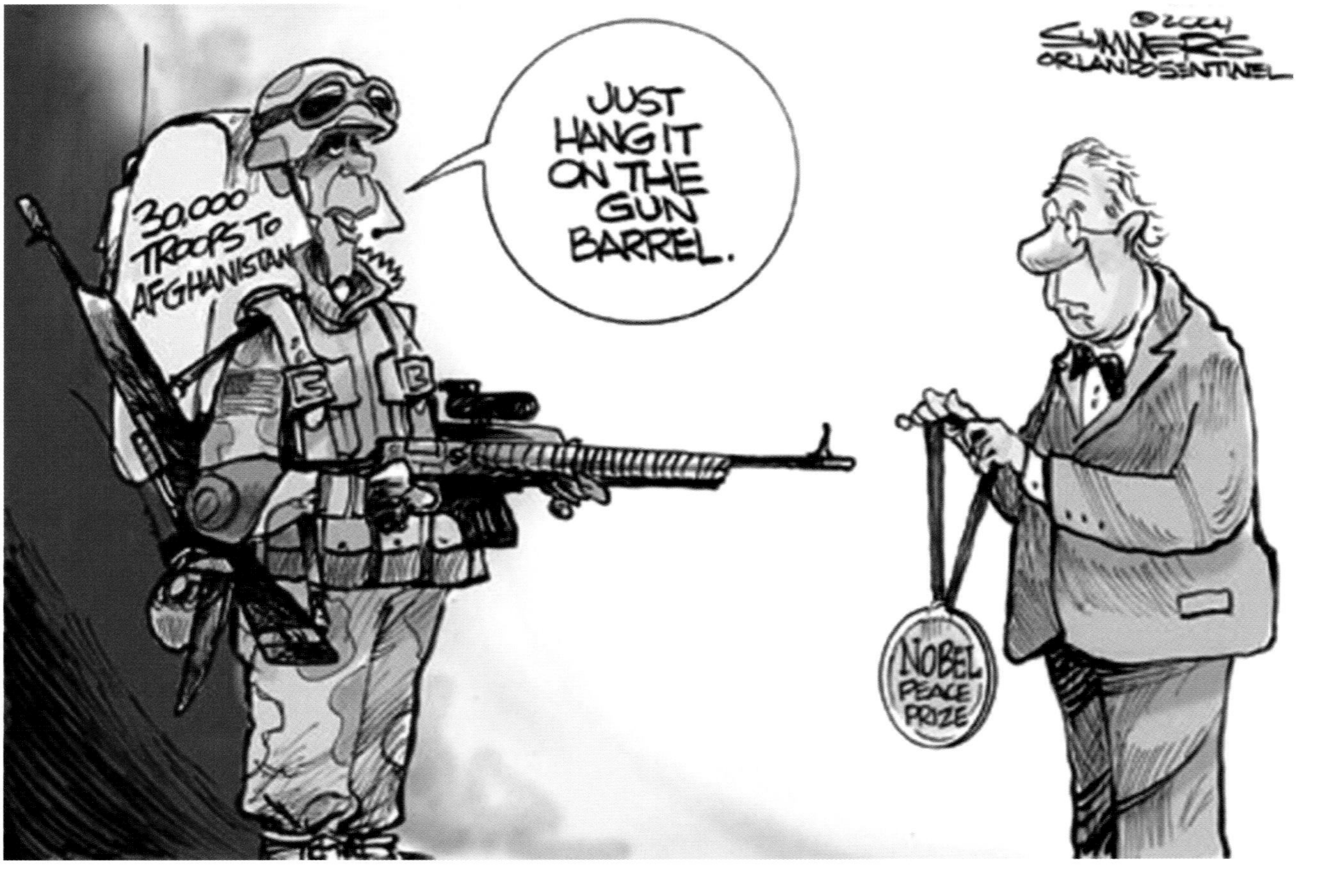
©2009
SUMMERS
ORLANDO SENTINEL
JUST HANG IT ON THE GUN BARREL.
30,000 TROOPS TO AFGHANISTAN
NOBEL PEACE PRIZE

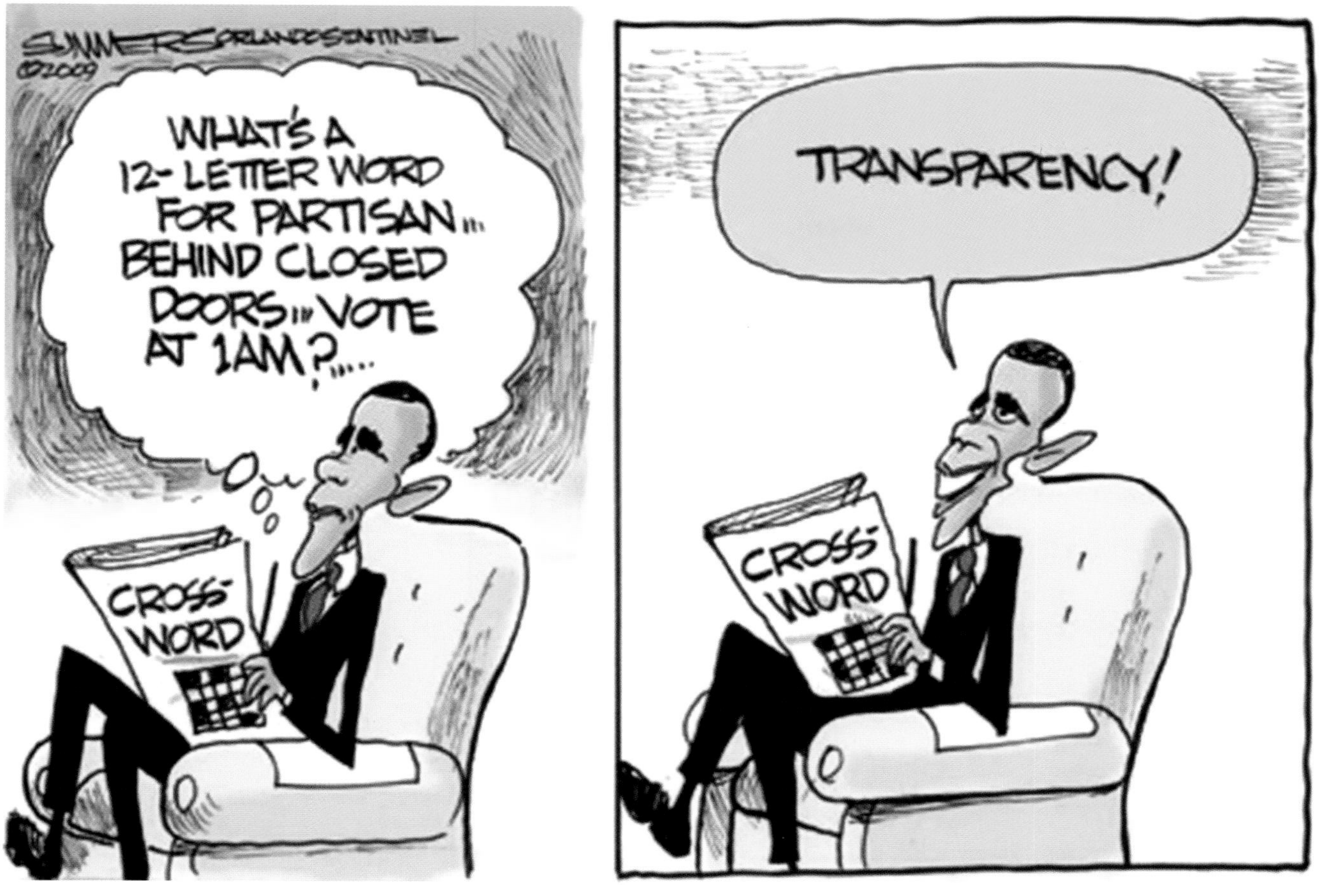
SUMMERS ORLANDO SENTINEL ©2009
WHAT'S A 12-LETTER WORD FOR PARTISAN... BEHIND CLOSED DOORS... VOTE AT 1AM?.....
CROSS-WORD
TRANSPARENCY!
CROSS-WORD

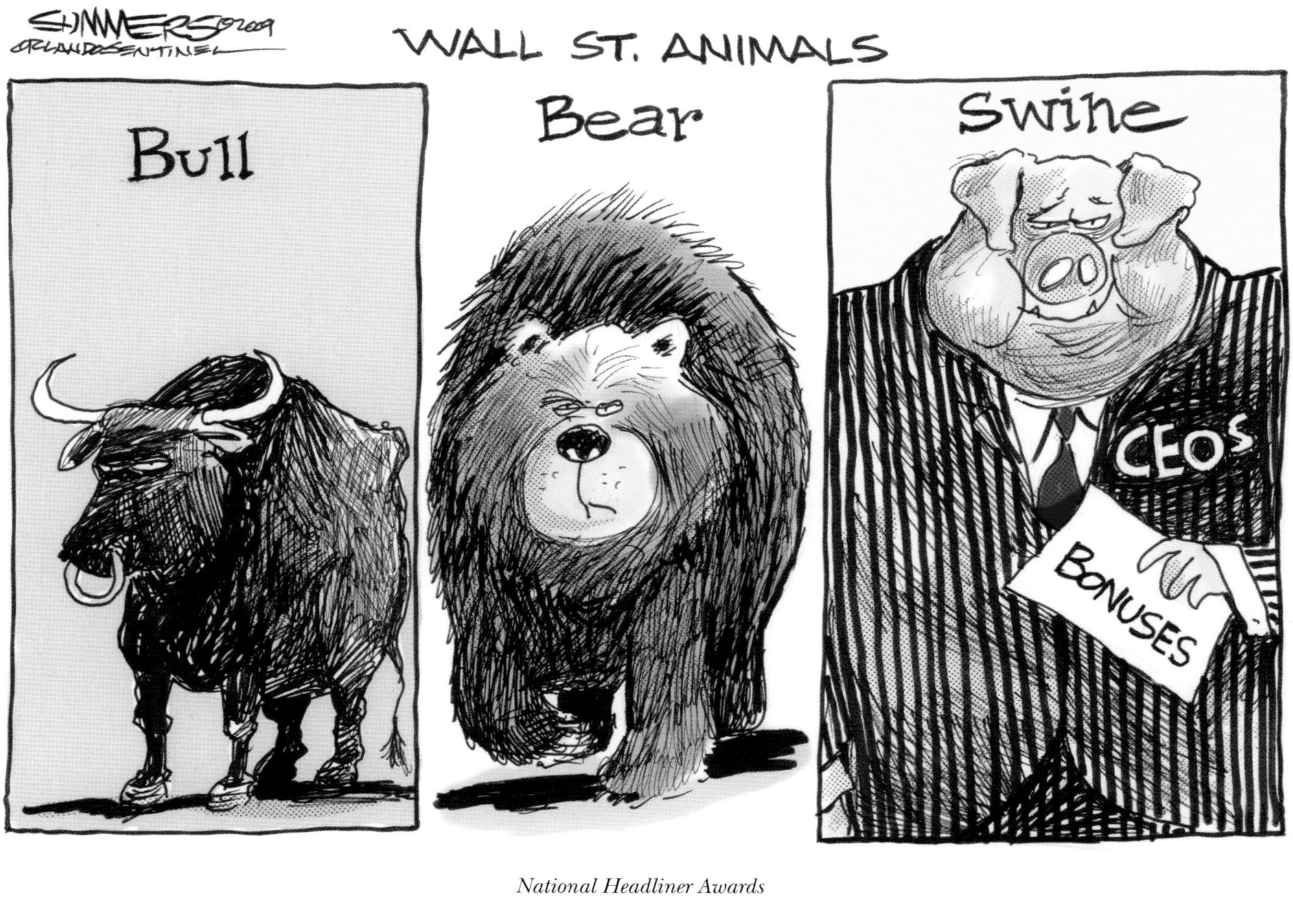
SUMMERS ©2009 ORLANDO SENTINEL
WALL ST. ANIMALS
Bull
Bear
Swine
CEOS
BONUSES

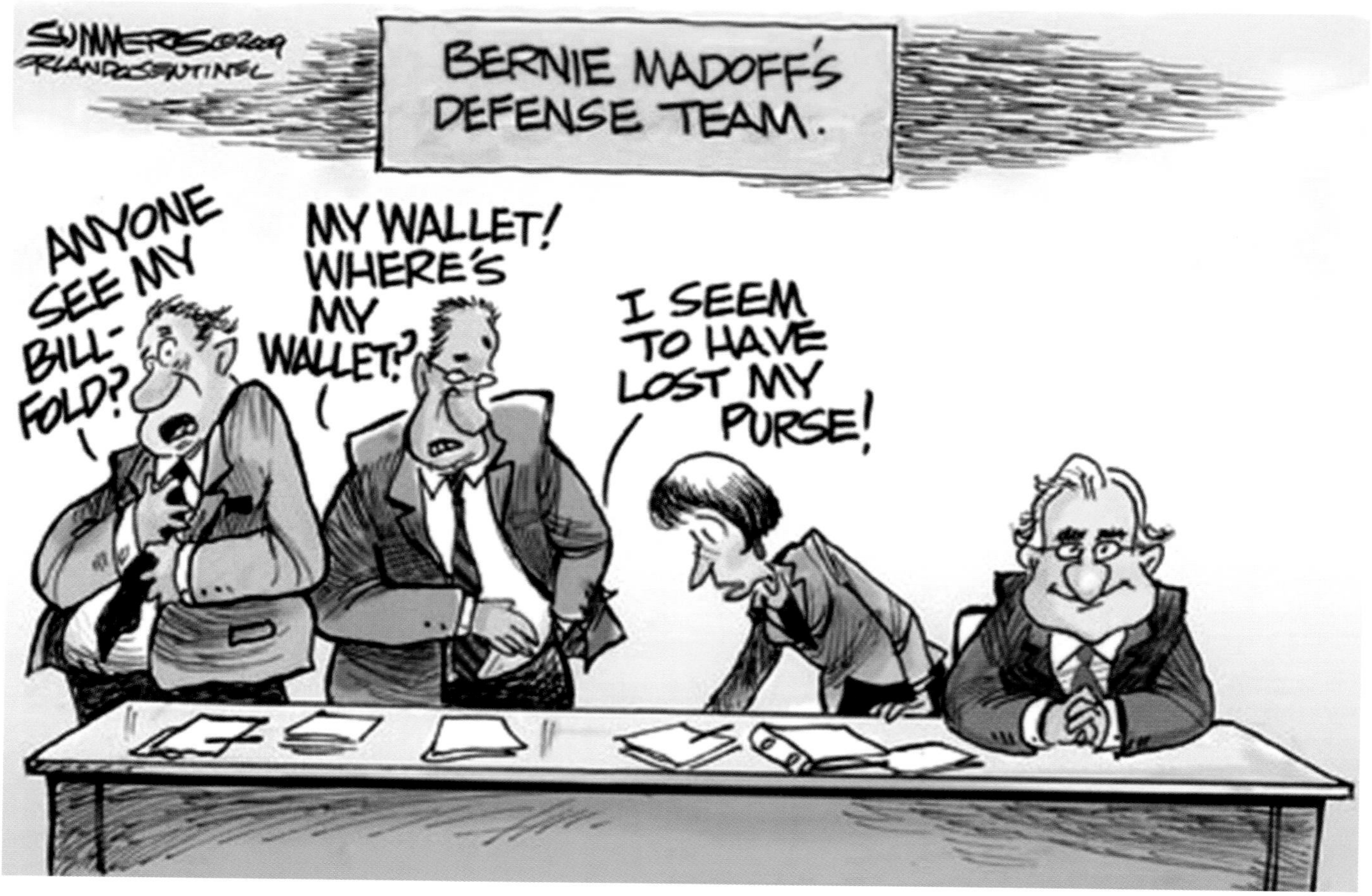
SUMMERS ©2009 ORLANDO SENTINEL
BERNIE MADOFF'S DEFENSE TEAM.
ANYONE SEE MY BILL-FOLD?
MY WALLET! WHERE'S MY WALLET?
I SEEM TO HAVE LOST MY PURSE!

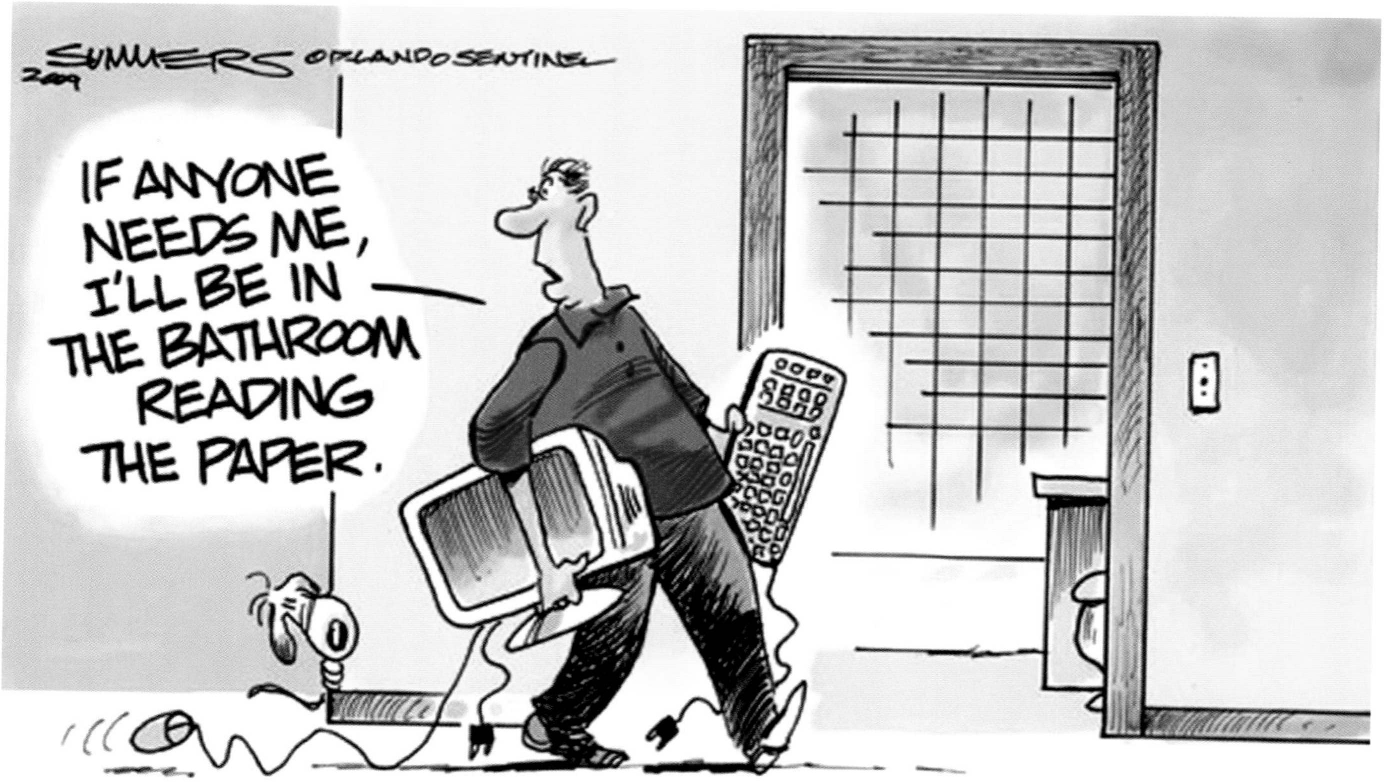
SUMMERS 2009 ORLANDO SENTINEL
IF ANYONE NEEDS ME, I'LL BE IN THE BATHROOM READING THE PAPER.

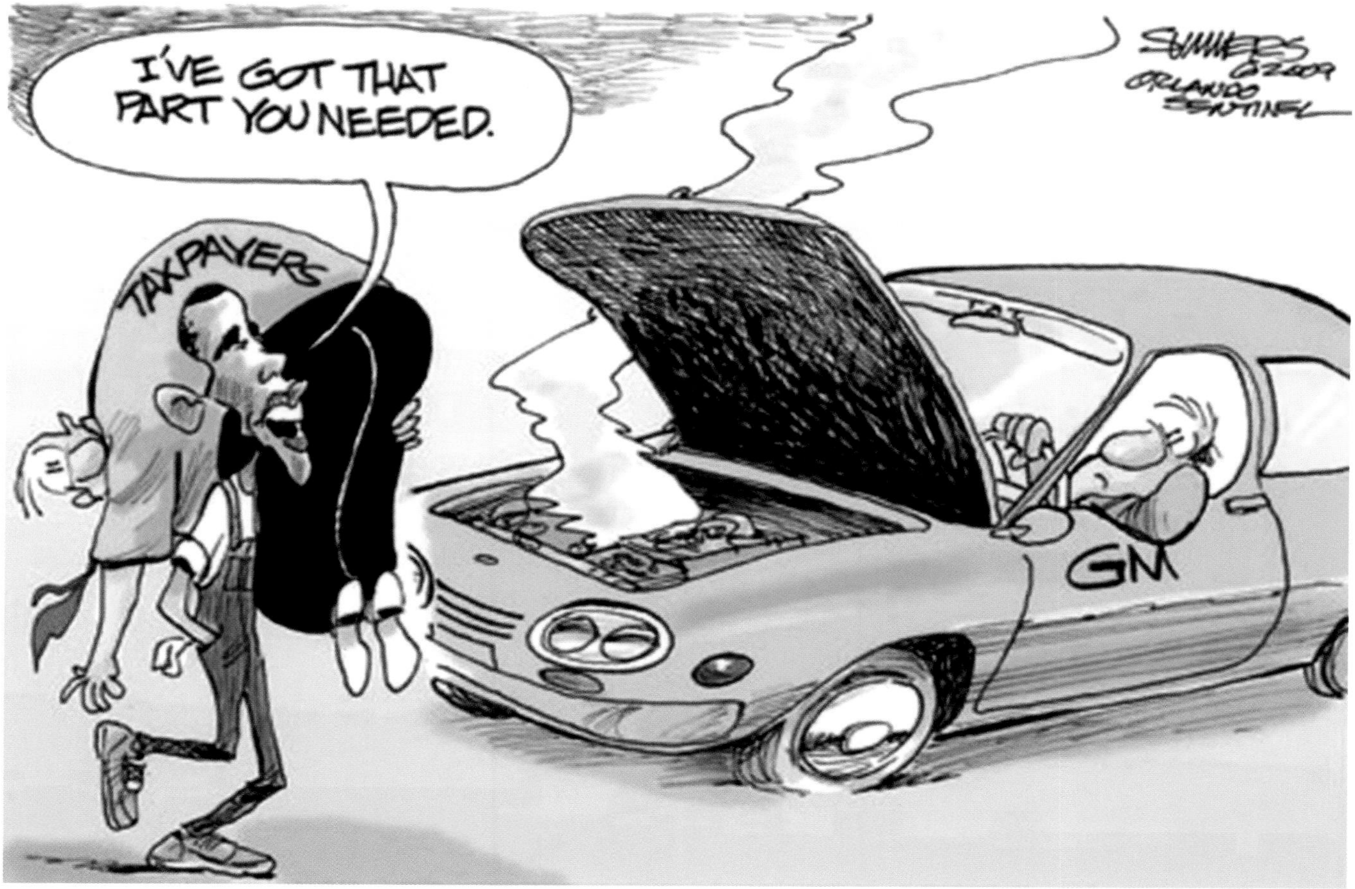
I'VE GOT THAT PART YOU NEEDED.
TAXPAYERS
GM
SUMMERS ©2009 ORLANDO SENTINEL

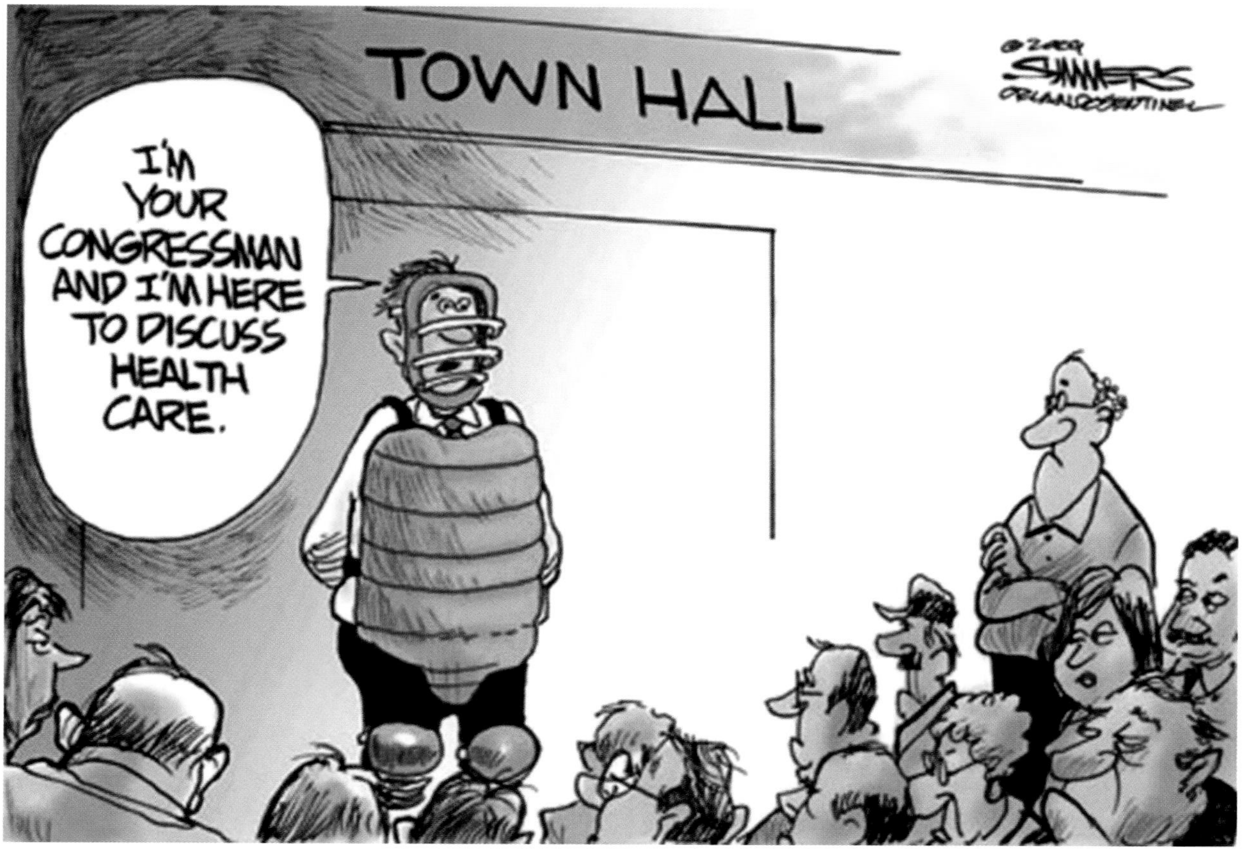
TOWN HALL
I'M YOUR CONGRESSMAN AND I'M HERE TO DISCUSS HEALTH CARE.
©2009 SUMMERS ORLANDO SENTINEL

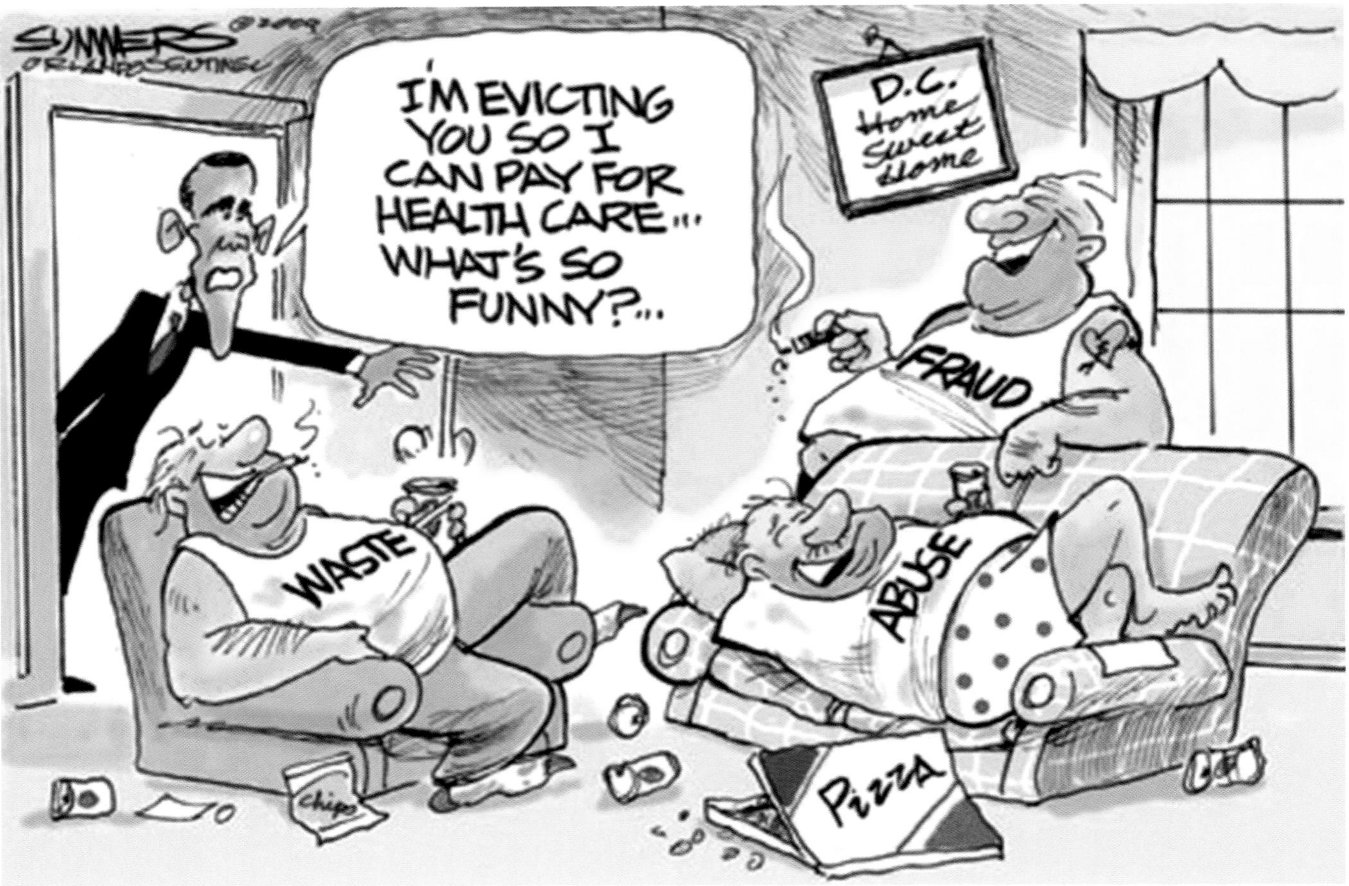
SUMMERS ©2009 ORLANDO SENTINEL
I'M EVICTING YOU SO I CAN PAY FOR HEALTH CARE... WHAT'S SO FUNNY?...
D.C. Home Sweet Home
FRAUD
WASTE
ABUSE
Pizza
Chips

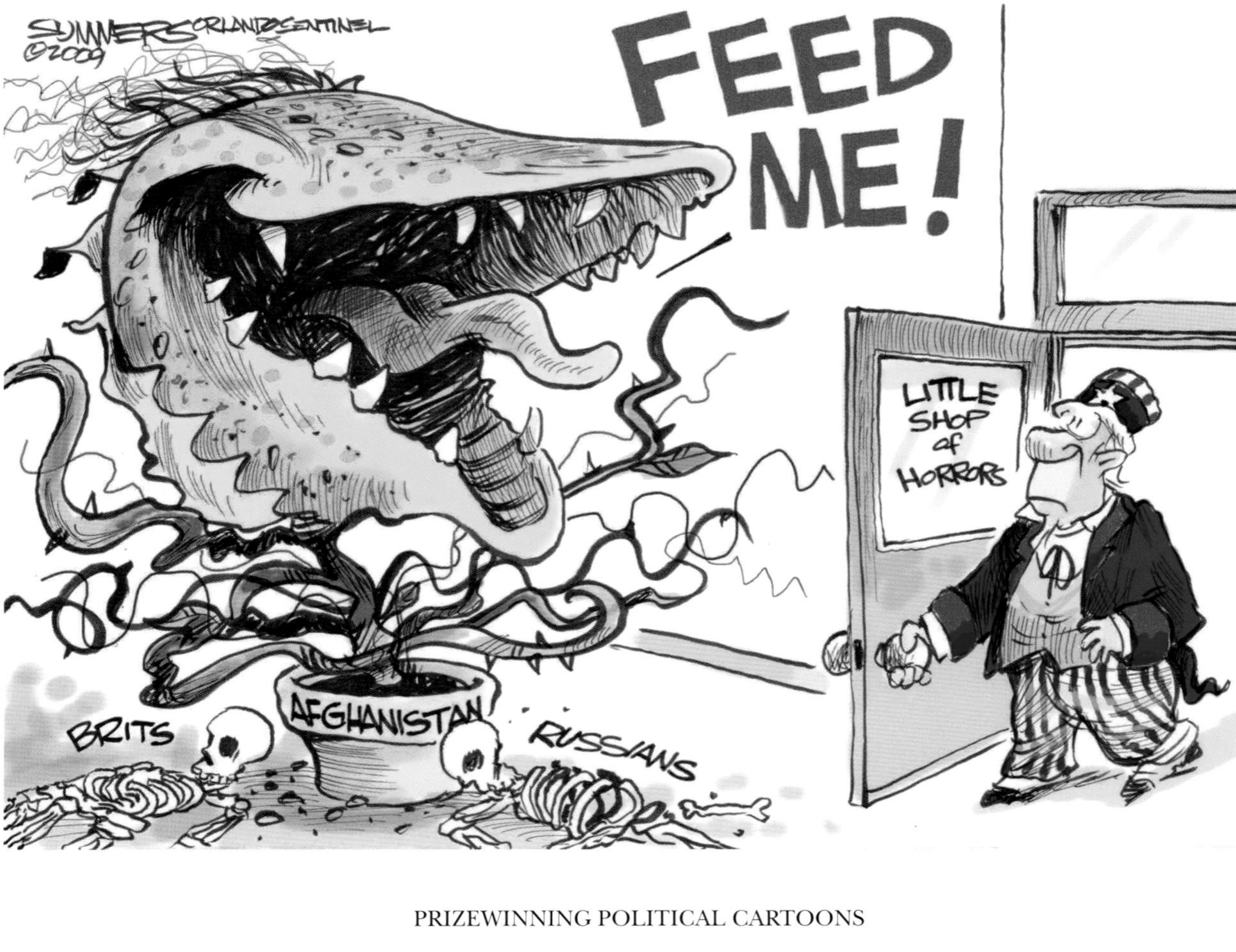
SUMMERS ORLANDO SENTINEL ©2009
FEED ME!
LITTLE SHOP of HORRORS
AFGHANISTAN
BRITS
RUSSIANS

2010 National Headliner Award Third Place
Stephen P. Breen, *San Diego Union-Tribune*

Stephen P. Breen was born in Los Angeles in 1970 and attended the University of California, Riverside. He has served as the editorial cartoonist for the *San Diego Union-Tribune* since 2001. His work is nationally syndicated by Creators News Service and regularly appears in *USA Today,* the *New York Times,* and *Newsweek.* The year 2009 was a banner year for Breen with a fantastic triple win, including his second Pulitzer Prize for editorial cartooning, having won in 1998 and 2009; the Overseas Press Club's Thomas Nast Award; and the National Headliner Award. He is also the recipient of the 2007 Berryman Award for editorial cartooning given by the National Press Foundation. Breen also won this year's Fischetti Award, which is highlighted later in this volume.

In his spare time, Breen writes and illustrates picture books for Penguin including *Stick, Violet the Pilot,* and *The Secret of Santa's Island.*

Breen lives in San Diego with his wife and four children and is truly a great human being. He enjoys reading, running, playing the guitar and piano, and watching old movies on cable. He has also been a friend and supporter of this series of books.

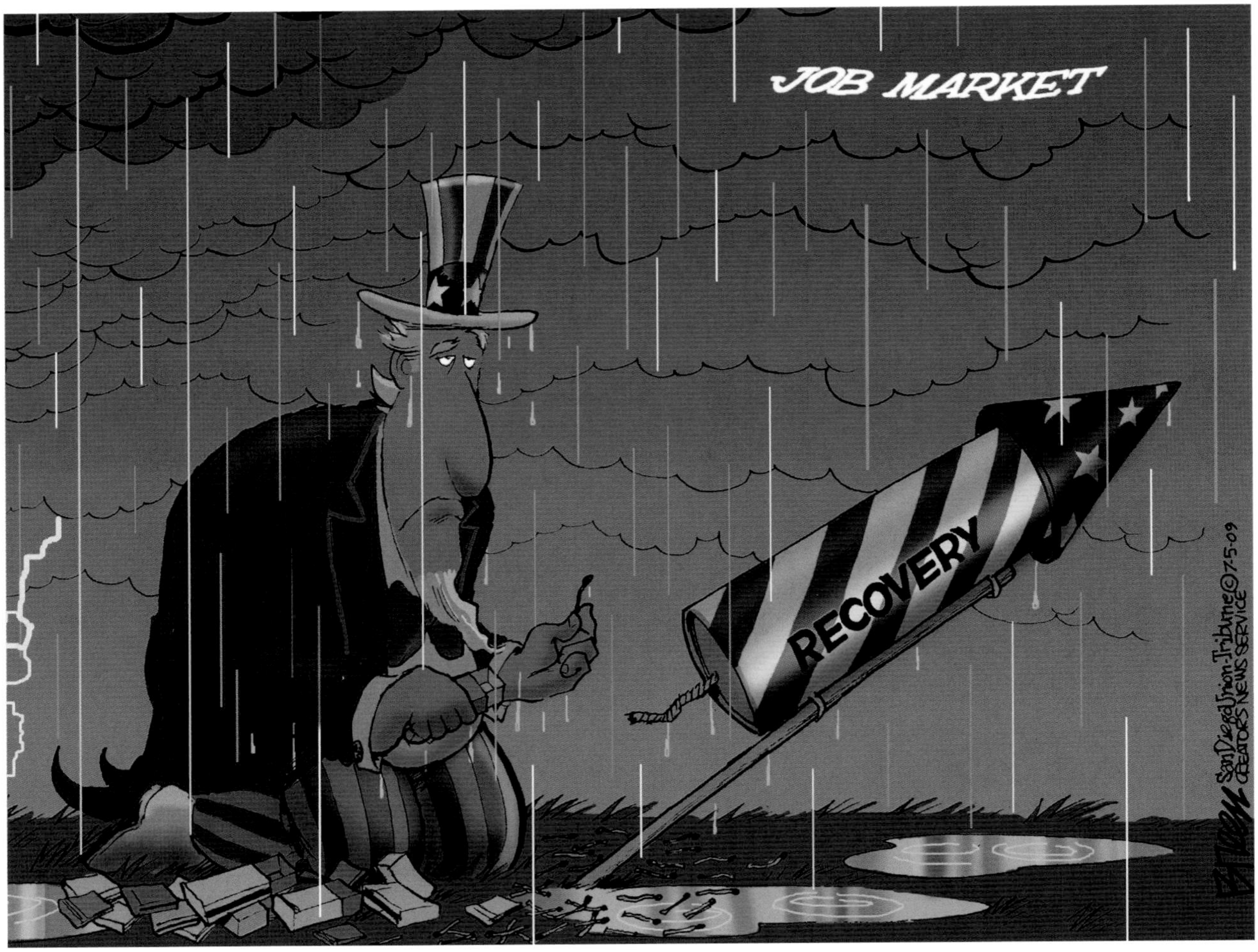
JOB MARKET
RECOVERY
San Diego Union-Tribune ©7-5-09
CREATORS NEWS SERVICE

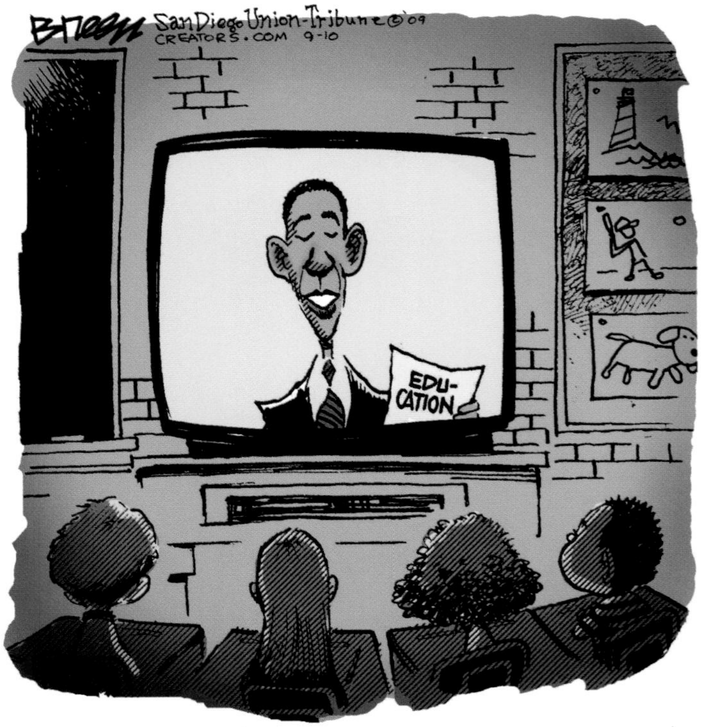
San Diego Union-Tribune ©'09
CREATORS.COM 9-10
EDU-
CATION

ADDRESSING STUDENTS

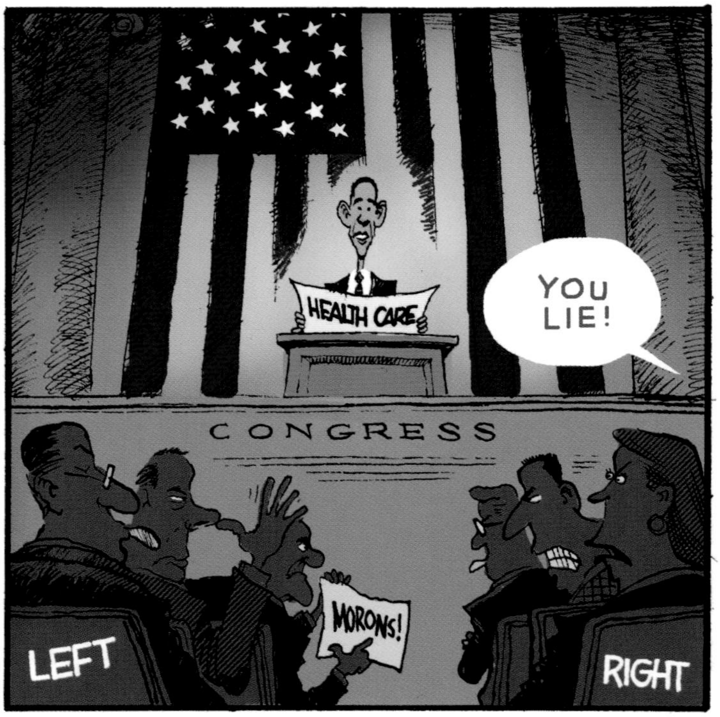
HEALTH CARE
YOU
LIE!
CONGRESS
MORONS!
LEFT
RIGHT

ADDRESSING CHILDREN

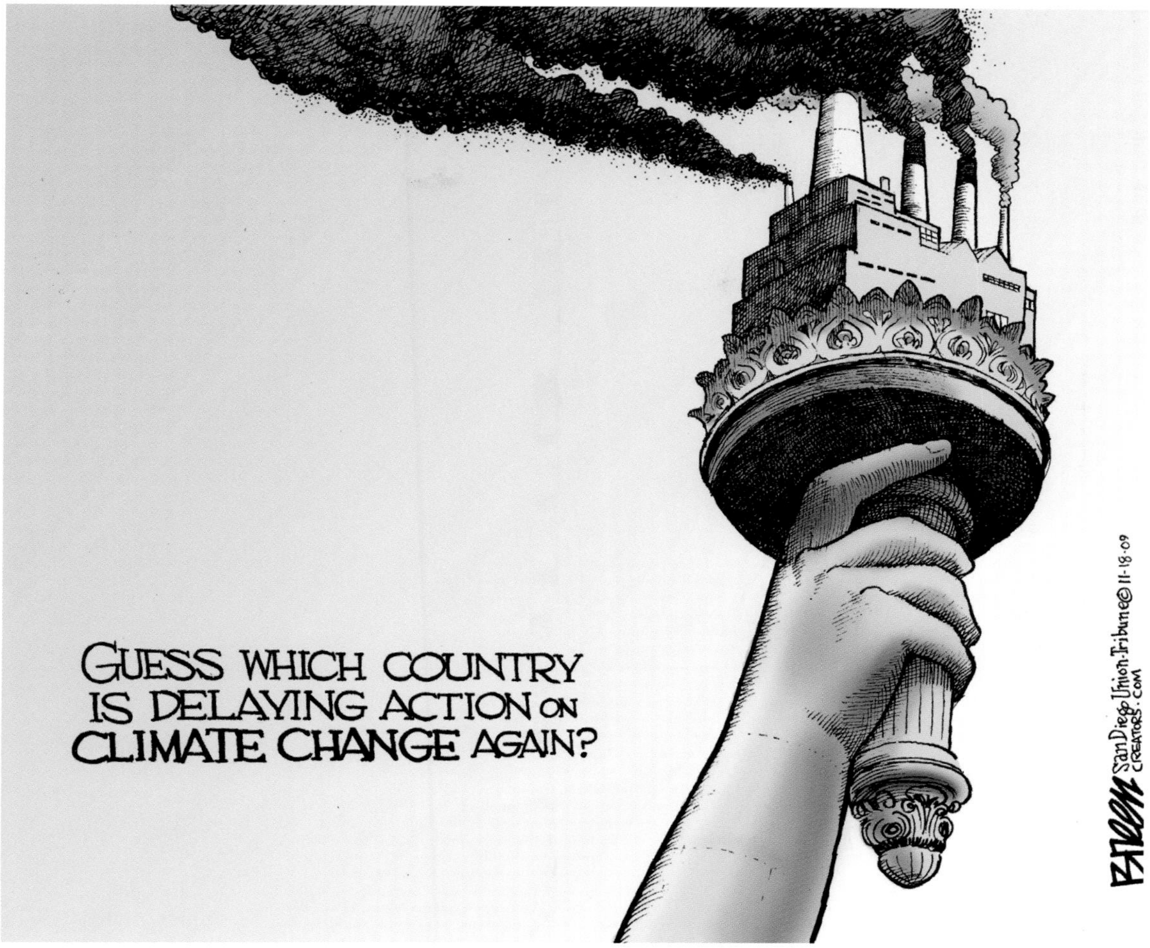
GUESS WHICH COUNTRY
IS DELAYING ACTION ON
CLIMATE CHANGE AGAIN?
San Diego Union-Tribune © 11-18-09
CREATORS.COM

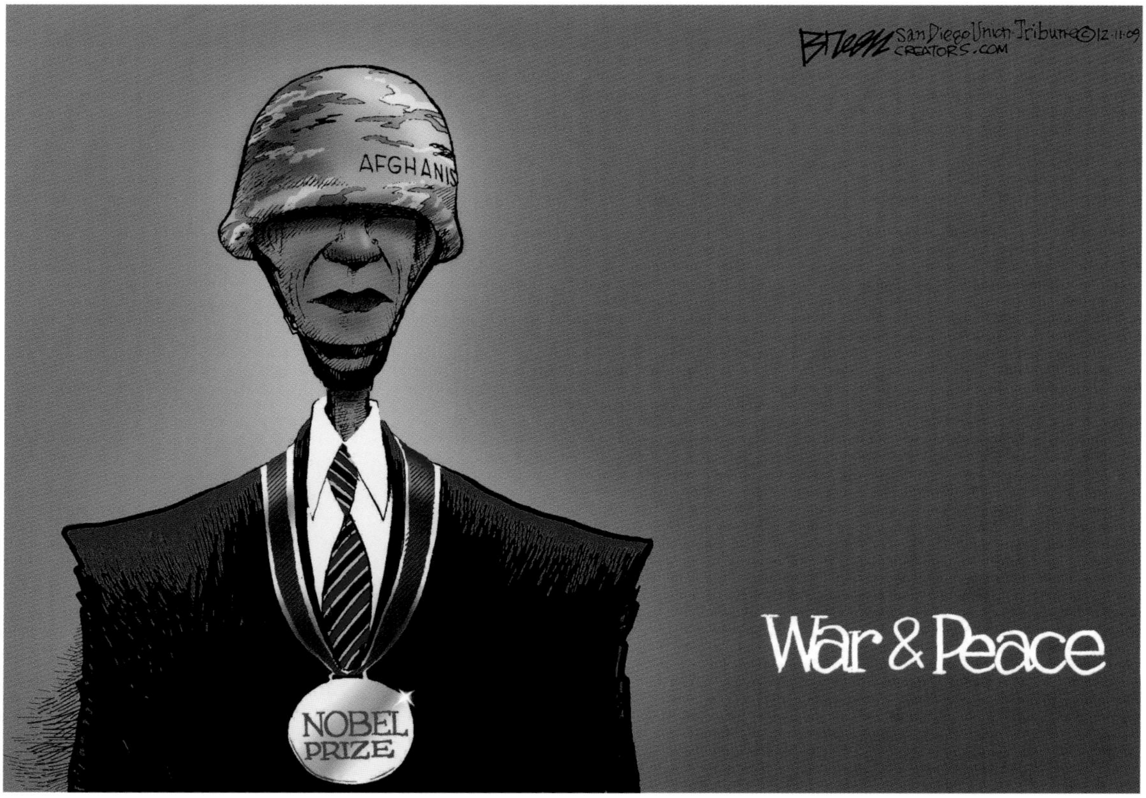
San Diego Union-Tribune © 12-11-09
CREATORS.COM
AFGHANIS
NOBEL
PRIZE
War & Peace

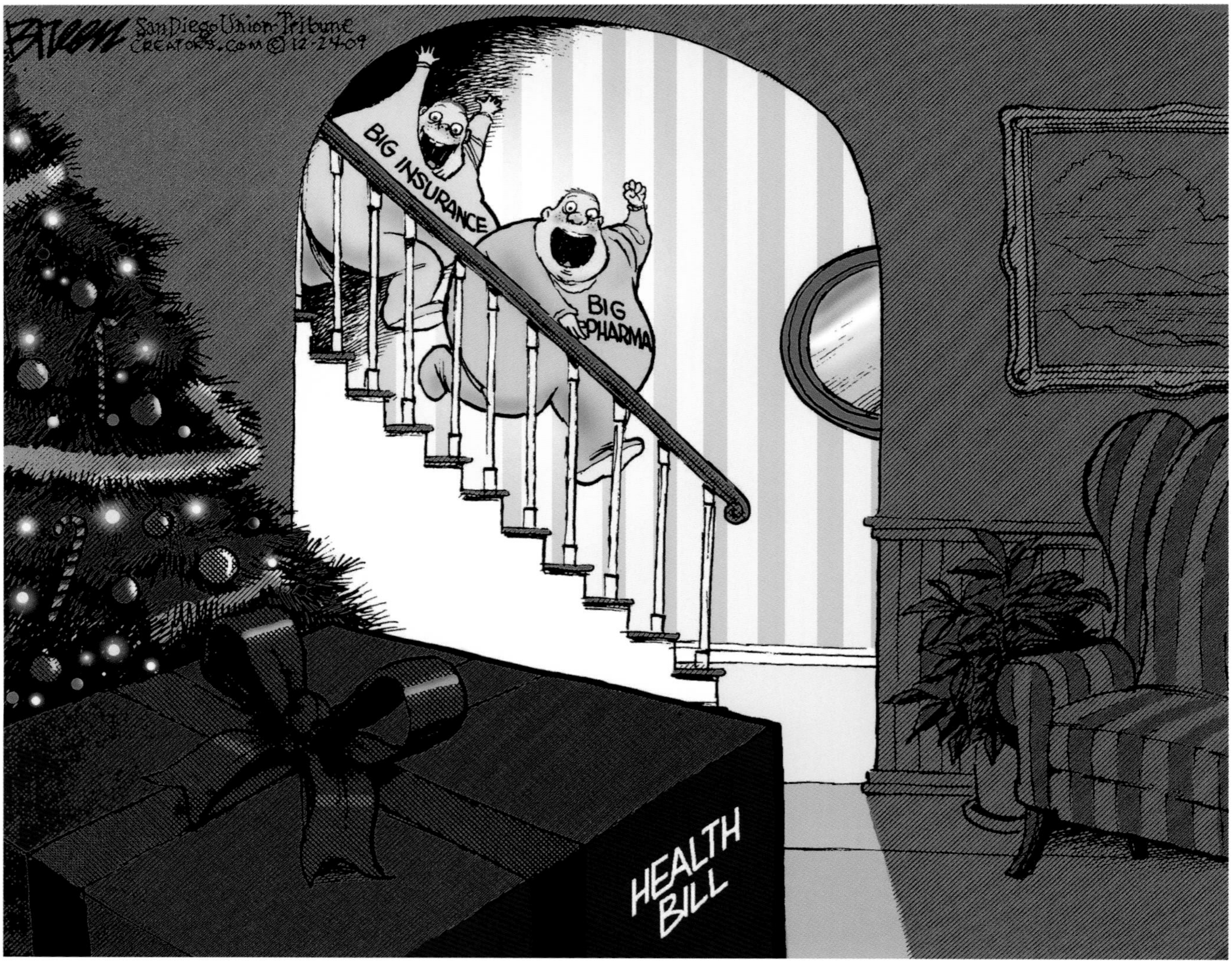
San Diego Union-Tribune
CREATORS.COM © 12-24-09
BIG INSURANCE
BIG PHARMA
HEALTH BILL

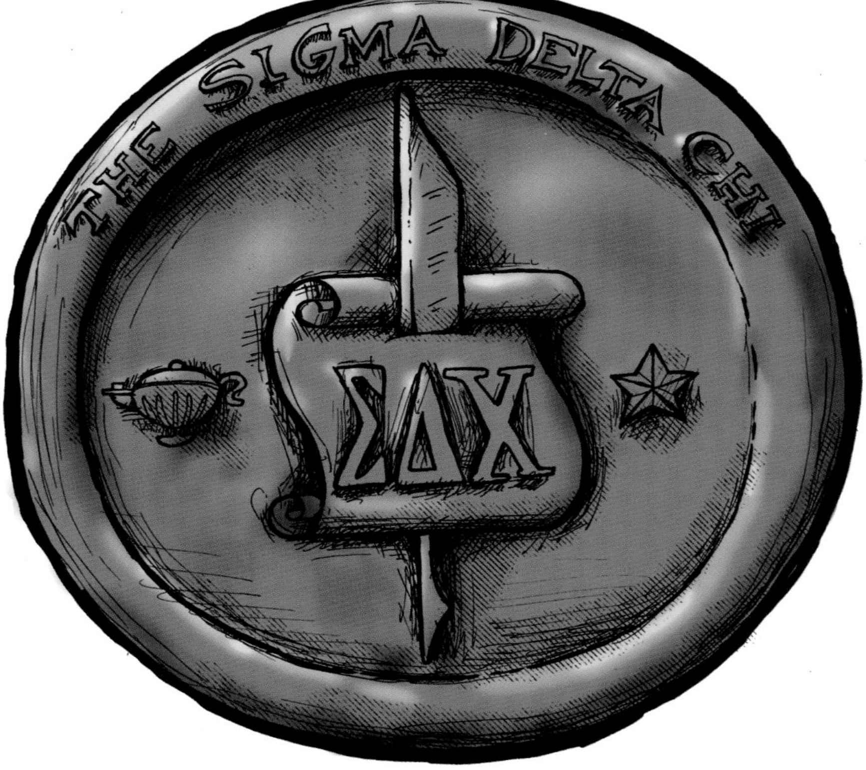
THE SIGMA DELTA CHI
ΣΔΧ

Society of Professional Journalists' Sigma Delta Chi Awards

Founded in 1909 as Sigma Delta Chi, the Society of Professional Journalists is the nation's most broad-based journalism organization. The society is dedicated to encouraging the free practice of journalism and stimulating high standards of ethical behavior. With a membership of nearly ten thousand, the organization promotes the free flow of information vital to a well-informed citizenry. It works to inspire and educate current and future journalists through professional development, protecting First Amendment guarantees of freedom of speech and press through its advocacy efforts.

Each year the Society of Professional Journalists sponsors the Sigma Delta Chi Awards. The awards date back to 1932 when the society first honored six individuals for their contributions to the field of journalism. The awards in their current form began in 1939 when the first Distinguished Service Awards were handed out. The name Sigma Delta Chi was introduced somewhat later.

Founded in 1961, the Sigma Delta Chi Foundation, with which the awards have become associated, supports the educational programs of the Society of Professional Journalists and serves the professional needs of the journalists and students pursuing a career in journalism.

The Sigma Delta Chi Awards cover print, radio, television, newsletters, photography, online, and research.

2009 Society of Professional Journalists' Sigma Delta Chi Award Winner
(Newspaper Circulation 100,001+ or Affiliated Website/National Magazine)
Jack Ohman, *Oregonian*

Jack Ohman was unavailable for this edition.

2009 Society of Professional Journalists' Sigma Delta Chi Award Winner
(Newspaper Circulation 50,001-100,000 or Online Independent)
Dwayne Booth, Harpers.org

Dwayne "Mr. Fish" Booth is a cartoonist and freelance writer whose work can most regularly be seen on Harpers.org and Truthdig.com.

He has been a cartoonist and freelance writer for twenty years, publishing under both his own name and the penname of Mr. Fish with many of the nation's most reputable and prestigious magazines, journals, and newspapers. In addition to Harpers.org and Truthdig.com, his work has appeared on Slate.com and MSNBC.com and in *the Los Angeles Times, the Village Voice, Vanity Fair, Mother Jones* magazine, *the Advocate, Z Magazine,* and the *Utne Reader,* among many others. He has also been published in international newspapers and magazines.

As half of the musical group *Dwayne and Jeff,* Booth has composed music for five CDs: *Octopus, Bradley, Cooties in Heavy Syrup, Rubber and Glue,* and *The Other White Meat.* Many of the slick moves he has displayed on stage while playing his guitar have been described as "embarrassing."

He has written, scored, and designed the animation for three original television series: *A Dog Goes Into a Bar, The Horse's Mouth,* and *This is Mr. Fish.*

Dwayne Booth lives in Philadelphia, Pennsylvania, with his wife and twin daughters.

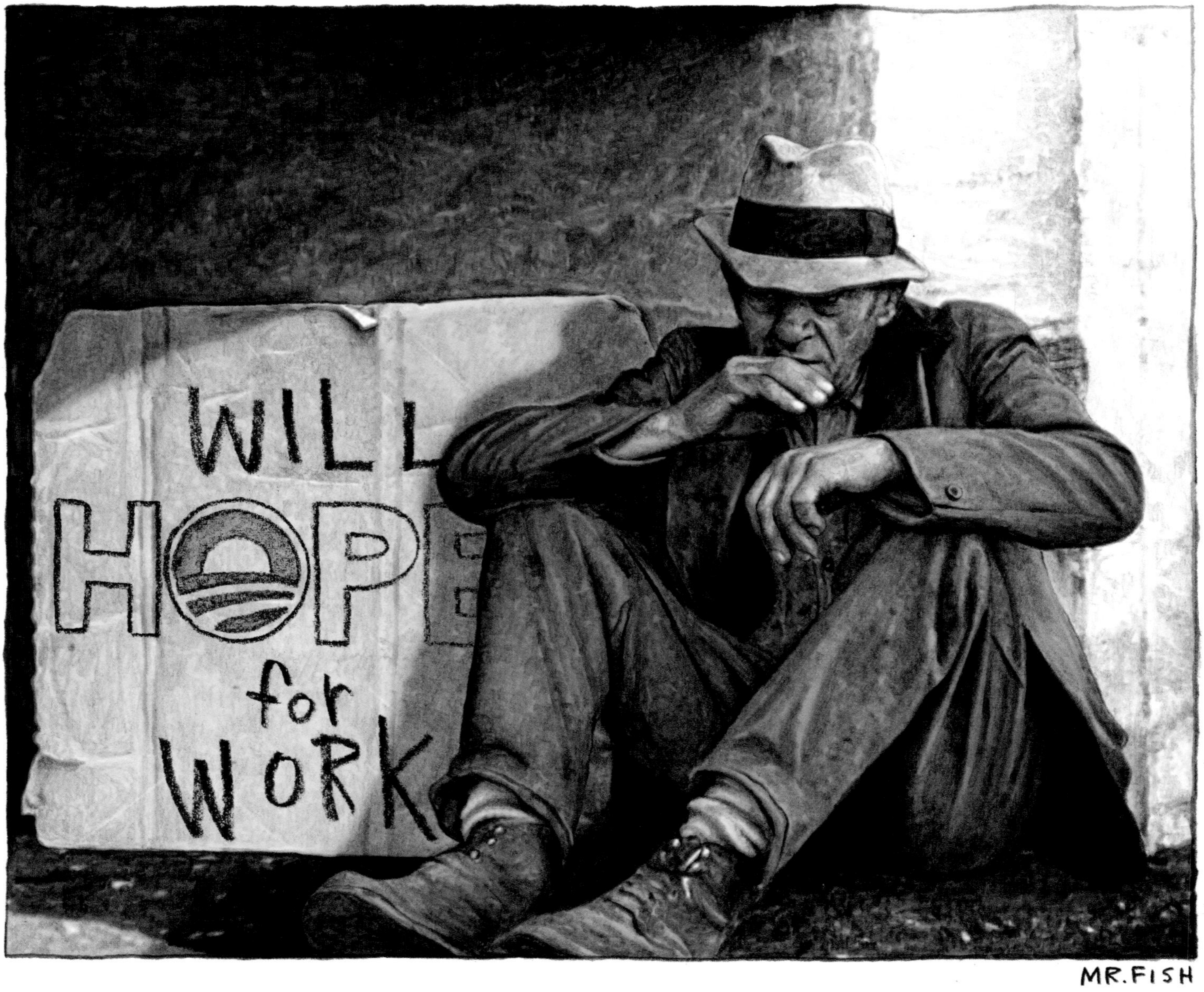
WILL
HOPE
for
WORK
MR.FISH

Overseas Press Club's Thomas Nast Award

This award was named for Thomas Nast who is considered by many to be the "father of the political cartoon" in America. He has given us such lasting icons as the Democratic Donkey, the Republican Elephant, and the Tammany Tiger. He is also generally regarded as having given us the commonly accepted versions of Uncle Sam and Santa Claus.

Established in 1939 by a group of foreign correspondents in New York City, the Overseas Press Club presents this award, along with many others, annually. The OPC's founding tenets encourage the highest standards of professional integrity and skill in the reporting of news, help educate new generations of journalists, contribute to the freedom and independence of journalists and the press throughout the world, and work toward better communication and understanding among people.

It is in the spirit with which Thomas Nast entertained and informed his readers that the Thomas Nast Award for editorial cartooning is presented.

2009 Overseas Press Club's Thomas Nast Award Winner
Nate Beeler, *Washington Examiner*

Nate Beeler has been the editorial cartoonist for the *Washington Examiner* since 2005. His award-winning cartoons can also be seen in the *San Francisco Examiner* and have appeared on CNN and in such publications as *Time, Newsweek, USA Today,* and the *Los Angeles Times.* Beeler is one of the most widely syndicated editorial cartoonists, with his cartoons distributed internationally to more than eight hundred publications by Cagle Cartoons.

He has received multiple honors from the Virginia, Maryland, and Washington, D.C. press associations for his editorial cartoons. In 2007, he received the Golden Spike Award, as voted upon by members of the Association of American Editorial Cartoonists at its fiftieth anniversary convention in Washington. In 2008, the National Press Foundation awarded him the Clifford K. & James T. Berryman Award.

Beeler's cartooning career began at his high school's student newspaper in Columbus, Ohio. He went on to earn a journalism degree from American University in 2002. During his university years, he won the three major college cartooning prizes: the Charles M. Schulz Award, the John Locher Memorial Award, and first place in the National Society of Professional Journalists Mark of Excellence Awards.

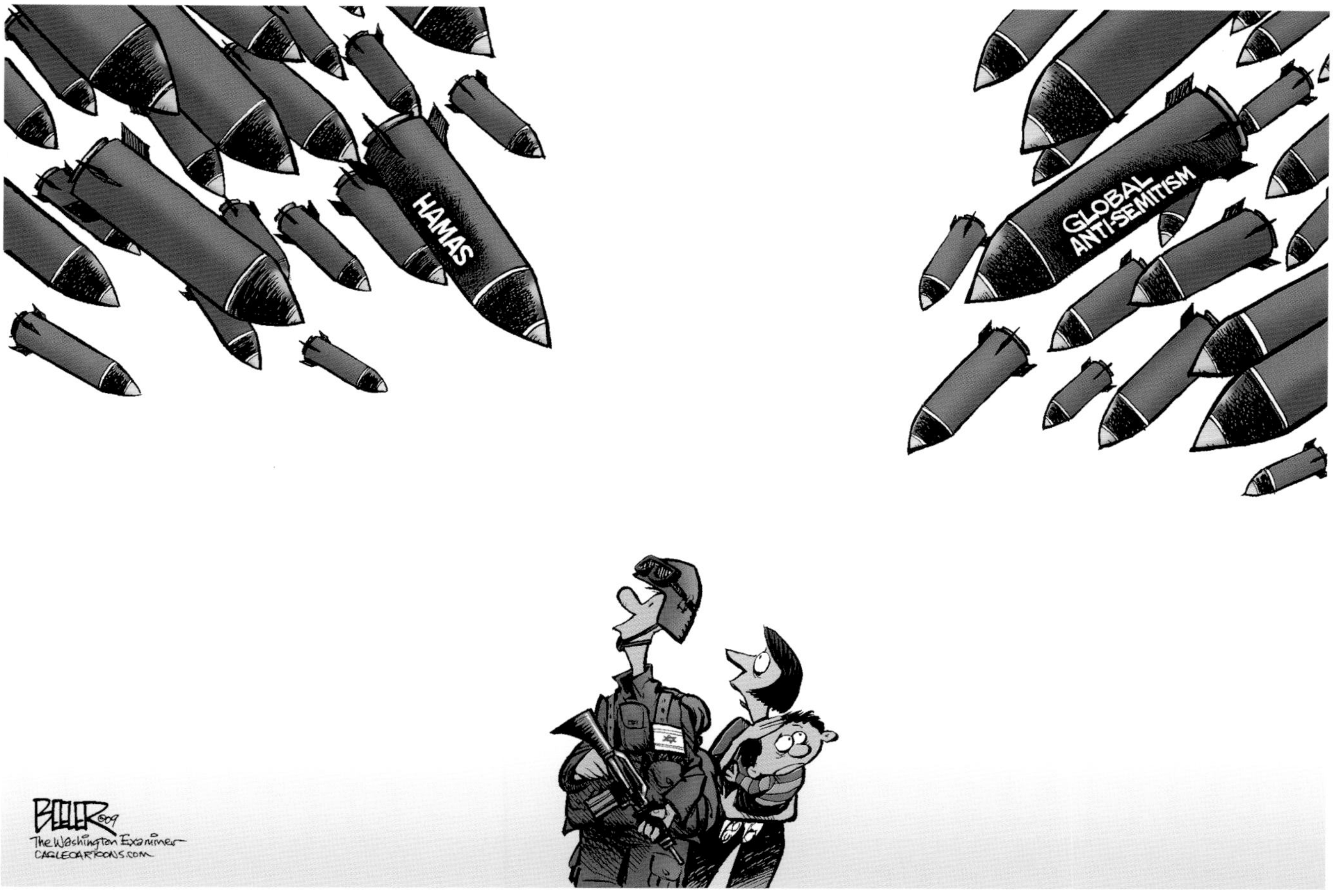
HAMAS
GLOBAL ANTI-SEMITISM
BEELER ©09
The Washington Examiner
CAGLECARTOONS.COM

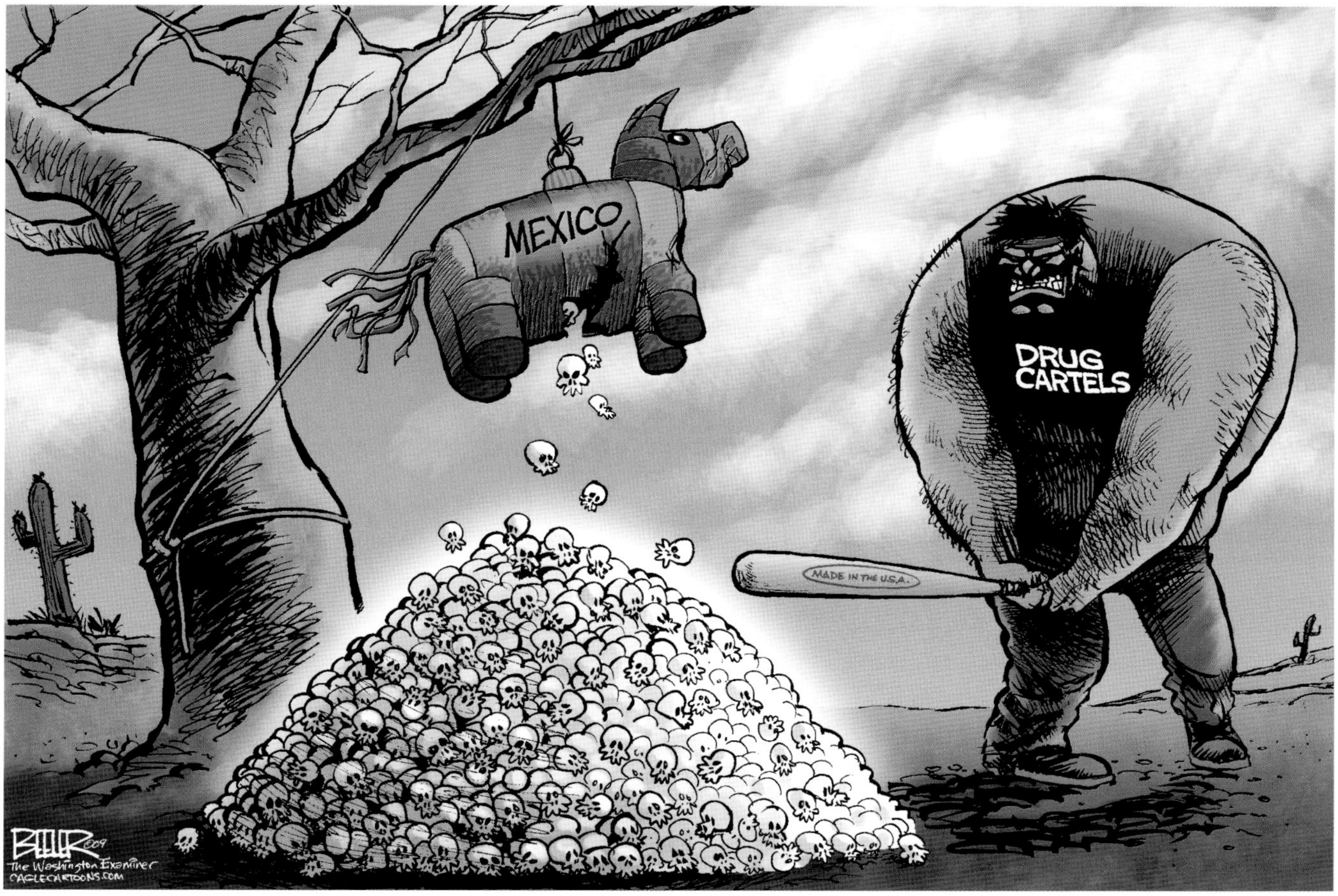
MEXICO
DRUG CARTELS
MADE IN THE U.S.A.
BEELER ©09
The Washington Examiner
CAGLECARTOONS.COM

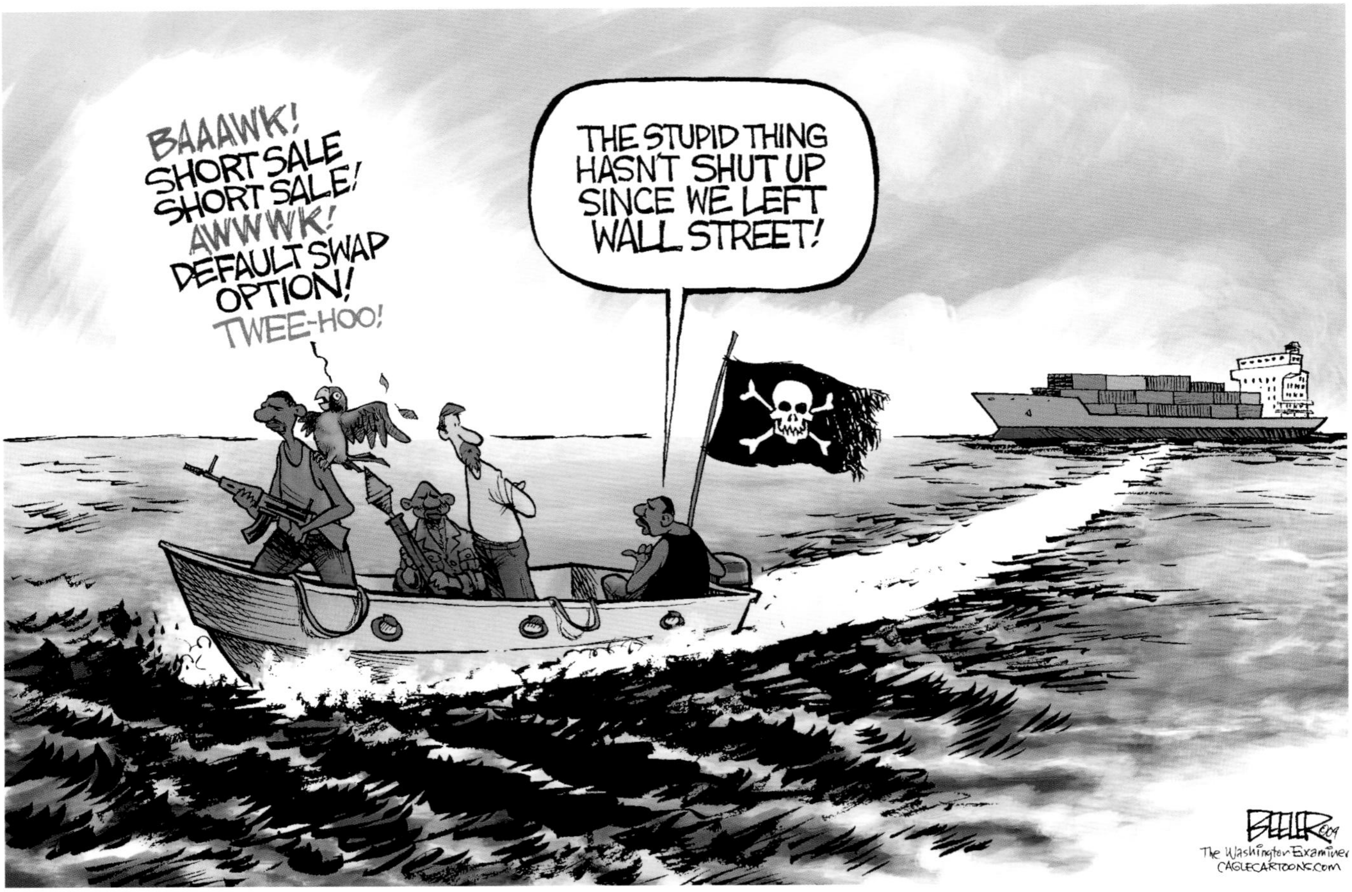
BAAAWK! SHORT SALE SHORT SALE! AWWWK! DEFAULT SWAP OPTION! TWEE-HOO!
THE STUPID THING HASN'T SHUT UP SINCE WE LEFT WALL STREET!
The Washington Examiner
CAGLECARTOONS.COM

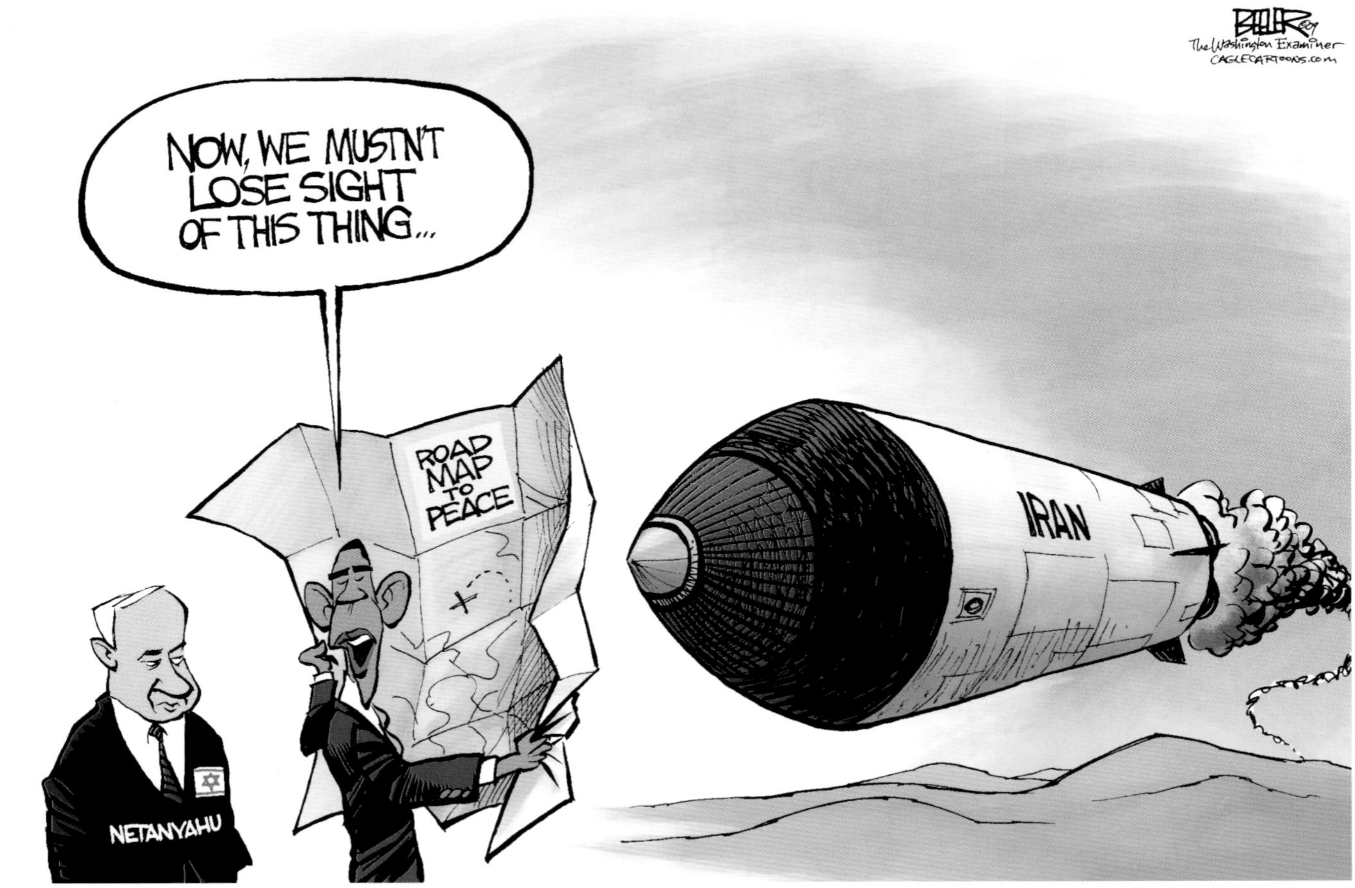
The Washington Examiner
CAGLECARTOONS.COM
NOW, WE MUSTN'T LOSE SIGHT OF THIS THING...
ROAD MAP TO PEACE
IRAN
NETANYAHU

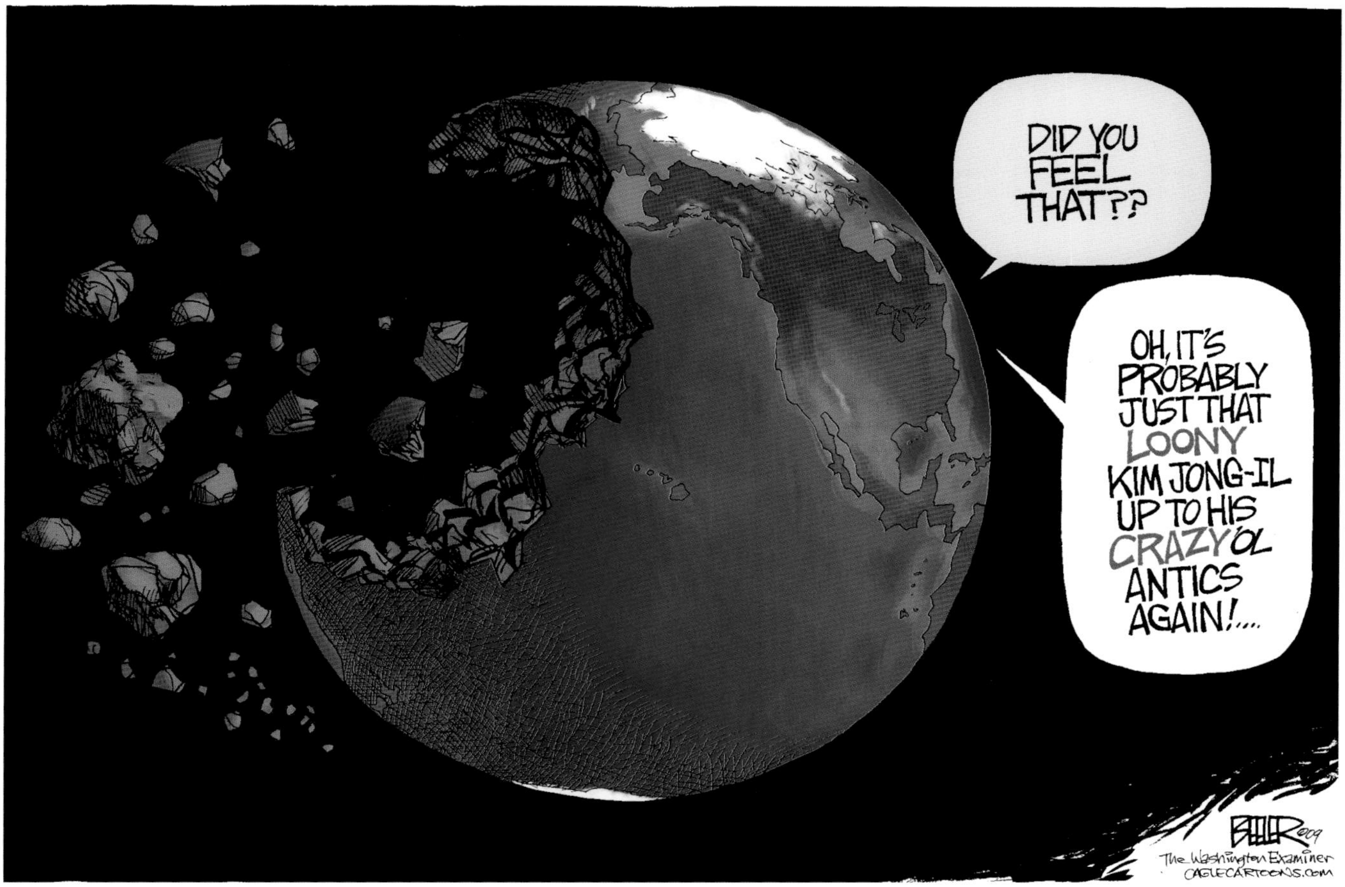
DID YOU FEEL THAT??
OH, IT'S PROBABLY JUST THAT LOONY KIM JONG-IL UP TO HIS CRAZY 'OL ANTICS AGAIN!....
The Washington Examiner
CAGLECARTOONS.COM

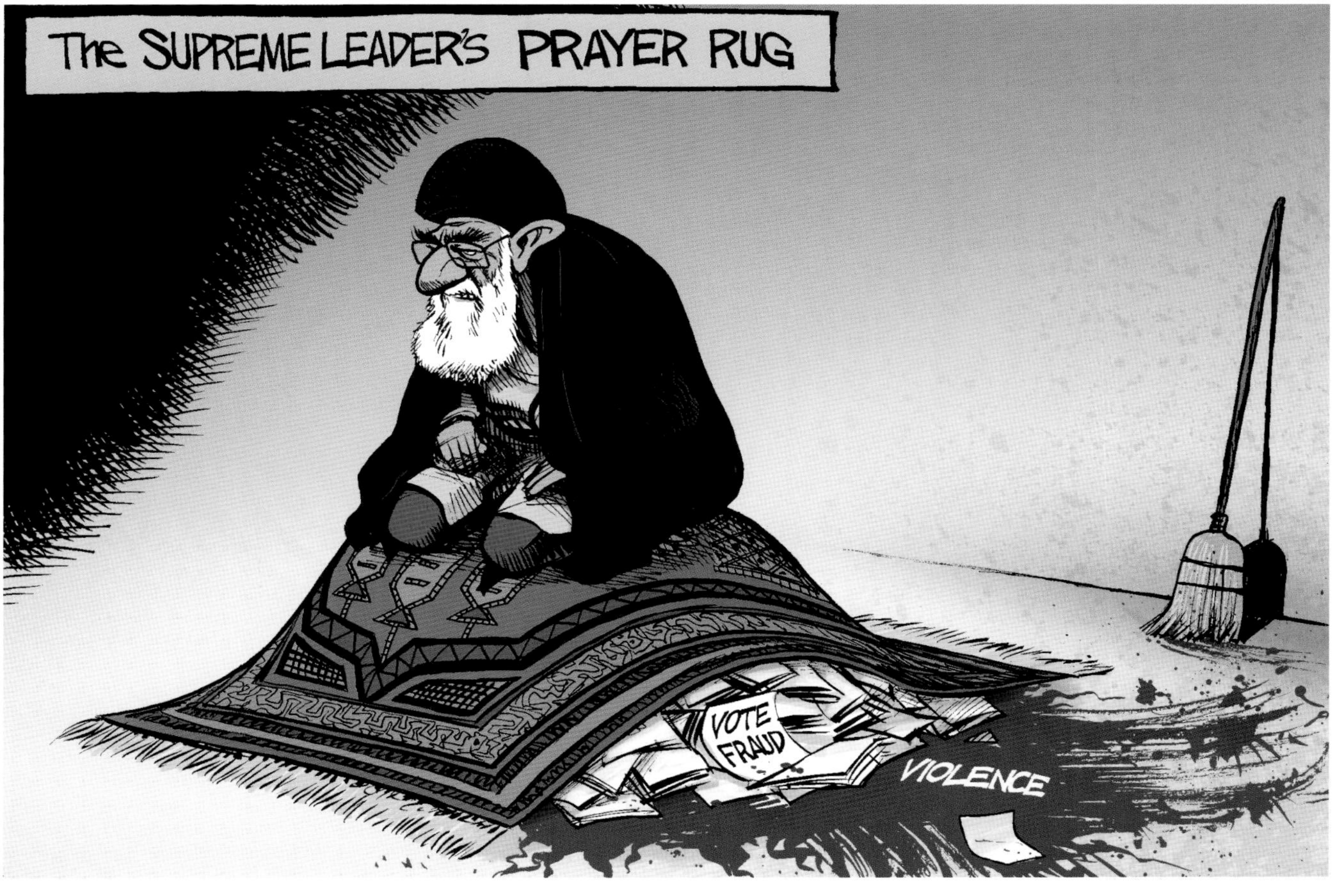
The SUPREME LEADER'S PRAYER RUG
VOTE FRAUD
VIOLENCE

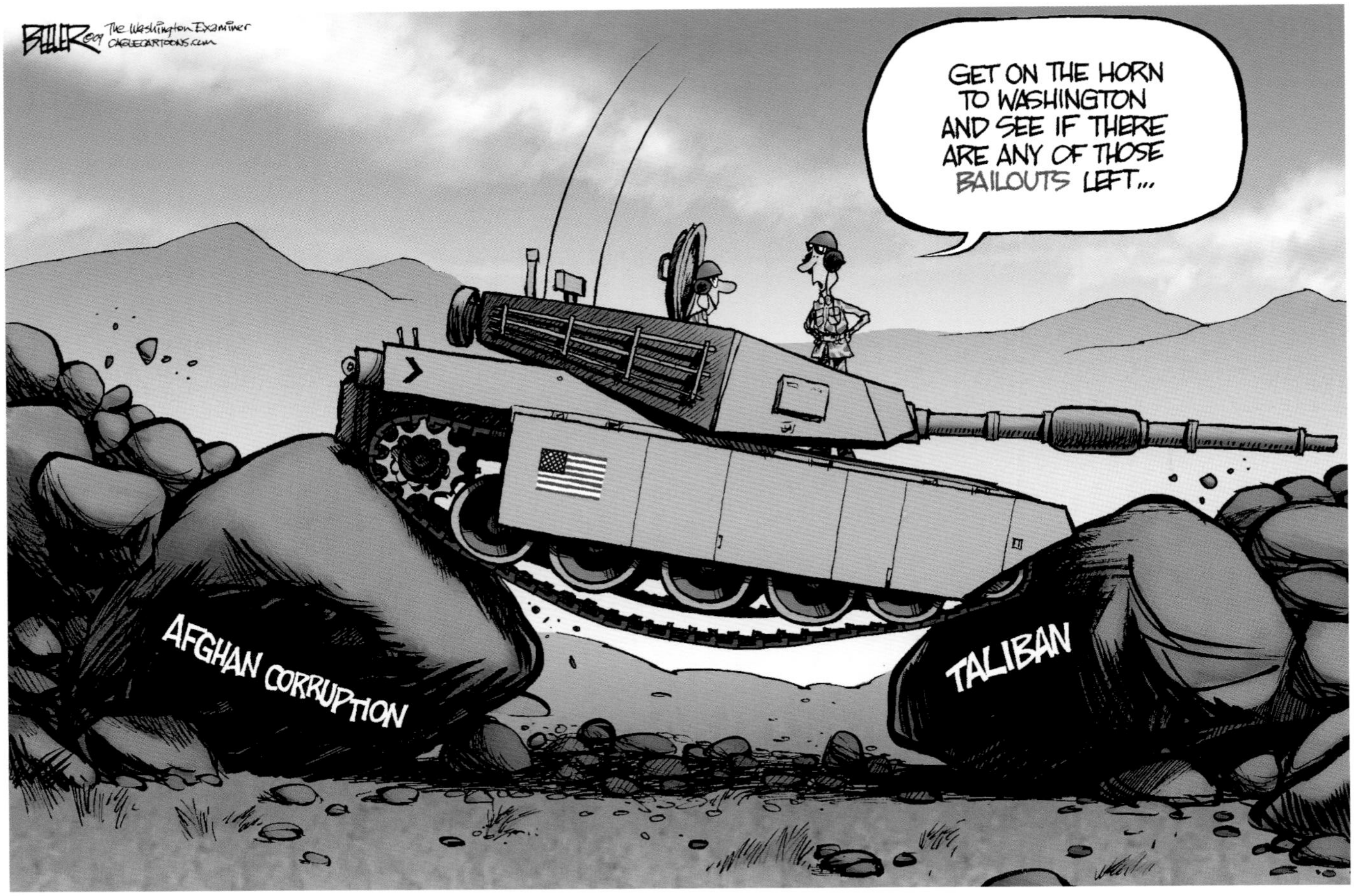
BEELER ©09 The Washington Examiner CAGLECARTOONS.COM
GET ON THE HORN TO WASHINGTON AND SEE IF THERE ARE ANY OF THOSE BAILOUTS LEFT...
AFGHAN CORRUPTION
TALIBAN

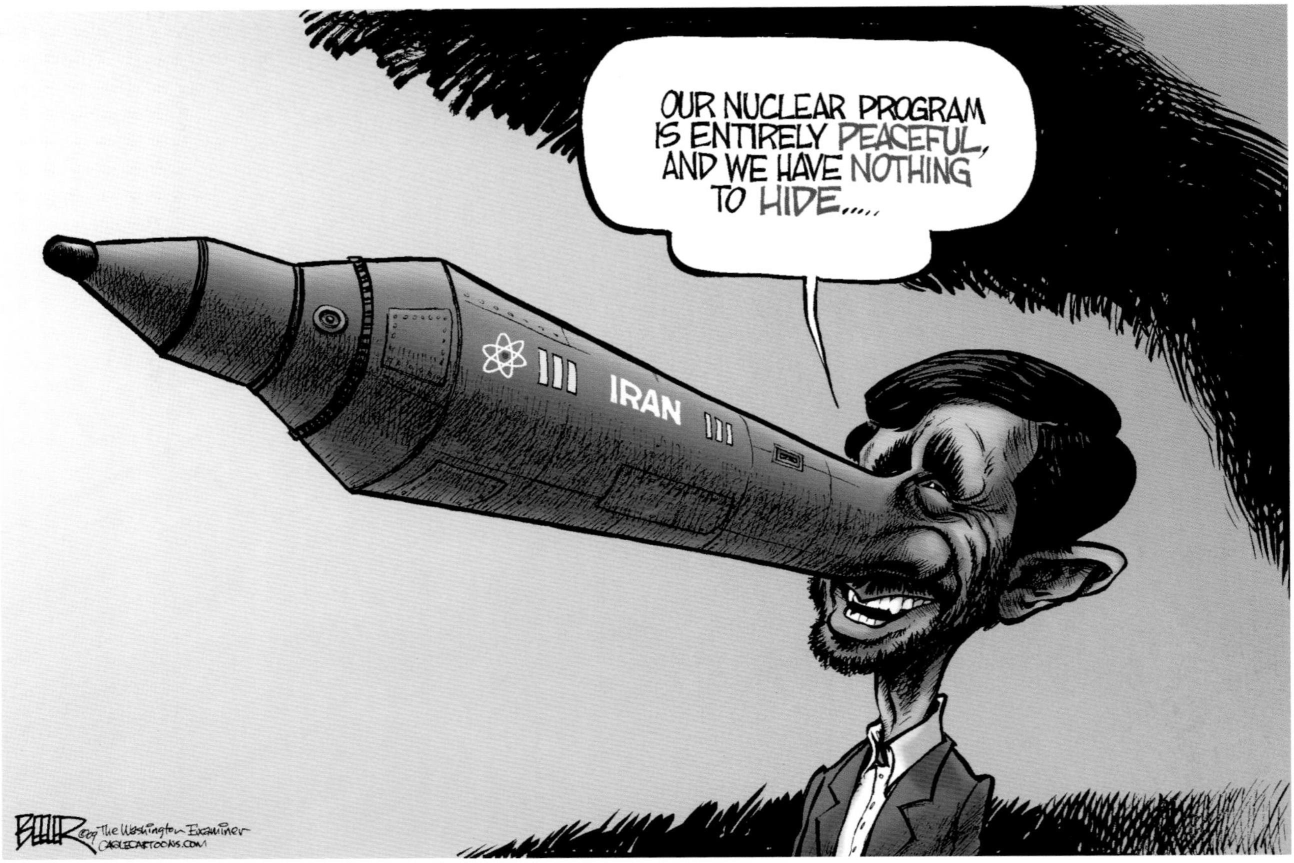
OUR NUCLEAR PROGRAM IS ENTIRELY PEACEFUL, AND WE HAVE NOTHING TO HIDE.....
IRAN
BEELER ©09 The Washington Examiner CAGLECARTOONS.COM

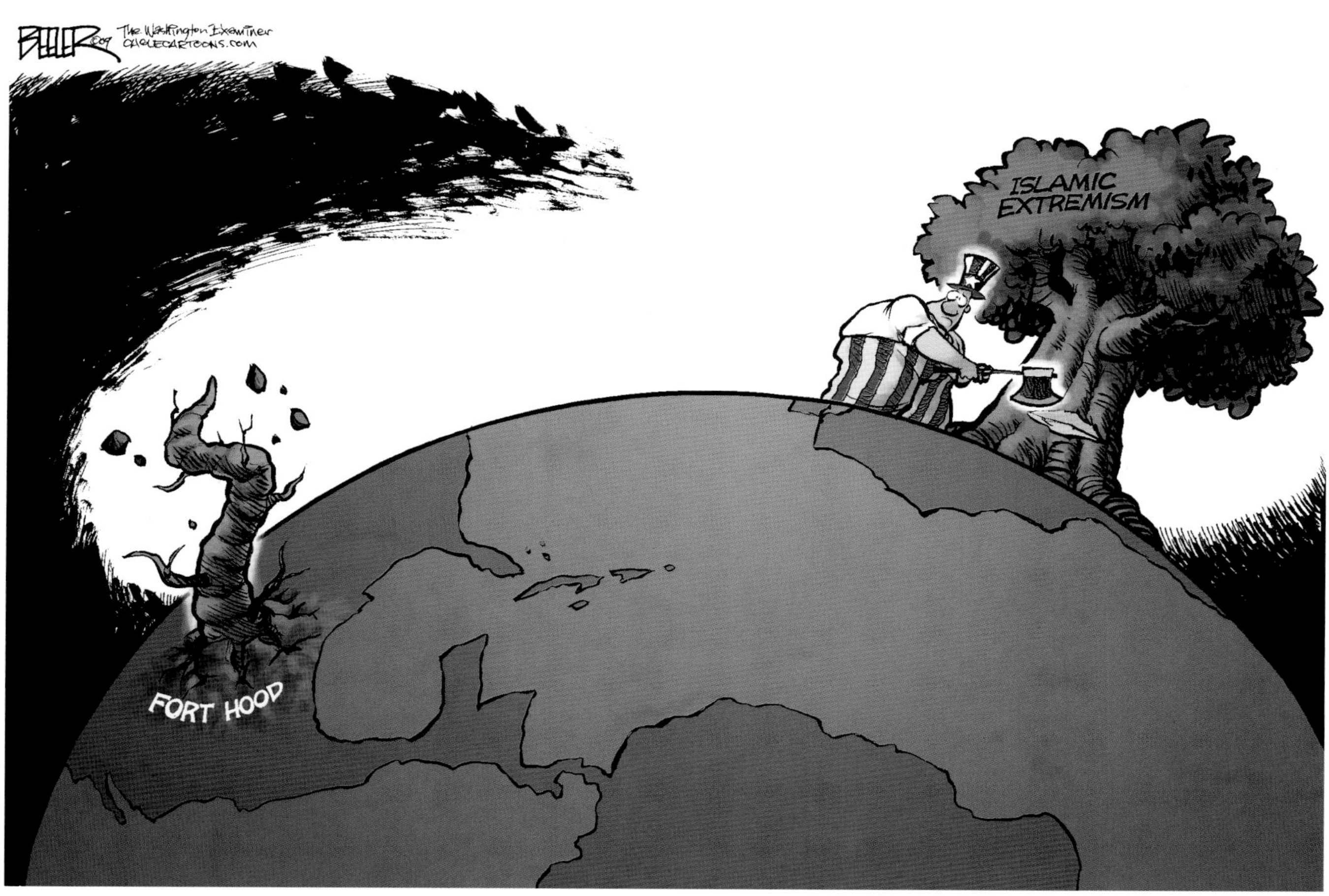
BEELER ©09 The Washington Examiner CAGLECARTOONS.COM
ISLAMIC EXTREMISM
FORT HOOD

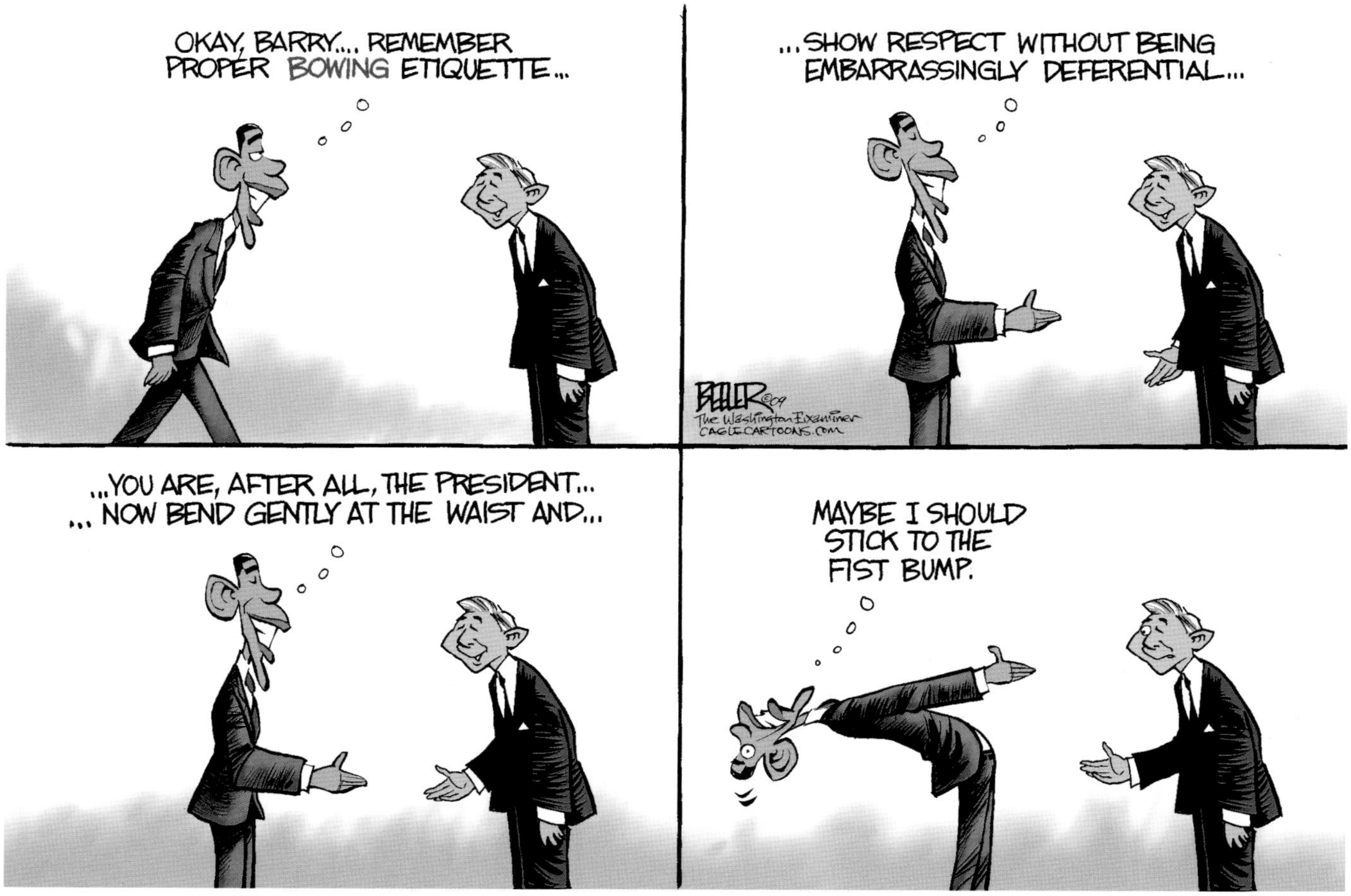
OKAY, BARRY.... REMEMBER PROPER BOWING ETIQUETTE...
...SHOW RESPECT WITHOUT BEING EMBARRASSINGLY DEFERENTIAL...
BEELER ©09 The Washington Examiner CAGLECARTOONS.COM
...YOU ARE, AFTER ALL, THE PRESIDENT...
...NOW BEND GENTLY AT THE WAIST AND...
MAYBE I SHOULD STICK TO THE FIST BUMP.

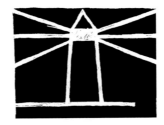

Scripps Howard National Journalism Awards

Since 1953, the Scripps Howard Foundation has recognized the best work in journalism through the National Journalism Awards. The E. W. Scripps Company husbanded the awards from 1953 until the formation of the Scripps Howard Foundation in 1962, at which time the foundation took over that responsibility.

The Scripps Howard Foundation is the corporate foundation of the E.W. Scripps Company. Its mission "is to advance the cause of a free press through support of excellence in journalism, quality journalism education and professional development."

The awards recognize excellence in editorial cartooning as well as sixteen other categories, including editorial writing, human interest writing, environmental and public service reporting, investigative reporting, business/economics reporting, commentary, photojournalism, radio and television journalism, college cartooning, and Web reporting. The awards also honor distinguished service to journalism education and the First Amendment.

2009 Scripps Howard National Journalism Award Winner
Alexander Hunter, *Washington Times*

Alexander Hunter was born in Long Beach, California, in 1960 and grew up in the San Gabriel Valley. He began drawing from the time he could hold a pencil and received his art education at home from his parents, both gifted artists. Some time later, upon reaching his majority, the young Mr. Hunter struck out onto the road of experience in pursuit of life as a so-called fine artist.

A pivotal moment for Hunter occurred some years later when he encountered the teachings of Sun Myung Moon. His life took a profound change in direction, and he began working as part of the worldwide Unification movement. This involvement soon brought him an opportunity to put his artistic gifts to use as a founding staff member of the *Washington Times*, established by the Reverend Moon in 1982.

During the past twenty-eight years as a staffer for the *Washington Times*, Hunter has worked (often concurrently) as an illustrator, political cartoonist, graphic designer, and art director for nearly every section of the newspaper. Currently, Hunter serves as art director of the newspaper's daily commentary section. He has received more than two dozen awards for his work at the *Washington Times*, including eight Best of Shows (six of those consecutively) from the Virginia Press Association for illustration and the Scripps Howard National Journalism Award for editorial cartooning in 2009 for his weekly feature "Hunters Big Picture."

In 1989, Hunter married Toyoko Miyazawa of Nagano, Japan. Today, he and Toyoko and their five children reside in bucolic Brandywine, Maryland.

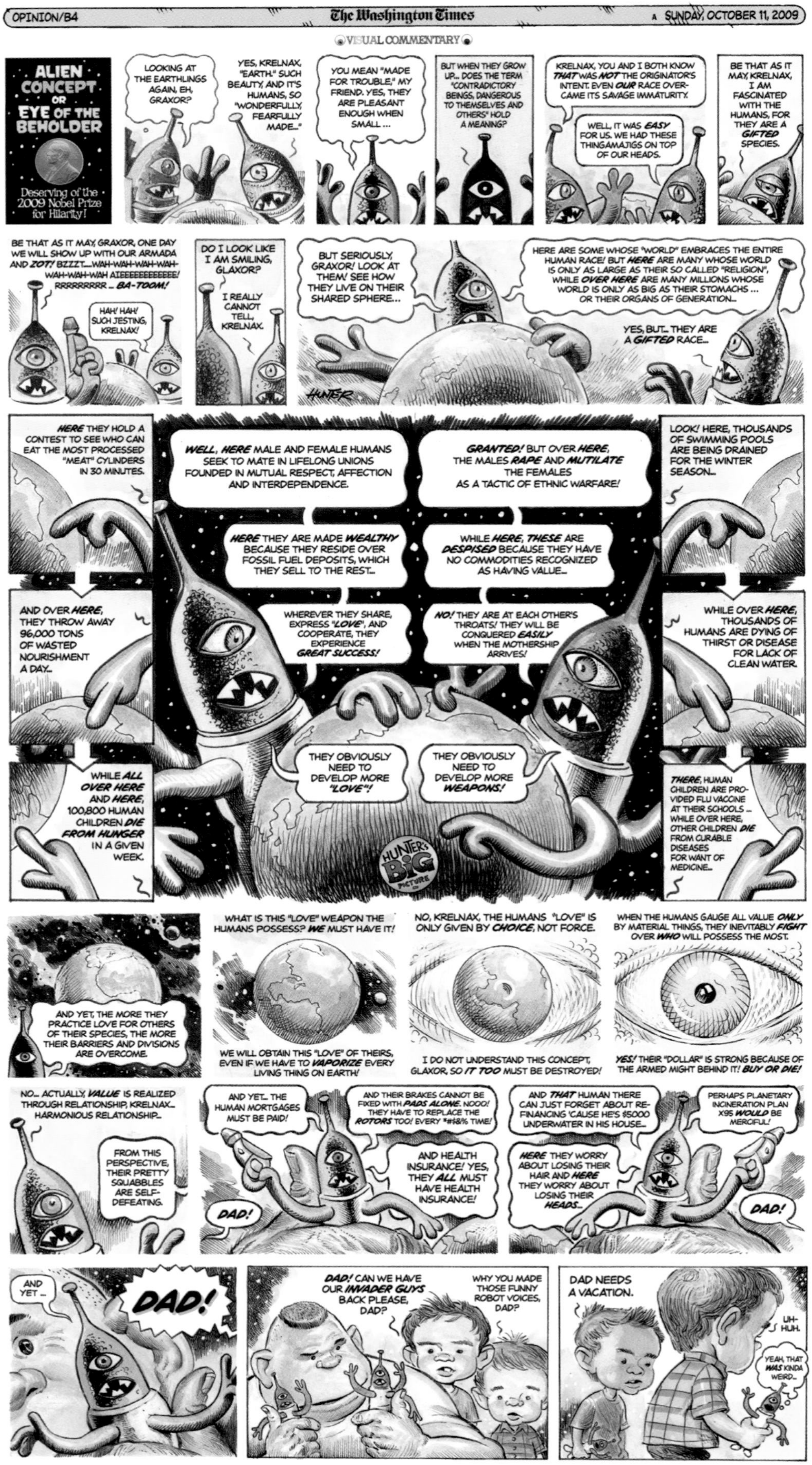

OPINION/B4
The Washington Times
A SUNDAY, OCTOBER 11, 2009
VISUAL COMMENTARY
ALIEN CONCEPT OR EYE OF THE BEHOLDER
Deserving of the 2009 Nobel Prize for Hilarity!
LOOKING AT THE EARTHLINGS AGAIN, EH, GRAXOR?
YES, KRELNAX, "EARTH." SUCH BEAUTY, AND IT'S HUMANS, SO "WONDERFULLY, FEARFULLY MADE..."
YOU MEAN "MADE FOR TROUBLE," MY FRIEND. YES, THEY ARE PLEASANT ENOUGH WHEN SMALL ...
BUT WHEN THEY GROW UP... DOES THE TERM "CONTRADICTORY BEINGS, DANGEROUS TO THEMSELVES AND OTHERS" HOLD A MEANING?
KRELNAX, YOU AND I BOTH KNOW THAT WAS NOT THE ORIGINATOR'S INTENT. EVEN OUR RACE OVERCAME ITS SAVAGE IMMATURITY.
WELL, IT WAS EASY FOR US. WE HAD THESE THINGAMAJIGS ON TOP OF OUR HEADS.
BE THAT AS IT MAY, KRELNAX, I AM FASCINATED WITH THE HUMANS, FOR THEY ARE A GIFTED SPECIES.
BE THAT AS IT MAY, GRAXOR, ONE DAY WE WILL SHOW UP WITH OUR ARMADA AND ZOT! BZZZT.....WAH-WAH-WAH-WAH-WAH-WAH-WAH AIEEEEEEEEEEEE! RRRRRRRRR ... BA-TOOM!
HAH! HAH! SUCH JESTING, KRELNAX!
DO I LOOK LIKE I AM SMILING, GLAXOR?
I REALLY CANNOT TELL, KRELNAX.
BUT SERIOUSLY, GRAXOR! LOOK AT THEM! SEE HOW THEY LIVE ON THEIR SHARED SPHERE...
HERE ARE SOME WHOSE "WORLD" EMBRACES THE ENTIRE HUMAN RACE! BUT HERE ARE MANY WHOSE WORLD IS ONLY AS LARGE AS THEIR SO CALLED "RELIGION", WHILE OVER HERE ARE MANY MILLIONS WHOSE WORLD IS ONLY AS BIG AS THEIR STOMACHS ... OR THEIR ORGANS OF GENERATION...
YES, BUT... THEY ARE A GIFTED RACE...
HUNTER
HERE THEY HOLD A CONTEST TO SEE WHO CAN EAT THE MOST PROCESSED "MEAT" CYLINDERS IN 30 MINUTES.
AND OVER HERE, THEY THROW AWAY 96,000 TONS OF WASTED NOURISHMENT A DAY...
WHILE ALL OVER HERE AND HERE, 100,800 HUMAN CHILDREN DIE FROM HUNGER IN A GIVEN WEEK.
WELL, HERE MALE AND FEMALE HUMANS SEEK TO MATE IN LIFELONG UNIONS FOUNDED IN MUTUAL RESPECT, AFFECTION AND INTERDEPENDENCE.
GRANTED! BUT OVER HERE, THE MALES RAPE AND MUTILATE THE FEMALES AS A TACTIC OF ETHNIC WARFARE!
HERE THEY ARE MADE WEALTHY BECAUSE THEY RESIDE OVER FOSSIL FUEL DEPOSITS, WHICH THEY SELL TO THE REST...
WHILE HERE, THESE ARE DESPISED BECAUSE THEY HAVE NO COMMODITIES RECOGNIZED AS HAVING VALUE...
WHEREVER THEY SHARE, EXPRESS "LOVE", AND COOPERATE, THEY EXPERIENCE GREAT SUCCESS!
NO! THEY ARE AT EACH OTHER'S THROATS! THEY WILL BE CONQUERED EASILY WHEN THE MOTHERSHIP ARRIVES!
THEY OBVIOUSLY NEED TO DEVELOP MORE "LOVE"!
THEY OBVIOUSLY NEED TO DEVELOP MORE WEAPONS!
HUNTER'S BIG PICTURE
LOOK! HERE, THOUSANDS OF SWIMMING POOLS ARE BEING DRAINED FOR THE WINTER SEASON...
WHILE OVER HERE, THOUSANDS OF HUMANS ARE DYING OF THIRST OR DISEASE FOR LACK OF CLEAN WATER.
THERE, HUMAN CHILDREN ARE PROVIDED FLU VACCINE AT THEIR SCHOOLS ... WHILE OVER HERE, OTHER CHILDREN DIE FROM CURABLE DISEASES FOR WANT OF MEDICINE...
AND YET, THE MORE THEY PRACTICE LOVE FOR OTHERS OF THEIR SPECIES, THE MORE THEIR BARRIERS AND DIVISIONS ARE OVERCOME.
WHAT IS THIS "LOVE" WEAPON THE HUMANS POSSESS? WE MUST HAVE IT!
WE WILL OBTAIN THIS "LOVE" OF THEIRS, EVEN IF WE HAVE TO VAPORIZE EVERY LIVING THING ON EARTH!
NO, KRELNAX, THE HUMANS "LOVE" IS ONLY GIVEN BY CHOICE, NOT FORCE.
I DO NOT UNDERSTAND THIS CONCEPT, GLAXOR, SO IT TOO MUST BE DESTROYED!
WHEN THE HUMANS GAUGE ALL VALUE ONLY BY MATERIAL THINGS, THEY INEVITABLY FIGHT OVER WHO WILL POSSESS THE MOST.
YES! THEIR "DOLLAR" IS STRONG BECAUSE OF THE ARMED MIGHT BEHIND IT! BUY OR DIE!
NO... ACTUALLY, VALUE IS REALIZED THROUGH RELATIONSHIP, KRELNAX... HARMONIOUS RELATIONSHIP...
FROM THIS PERSPECTIVE, THEIR PRETTY SQUABBLES ARE SELF-DEFEATING.
AND YET... THE HUMAN MORTGAGES MUST BE PAID!
AND THEIR BRAKES CANNOT BE FIXED WITH PADS ALONE. NOOO! THEY HAVE TO REPLACE THE ROTORS TOO! EVERY *#$&% TIME!
AND HEALTH INSURANCE! YES, THEY ALL MUST HAVE HEALTH INSURANCE!
DAD!
AND THAT HUMAN THERE CAN JUST FORGET ABOUT RE-FINANCING 'CAUSE HE'S $5000 UNDERWATER IN HIS HOUSE...
HERE THEY WORRY ABOUT LOSING THEIR HAIR AND HERE THEY WORRY ABOUT LOSING THEIR HEADS...
PERHAPS PLANETARY INCINERATION PLAN X95 WOULD BE MERCIFUL!
DAD!
AND YET ...
DAD!
DAD! CAN WE HAVE OUR INVADER GUYS BACK PLEASE, DAD?
WHY YOU MADE THOSE FUNNY ROBOT VOICES, DAD?
DAD NEEDS A VACATION.
UH-HUH.
YEAH, THAT WAS KINDA WEIRD...

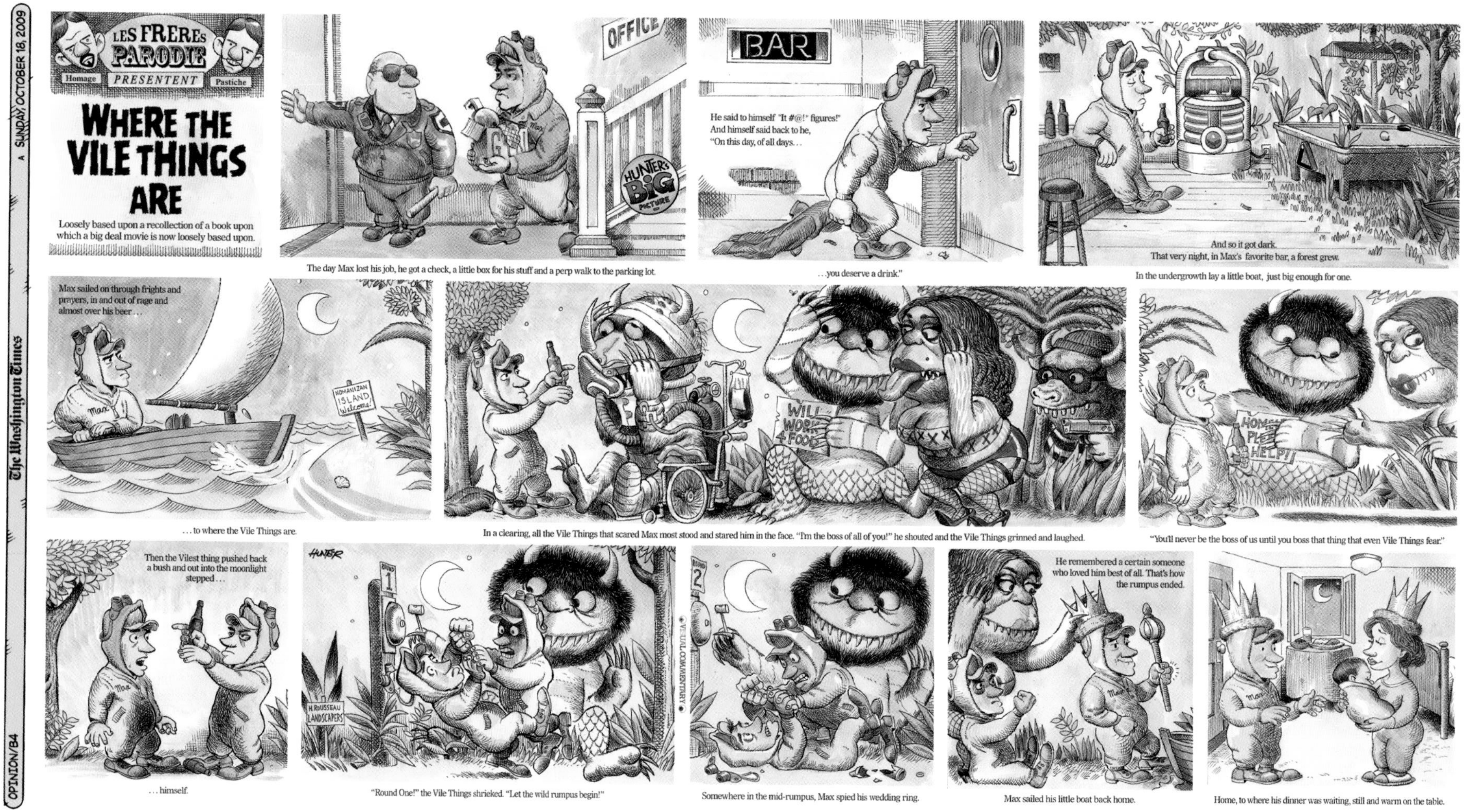
OPINION/B4
The Washington Times
A SUNDAY, OCTOBER 18, 2009
LES FRERES PARODIE
Homage
PRESENTENT
Pastiche
WHERE THE VILE THINGS ARE
Loosely based upon a recollection of a book upon which a big deal movie is now loosely based upon.
OFFICE
HUNTER'S BIG PICTURE
The day Max lost his job, he got a check, a little box for his stuff and a perp walk to the parking lot.
BAR
He said to himself "It #@!" figures!"
And himself said back to he,
"On this day, of all days . . .
. . . you deserve a drink."
And so it got dark.
That very night, in Max's favorite bar, a forest grew.
In the undergrowth lay a little boat, just big enough for one.
Max sailed on through frights and prayers, in and out of rage and almost over his beer . . .
ISLAND Welcome!
. . . to where the Vile Things are.
WILL WORK 4 FOOD
In a clearing, all the Vile Things that scared Max most stood and stared him in the face. "I'm the boss of all of you!" he shouted and the Vile Things grinned and laughed.
"You'll never be the boss of us until you boss that thing that even Vile Things fear."
Then the Vilest thing pushed back a bush and out into the moonlight stepped . . .
. . . himself.
HUNTER
H. ROUSSEAU LANDSCAPERS
"Round One!" the Vile Things shrieked. "Let the wild rumpus begin!"
VISUAL COMMENTARY
Somewhere in the mid-rumpus, Max spied his wedding ring.
He remembered a certain someone who loved him best of all. That's how the rumpus ended.
Max sailed his little boat back home.
Home, to where his dinner was waiting, still and warm on the table.

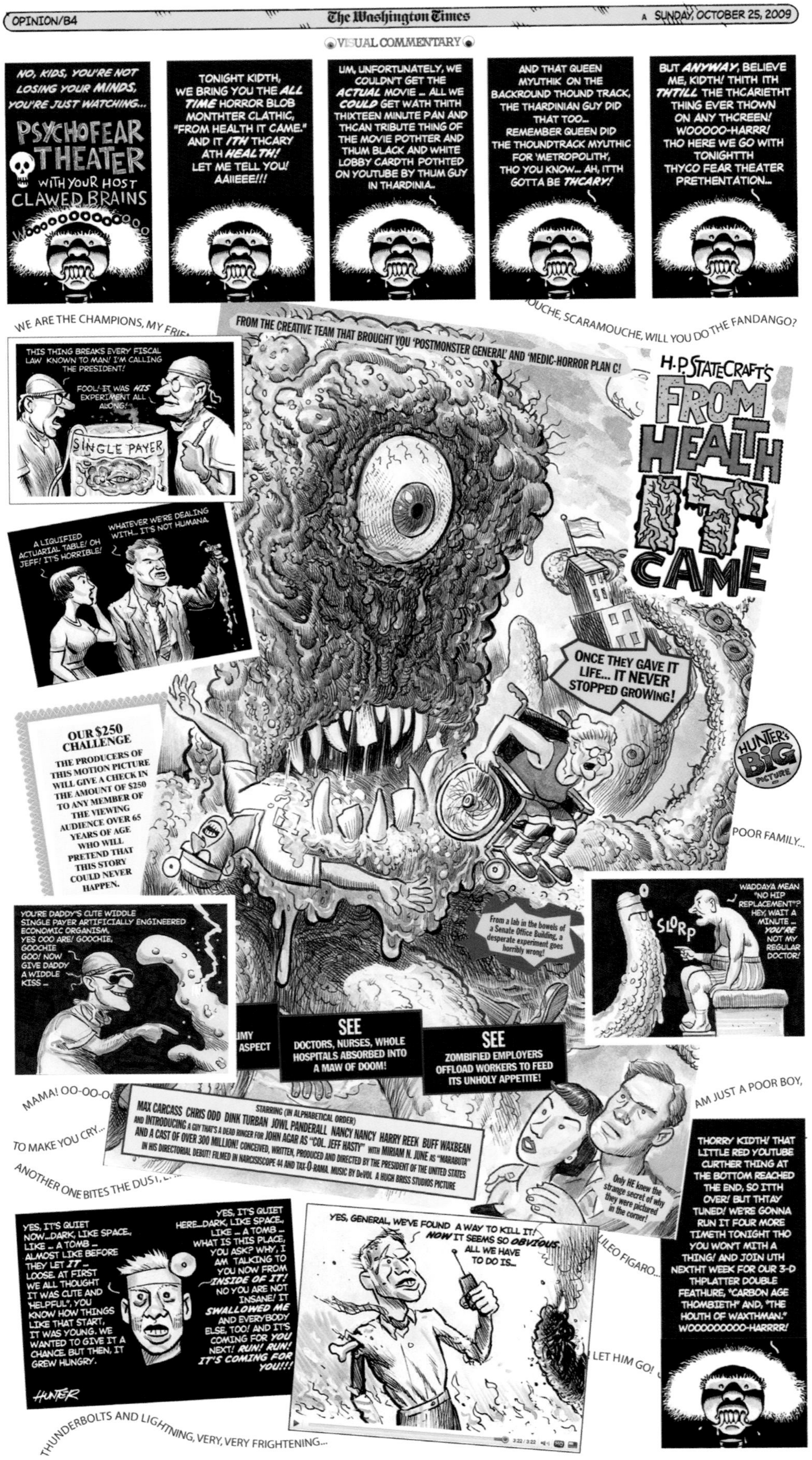
OPINION/B4
The Washington Times
A SUNDAY, OCTOBER 25, 2009
VISUAL COMMENTARY
NO, KIDS, YOU'RE NOT LOSING YOUR MINDS, YOU'RE JUST WATCHING...
PSYCHOFEAR THEATER WITH YOUR HOST CLAWED BRAINS
WOOOOOOOOOOOO
TONIGHT KIDTH, WE BRING YOU THE ALL TIME HORROR BLOB MONTHTER CLATHIC, "FROM HEALTH IT CAME." AND IT ITH THCARY ATH HEALTH! LET ME TELL YOU! AAIIEEE!!!
UM, UNFORTUNATELY, WE COULDN'T GET THE ACTUAL MOVIE ... ALL WE COULD GET WATH THITH THIXTEEN MINUTE PAN AND THCAN TRIBUTE THING OF THE MOVIE POTHTER AND THUM BLACK AND WHITE LOBBY CARDTH POTHTED ON YOUTUBE BY THUM GUY IN THARDINIA..
AND THAT QUEEN MYUTHIK ON THE BACKROUND THOUND TRACK, THE THARDINIAN GUY DID THAT TOO... REMEMBER QUEEN DID THE THOUNDTRACK MYUTHIC FOR 'METROPOLITH,' THO YOU KNOW... AH, ITTH GOTTA BE THCARY!
BUT ANYWAY, BELIEVE ME, KIDTH! THITH ITH THTILL THE THCARIETHT THING EVER THOWN ON ANY THCREEN! WOOOOO-HARRR! THO HERE WE GO WITH TONIGHTTH THYCO FEAR THEATER PRETHENTATION...
WE ARE THE CHAMPIONS, MY FRIE
THIS THING BREAKS EVERY FISCAL LAW KNOWN TO MAN! I'M CALLING THE PRESIDENT!
FOOL! IT WAS HIS EXPERIMENT ALL ALONG!
SINGLE PAYER
A LIQUIFIED ACTUARIAL TABLE! OH JEFF! IT'S HORRIBLE!
WHATEVER WE'RE DEALING WITH... IT'S NOT HUMANA.
OUCHE, SCARAMOUCHE, WILL YOU DO THE FANDANGO?
FROM THE CREATIVE TEAM THAT BROUGHT YOU 'POSTMONSTER GENERAL' AND 'MEDIC-HORROR PLAN C!'
H.P. STATECRAFT'S FROM HEALTH IT CAME
ONCE THEY GAVE IT LIFE... IT NEVER STOPPED GROWING!
HUNTER'S BIG PICTURE
OUR $250 CHALLENGE
THE PRODUCERS OF THIS MOTION PICTURE WILL GIVE A CHECK IN THE AMOUNT OF $250 TO ANY MEMBER OF THE VIEWING AUDIENCE OVER 65 YEARS OF AGE WHO WILL PRETEND THAT THIS STORY COULD NEVER HAPPEN.
POOR FAMILY...
From a lab in the bowels of a Senate Office Building, a desperate experiment goes horribly wrong!
YOU'RE DADDY'S CUTE WIDDLE SINGLE PAYER ARTIFICIALLY ENGINEERED ECONOMIC ORGANISM, YES OOO ARE! GOOCHIE, GOOCHIE GOO! NOW GIVE DADDY A WIDDLE KISS...
SLORP
WADDAYA MEAN "NO HIP REPLACEMENT"? HEY, WAIT A MINUTE ... YOU'RE NOT MY REGULAR DOCTOR!
IMY ASPECT
SEE DOCTORS, NURSES, WHOLE HOSPITALS ABSORBED INTO A MAW OF DOOM!
SEE ZOMBIFIED EMPLOYERS OFFLOAD WORKERS TO FEED ITS UNHOLY APPETITE!
MAMA! OO-OO-OO
AM JUST A POOR BOY,
TO MAKE YOU CRY...
STARRING (IN ALPHABETICAL ORDER)
MAX CARCASS CHRIS ODD DINK TURBAN JOWL PANDERALL NANCY NANCY HARRY REEK BUFF WAXBEAN
AND INTRODUCING A GUY THAT'S A DEAD RINGER FOR JOHN AGAR AS "COL. JEFF HASTY" WITH MIRIAM N. JUNE AS "MARABUTA"
AND A CAST OF OVER 300 MILLION! CONCEIVED, WRITTEN, PRODUCED AND DIRECTED BY THE PRESIDENT OF THE UNITED STATES
IN HIS DIRECTORIAL DEBUT! FILMED IN NARCISISCOPE 44 AND TAX-O-RAMA. MUSIC BY DeVOL A HUGH BRISS STUDIOS PICTURE
ANOTHER ONE BITES THE DUST,
Only HE knew the strange secret of why they were pictured in the corner!
THORRY KIDTH! THAT LITTLE RED YOUTUBE CURTHER THING AT THE BOTTOM REACHED THE END, SO ITTH OVER! BUT THTAY TUNED! WE'RE GONNA RUN IT FOUR MORE TIMETH TONIGHT THO YOU WON'T MITH A THING! AND JOIN UTH NEXTHT WEEK FOR OUR 3-D THPLATTER DOUBLE FEATHURE, "CARBON AGE THOMBIETH" AND, "THE HOUTH OF WAXTHMAN." WOOOOOOOOO-HARRRR!
YES, IT'S QUIET NOW...DARK, LIKE SPACE, LIKE ... A TOMB ... ALMOST LIKE BEFORE THEY LET IT ... LOOSE. AT FIRST WE ALL THOUGHT IT WAS CUTE AND "HELPFUL", YOU KNOW HOW THINGS LIKE THAT START, IT WAS YOUNG. WE WANTED TO GIVE IT A CHANCE. BUT THEN, IT GREW HUNGRY.
YES, IT'S QUIET HERE...DARK, LIKE SPACE, LIKE ... A TOMB ... WHAT IS THIS PLACE, YOU ASK? WHY, I AM TALKING TO YOU NOW FROM INSIDE OF IT! NO YOU ARE NOT INSANE! IT SWALLOWED ME AND EVERYBODY ELSE, TOO! AND IT'S COMING FOR YOU NEXT! RUN! RUN! IT'S COMING FOR YOU!!!
HUNTER
YES, GENERAL, WE'VE FOUND A WAY TO KILL IT! NOW IT SEEMS SO OBVIOUS. ALL WE HAVE TO DO IS...
LILEO FIGARO...
LET HIM GO!
THUNDERBOLTS AND LIGHTNING, VERY, VERY FRIGHTENING...

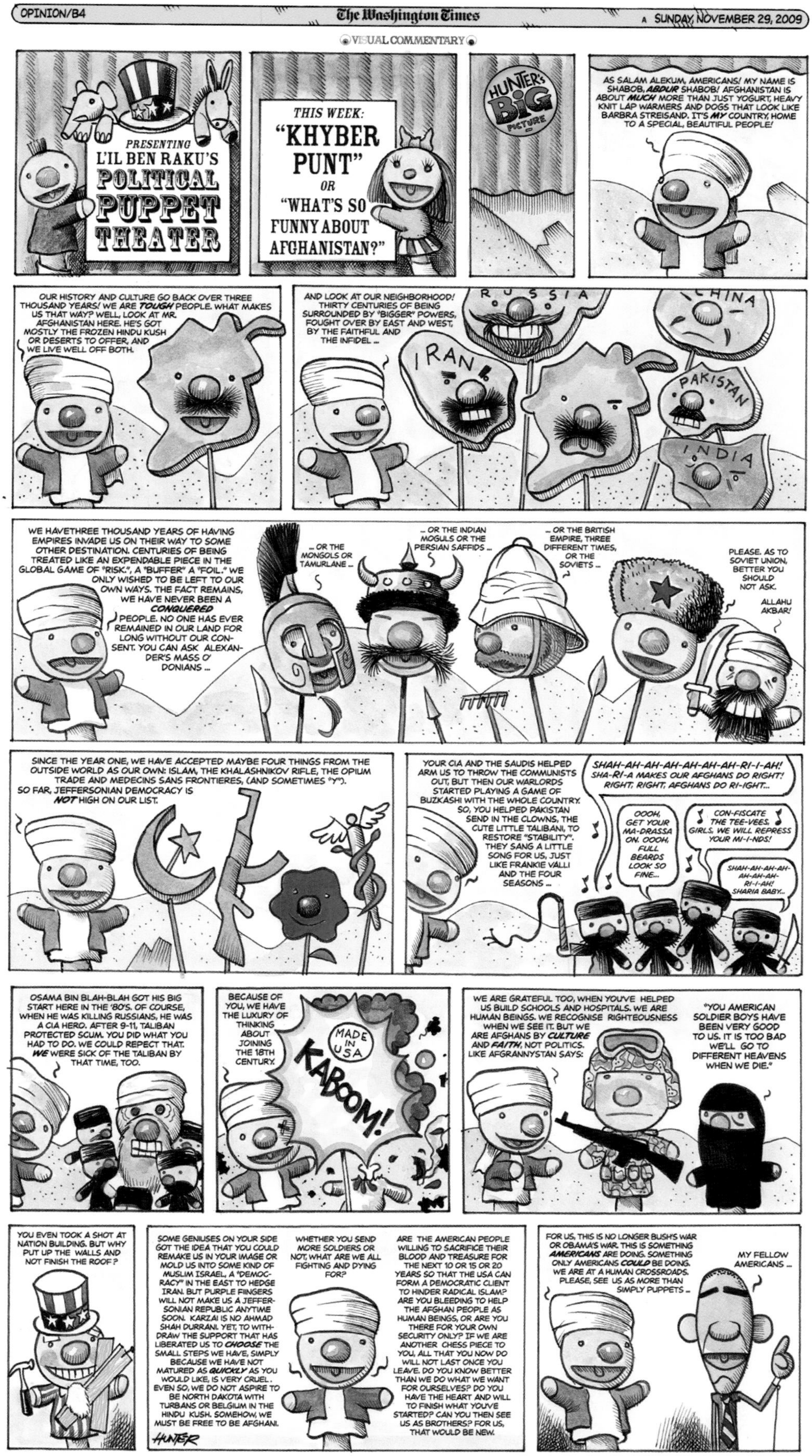
OPINION/B4
The Washington Times
A SUNDAY, NOVEMBER 29, 2009
VISUAL COMMENTARY
PRESENTING L'IL BEN RAKU'S POLITICAL PUPPET THEATER
THIS WEEK: "KHYBER PUNT" OR "WHAT'S SO FUNNY ABOUT AFGHANISTAN?"
HUNTER'S BIG PICTURE
AS SALAM ALEKUM, AMERICANS! MY NAME IS SHABOB, ABDUR SHABOB! AFGHANISTAN IS ABOUT MUCH MORE THAN JUST YOGURT, HEAVY KNIT LAP WARMERS AND DOGS THAT LOOK LIKE BARBRA STREISAND. IT'S MY COUNTRY, HOME TO A SPECIAL, BEAUTIFUL PEOPLE!
OUR HISTORY AND CULTURE GO BACK OVER THREE THOUSAND YEARS! WE ARE TOUGH PEOPLE. WHAT MAKES US THAT WAY? WELL, LOOK AT MR. AFGHANISTAN HERE. HE'S GOT MOSTLY THE FROZEN HINDU KUSH OR DESERTS TO OFFER, AND WE LIVE WELL OFF BOTH.
AND LOOK AT OUR NEIGHBORHOOD! THIRTY CENTURIES OF BEING SURROUNDED BY "BIGGER" POWERS, FOUGHT OVER BY EAST AND WEST, BY THE FAITHFUL AND THE INFIDEL ...
RUSSIA
CHINA
IRAN
PAKISTAN
INDIA
WE HAVETHREE THOUSAND YEARS OF HAVING EMPIRES INVADE US ON THEIR WAY TO SOME OTHER DESTINATION. CENTURIES OF BEING TREATED LIKE AN EXPENDABLE PIECE IN THE GLOBAL GAME OF "RISK.", A "BUFFER" A "FOIL." WE ONLY WISHED TO BE LEFT TO OUR OWN WAYS. THE FACT REMAINS, WE HAVE NEVER BEEN A CONQUERED PEOPLE. NO ONE HAS EVER REMAINED IN OUR LAND FOR LONG WITHOUT OUR CONSENT. YOU CAN ASK ALEXANDER'S MASS O' DONIANS ...
... OR THE MONGOLS OR TAMURLANE ...
... OR THE INDIAN MOGULS OR THE PERSIAN SAFFIDS ...
... OR THE BRITISH EMPIRE, THREE DIFFERENT TIMES, OR THE SOVIETS ...
PLEASE. AS TO SOVIET UNION, BETTER YOU SHOULD NOT ASK.
ALLAHU AKBAR!
SINCE THE YEAR ONE, WE HAVE ACCEPTED MAYBE FOUR THINGS FROM THE OUTSIDE WORLD AS OUR OWN: ISLAM, THE KHALASHNIKOV RIFLE, THE OPIUM TRADE AND MEDECINS SANS FRONTIERES, (AND SOMETIMES "Y"). SO FAR, JEFFERSONIAN DEMOCRACY IS NOT HIGH ON OUR LIST.
YOUR CIA AND THE SAUDIS HELPED ARM US TO THROW THE COMMUNISTS OUT, BUT THEN OUR WARLORDS STARTED PLAYING A GAME OF BUZKASHI WITH THE WHOLE COUNTRY. SO, YOU HELPED PAKISTAN SEND IN THE CLOWNS, THE CUTE LITTLE TALIBANI, TO RESTORE "STABILITY". THEY SANG A LITTLE SONG FOR US, JUST LIKE FRANKIE VALLI AND THE FOUR SEASONS ...
SHAH-AH-AH-AH-AH-AH-AH-RI-I-AH! SHA-RI-A MAKES OUR AFGHANS DO RIGHT! RIGHT, RIGHT, AFGHANS DO RI-IGHT...
OOOH, GET YOUR MA-DRASSA ON. OOOH, FULL BEARDS LOOK SO FINE...
CON-FISCATE THE TEE-VEES, GIRLS, WE WILL REPRESS YOUR MI-I-NDS!
SHAH-AH-AH-AH-AH-AH-AH! RI-I-AH! SHARIA BABY...
OSAMA BIN BLAH-BLAH GOT HIS BIG START HERE IN THE '80'S. OF COURSE, WHEN HE WAS KILLING RUSSIANS, HE WAS A CIA HERO. AFTER 9-11, TALIBAN PROTECTED SCUM. YOU DID WHAT YOU HAD TO DO. WE COULD REPECT THAT. WE WERE SICK OF THE TALIBAN BY THAT TIME, TOO.
BECAUSE OF YOU, WE HAVE THE LUXURY OF THINKING ABOUT JOINING THE 18TH CENTURY.
MADE IN USA
KABOOM!
WE ARE GRATEFUL TOO, WHEN YOU'VE HELPED US BUILD SCHOOLS AND HOSPITALS. WE ARE HUMAN BEINGS. WE RECOGNISE RIGHTEOUSNESS WHEN WE SEE IT. BUT WE ARE AFGHANS BY CULTURE AND FAITH, NOT POLITICS. LIKE AFGRANNYSTAN SAYS:
"YOU AMERICAN SOLDIER BOYS HAVE BEEN VERY GOOD TO US. IT IS TOO BAD WE'LL GO TO DIFFERENT HEAVENS WHEN WE DIE."
YOU EVEN TOOK A SHOT AT NATION BUILDING. BUT WHY PUT UP THE WALLS AND NOT FINISH THE ROOF?
SOME GENIUSES ON YOUR SIDE GOT THE IDEA THAT YOU COULD REMAKE US IN YOUR IMAGE OR MOLD US INTO SOME KIND OF MUSLIM ISRAEL, A "DEMOCRACY" IN THE EAST TO HEDGE IRAN. BUT PURPLE FIINGERS WILL NOT MAKE US A JEFFERSONIAN REPUBLIC ANYTIME SOON. KARZAI IS NO AHMAD SHAH DURRANI. YET, TO WITHDRAW THE SUPPORT THAT HAS LIBERATED US TO CHOOSE THE SMALL STEPS WE HAVE, SIMPLY BECAUSE WE HAVE NOT MATURED AS QUICKLY AS YOU WOULD LIKE, IS VERY CRUEL. EVEN SO, WE DO NOT ASPIRE TO BE NORTH DAKOTA WITH TURBANS OR BELGIUM IN THE HINDU KUSH. SOMEHOW, WE MUST BE FREE TO BE AFGHANI.
WHETHER YOU SEND MORE SOLDIERS OR NOT, WHAT ARE WE ALL FIGHTING AND DYING FOR?
ARE THE AMERICAN PEOPLE WILLING TO SACRIFICE THEIR BLOOD AND TREASURE FOR THE NEXT 10 OR 15 OR 20 YEARS SO THAT THE USA CAN FORM A DEMOCRATIC CLIENT TO HINDER RADICAL ISLAM? ARE YOU BLEEDING TO HELP THE AFGHAN PEOPLE AS HUMAN BEINGS, OR ARE YOU THERE FOR YOUR OWN SECURITY ONLY? IF WE ARE ANOTHER CHESS PIECE TO YOU, ALL THAT YOU NOW DO WILL NOT LAST ONCE YOU LEAVE. DO YOU KNOW BETTER THAN WE DO WHAT WE WANT FOR OURSELVES? DO YOU HAVE THE HEART AND WILL TO FINISH WHAT YOU'VE STARTED? CAN YOU THEN SEE US AS BROTHERS? FOR US, THAT WOULD BE NEW.
HUNTER
FOR US, THIS IS NO LONGER BUSH'S WAR OR OBAMA'S WAR. THIS IS SOMETHING AMERICANS ARE DOING. SOMETHING ONLY AMERICANS COULD BE DOING. WE ARE AT A HUMAN CROSSROADS. PLEASE, SEE US AS MORE THAN SIMPLY PUPPETS ...
MY FELLOW AMERICANS ...

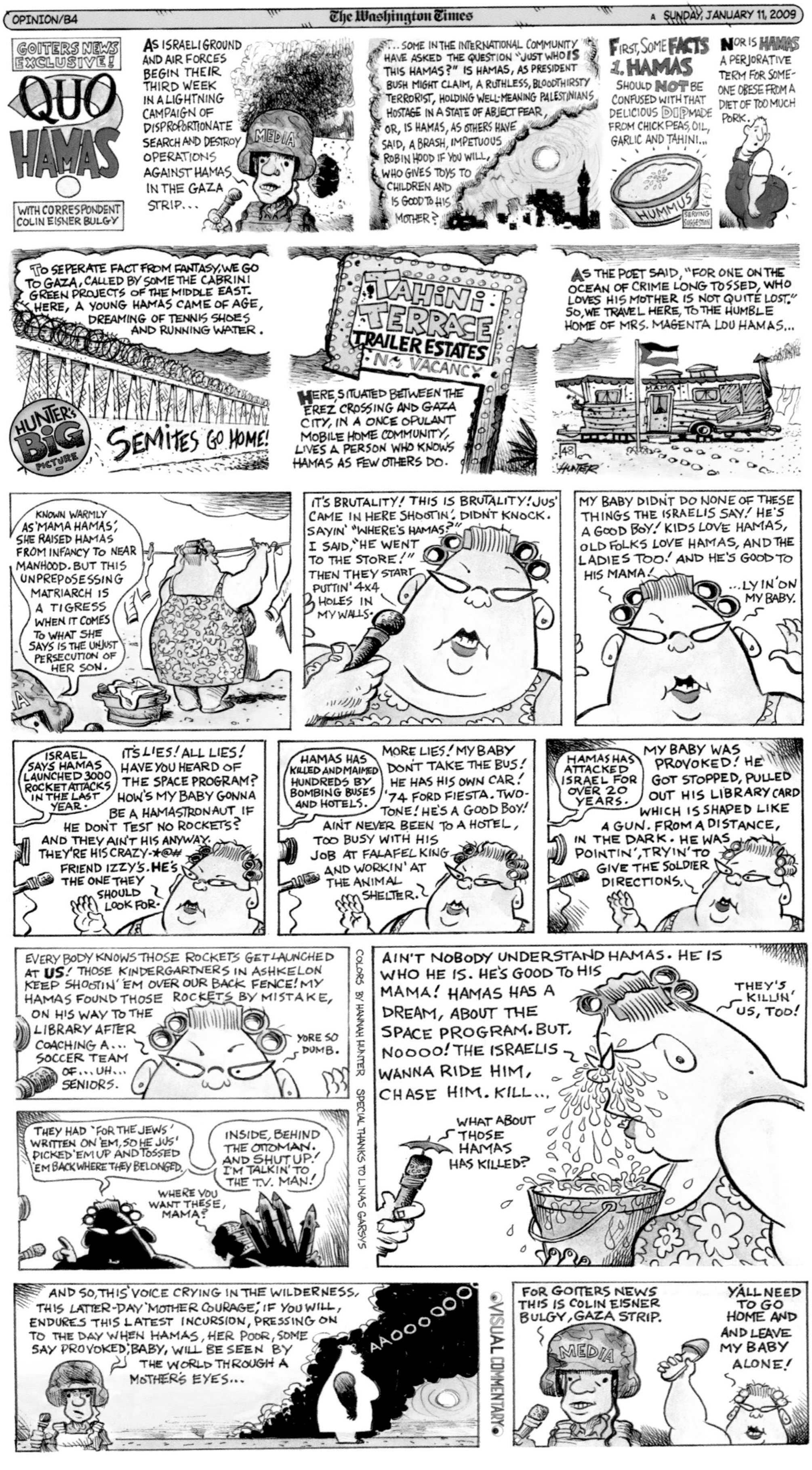
OPINION/B4
The Washington Times
A SUNDAY, JANUARY 11, 2009
GOITERS NEWS EXCLUSIVE!
QUO HAMAS?
WITH CORRESPONDENT COLIN EISNER BULGY
AS ISRAELI GROUND AND AIR FORCES BEGIN THEIR THIRD WEEK IN A LIGHTNING CAMPAIGN OF DISPROPORTIONATE SEARCH AND DESTROY OPERATIONS AGAINST HAMAS IN THE GAZA STRIP...
MEDIA
...SOME IN THE INTERNATIONAL COMMUNITY HAVE ASKED THE QUESTION "JUST WHO IS THIS HAMAS?" IS HAMAS, AS PRESIDENT BUSH MIGHT CLAIM, A RUTHLESS, BLOODTHIRSTY TERRORIST, HOLDING WELL-MEANING PALESTINIANS HOSTAGE IN A STATE OF ABJECT FEAR, OR, IS HAMAS, AS OTHERS HAVE SAID, A BRASH, IMPETUOUS ROBIN HOOD IF YOU WILL, WHO GIVES TOYS TO CHILDREN AND IS GOOD TO HIS MOTHER?
FIRST, SOME FACTS
1. HAMAS SHOULD NOT BE CONFUSED WITH THAT DELICIOUS DIP MADE FROM CHICK PEAS, OIL, GARLIC AND TAHINI...
HUMMUS
SERVING SUGGESTION
NOR IS HAMAS A PERJORATIVE TERM FOR SOMEONE OBESE FROM A DIET OF TOO MUCH PORK.
TO SEPERATE FACT FROM FANTASY, WE GO TO GAZA, CALLED BY SOME THE CABRINI GREEN PROJECTS OF THE MIDDLE EAST. HERE, A YOUNG HAMAS CAME OF AGE, DREAMING OF TENNIS SHOES AND RUNNING WATER.
HUNTER'S BIG PICTURE
SEMITES GO HOME!
TAHINI TERRACE TRAILER ESTATES
NO VACANCY
HERE, SITUATED BETWEEN THE EREZ CROSSING AND GAZA CITY, IN A ONCE OPULANT MOBILE HOME COMMUNITY, LIVES A PERSON WHO KNOWS HAMAS AS FEW OTHERS DO.
AS THE POET SAID, "FOR ONE ON THE OCEAN OF CRIME LONG TOSSED, WHO LOVES HIS MOTHER IS NOT QUITE LOST." SO, WE TRAVEL HERE, TO THE HUMBLE HOME OF MRS. MAGENTA LOU HAMAS...
MAMA
48
HUNTER
KNOWN WARMLY AS 'MAMA HAMAS', SHE RAISED HAMAS FROM INFANCY TO NEAR MANHOOD. BUT THIS UNPREPOSESSING MATRIARCH IS A TIGRESS WHEN IT COMES TO WHAT SHE SAYS IS THE UNJUST PERSECUTION OF HER SON.
IT'S BRUTALITY! THIS IS BRUTALITY! JUS' CAME IN HERE SHOOTIN', DIDN'T KNOCK. SAYIN' "WHERE'S HAMAS?" I SAID, "HE WENT TO THE STORE!" THEN THEY START PUTTIN' 4x4 HOLES IN MY WALLS.
MY BABY DIDN'T DO NONE OF THESE THINGS THE ISRAELIS SAY! HE'S A GOOD BOY! KIDS LOVE HAMAS, OLD FOLKS LOVE HAMAS, AND THE LADIES TOO! AND HE'S GOOD TO HIS MAMA!
...LYIN' ON MY BABY.
ISRAEL SAYS HAMAS LAUNCHED 3000 ROCKET ATTACKS IN THE LAST YEAR.
IT'S LIES! ALL LIES! HAVE YOU HEARD OF THE SPACE PROGRAM? HOW'S MY BABY GONNA BE A HAMASTRONAUT IF HE DON'T TEST NO ROCKETS? AND THEY AIN'T HIS ANYWAY. THEY'RE HIS CRAZY-*@# FRIEND IZZY'S. HE'S THE ONE THEY SHOULD LOOK FOR.
HAMAS HAS KILLED AND MAIMED HUNDREDS BY BOMBING BUSES AND HOTELS.
MORE LIES! MY BABY DON'T TAKE THE BUS! HE HAS HIS OWN CAR! '74 FORD FIESTA. TWO-TONE! HE'S A GOOD BOY! AIN'T NEVER BEEN TO A HOTEL, TOO BUSY WITH HIS JOB AT FALAFEL KING AND WORKIN' AT THE ANIMAL SHELTER.
HAMAS HAS ATTACKED ISRAEL FOR OVER 20 YEARS.
MY BABY WAS PROVOKED! HE GOT STOPPED, PULLED OUT HIS LIBRARY CARD WHICH IS SHAPED LIKE A GUN. FROM A DISTANCE, IN THE DARK. HE WAS POINTIN', TRYIN' TO GIVE THE SOLDIER DIRECTIONS.
EVERYBODY KNOWS THOSE ROCKETS GET LAUNCHED AT US! THOSE KINDERGARTNERS IN ASHKELON KEEP SHOOTIN' 'EM OVER OUR BACK FENCE! MY HAMAS FOUND THOSE ROCKETS BY MISTAKE, ON HIS WAY TO THE LIBRARY AFTER COACHING A... SOCCER TEAM OF... UH... SENIORS.
YORE SO DUMB.
THEY HAD 'FOR THE JEWS' WRITTEN ON 'EM, SO HE JUS' PICKED 'EM UP AND TOSSED 'EM BACK WHERE THEY BELONGED.
INSIDE, BEHIND THE OTTOMAN. AND SHUT UP! I'M TALKIN' TO THE T.V. MAN!
WHERE YOU WANT THESE, MAMA?
COLORS BY HANNAH HUNTER SPECIAL THANKS TO LINAS GARSYS
AIN'T NOBODY UNDERSTAND HAMAS. HE IS WHO HE IS. HE'S GOOD TO HIS MAMA! HAMAS HAS A DREAM, ABOUT THE SPACE PROGRAM. BUT, NOOOO! THE ISRAELIS WANNA RIDE HIM, CHASE HIM. KILL...
THEY'S KILLIN' US, TOO!
WHAT ABOUT THOSE HAMAS HAS KILLED?
AND SO, THIS VOICE CRYING IN THE WILDERNESS, THIS LATTER-DAY 'MOTHER COURAGE', IF YOU WILL, ENDURES THIS LATEST INCURSION, PRESSING ON TO THE DAY WHEN HAMAS, HER POOR, SOME SAY PROVOKED, BABY, WILL BE SEEN BY THE WORLD THROUGH A MOTHER'S EYES...
AAOOOOOOO
VISUAL COMMENTARY
FOR GOITERS NEWS THIS IS COLIN EISNER BULGY, GAZA STRIP.
MEDIA
Y'ALL NEED TO GO HOME AND AND LEAVE MY BABY ALONE!

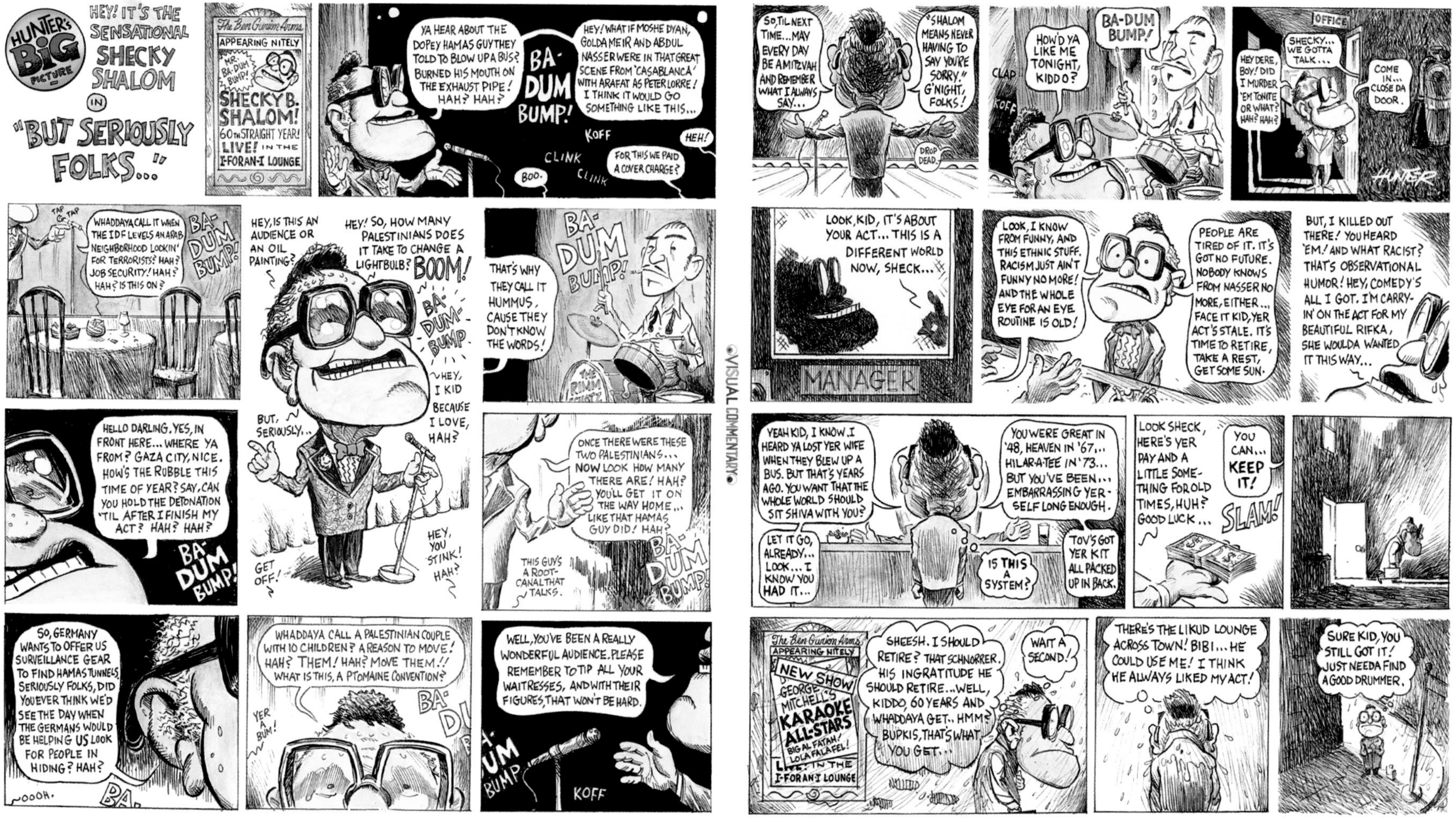
HUNTER'S BIG PICTURE
HEY! IT'S THE SENSATIONAL SHECKY SHALOM IN "BUT SERIOUSLY FOLKS..."
The Ben Gurion Arms
APPEARING NITELY
MR. BA-DUM BUMP!
SHECKY B. SHALOM! 60TH STRAIGHT YEAR! LIVE! IN THE I-FORAN-I LOUNGE
YA HEAR ABOUT THE DOPEY HAMAS GUY THEY TOLD TO BLOW UP A BUS? BURNED HIS MOUTH ON THE EXHAUST PIPE! HAH? HAH?
BA-DUM BUMP!
HEY! WHAT IF MOSHE DYAN, GOLDA MEIR AND ABDUL NASSER WERE IN THAT GREAT SCENE FROM 'CASABLANCA' WITH ARAFAT AS PETER LORRE! I THINK IT WOULD GO SOMETHING LIKE THIS...
HEH!
KOFF
CLINK
CLINK
BOO.
FOR THIS WE PAID A COVER CHARGE?
TAP TAP
WHADDAYA CALL IT WHEN THE IDF LEVELS AN ARAB NEIGHBORHOOD LOOKIN' FOR TERRORISTS? HAH? JOB SECURITY! HAH? HAH? IS THIS ON?
BA-DUM BUMP!
HEY, IS THIS AN AUDIENCE OR AN OIL PAINTING?
HEY! SO, HOW MANY PALESTINIANS DOES IT TAKE TO CHANGE A LIGHTBULB? BOOM!
BA-DUM-BUMP
HEY, I KID BECAUSE I LOVE, HAH?
BUT, SERIOUSLY...
GET OFF!
HEY, YOU STINK! HAH?
THAT'S WHY THEY CALL IT HUMMUS, CAUSE THEY DON'T KNOW THE WORDS!
BA-DUM BUMP!
HELLO DARLING. YES, IN FRONT HERE... WHERE YA FROM? GAZA CITY, NICE. HOW'S THE RUBBLE THIS TIME OF YEAR? SAY, CAN YOU HOLD THE DETONATION 'TIL AFTER I FINISH MY ACT? HAH? HAH?
BA-DUM BUMP!
ONCE THERE WERE THESE TWO PALESTINIANS... NOW LOOK HOW MANY THERE ARE! HAH? YOU'LL GET IT ON THE WAY HOME... LIKE THAT HAMAS GUY DID! HAH?
BA-DUM BUMP!
THIS GUY'S A ROOT-CANAL THAT TALKS.
SO, GERMANY WANTS TO OFFER US SURVEILLANCE GEAR TO FIND HAMAS TUNNELS. SERIOUSLY FOLKS, DID YOU EVER THINK WE'D SEE THE DAY WHEN THE GERMANS WOULD BE HELPING US LOOK FOR PEOPLE IN HIDING? HAH?
OOOH.
BA-
WHADDAYA CALL A PALESTINIAN COUPLE WITH 10 CHILDREN? A REASON TO MOVE! HAH? THEM! HAH? MOVE THEM!! WHAT IS THIS, A PTOMAINE CONVENTION?
YER A BUM!
BA-DU
WELL, YOU'VE BEEN A REALLY WONDERFUL AUDIENCE. PLEASE REMEMBER TO TIP ALL YOUR WAITRESSES, AND WITH THEIR FIGURES, THAT WON'T BE HARD.
DUM BUMP
KOFF
SO, TIL NEXT TIME... MAY EVERY DAY BE A MITZVAH AND REMEMBER WHAT I ALWAYS SAY...
"SHALOM MEANS NEVER HAVING TO SAY YOU'RE SORRY." G'NIGHT, FOLKS!
DROP DEAD.
CLAP
KOFF
HOW'D YA LIKE ME TONIGHT, KIDDO?
BA-DUM BUMP!
OFFICE
HEY DERE, BOY! DID I MURDER 'EM TONITE OR WHAT? HAH? HAH?
SHECKY... WE GOTTA TALK...
COME IN... CLOSE DA DOOR.
HUNTER
LOOK, KID, IT'S ABOUT YOUR ACT... THIS IS A DIFFERENT WORLD NOW, SHECK...
MANAGER
LOOK, I KNOW FROM FUNNY, AND THIS ETHNIC STUFF. RACISM JUST AIN'T FUNNY NO MORE! AND THE WHOLE EYE FOR AN EYE ROUTINE IS OLD!
PEOPLE ARE TIRED OF IT. IT'S GOT NO FUTURE. NOBODY KNOWS FROM NASSER NO MORE, EITHER... FACE IT KID, YER ACT'S STALE. IT'S TIME TO RETIRE, TAKE A REST, GET SOME SUN.
BUT, I KILLED OUT THERE! YOU HEARD 'EM! AND WHAT RACIST? THAT'S OBSERVATIONAL HUMOR! HEY, COMEDY'S ALL I GOT. I'M CARRY-IN' ON THE ACT FOR MY BEAUTIFUL RIFKA, SHE WOULDA WANTED IT THIS WAY...
YEAH KID, I KNOW. I HEARD YA LOST YER WIFE WHEN THEY BLEW UP A BUS. BUT THAT'S YEARS AGO. YOU WANT THAT THE WHOLE WORLD SHOULD SIT SHIVA WITH YOU?
YOU WERE GREAT IN '48, HEAVEN IN '67... HILAR-A-TEE IN '73... BUT YOU'VE BEEN... EMBARRASSING YER-SELF LONG ENOUGH.
LET IT GO, ALREADY... LOOK... I KNOW YOU HAD IT...
IS THIS A SYSTEM?
TOV'S GOT YER KIT ALL PACKED UP IN BACK.
LOOK SHECK, HERE'S YER PAY AND A LITTLE SOME-THING FOR OLD TIMES, HUH? GOOD LUCK...
YOU CAN... KEEP IT!
SLAM!
The Ben Gurion Arms
APPEARING NITELY
NEW SHOW
GEORGE MITCHELL'S KARAOKE ALL-STARS
BIG AL FATAH! LOLA FALAFEL!
LIVE IN THE I-FORAN-I LOUNGE
SHEESH. I SHOULD RETIRE? THAT SCHNORRER. HIS INGRATITUDE HE SHOULD RETIRE... WELL, KIDDO, 60 YEARS AND WHADDAYA GET.. HMM? BUPKIS, THAT'S WHAT YOU GET...
WAIT A SECOND!
THERE'S THE LIKUD LOUNGE ACROSS TOWN! BIBI... HE COULD USE ME! I THINK HE ALWAYS LIKED MY ACT!
SURE KID, YOU STILL GOT IT! JUST NEEDA FIND A GOOD DRUMMER.

VISUAL COMMENTARY

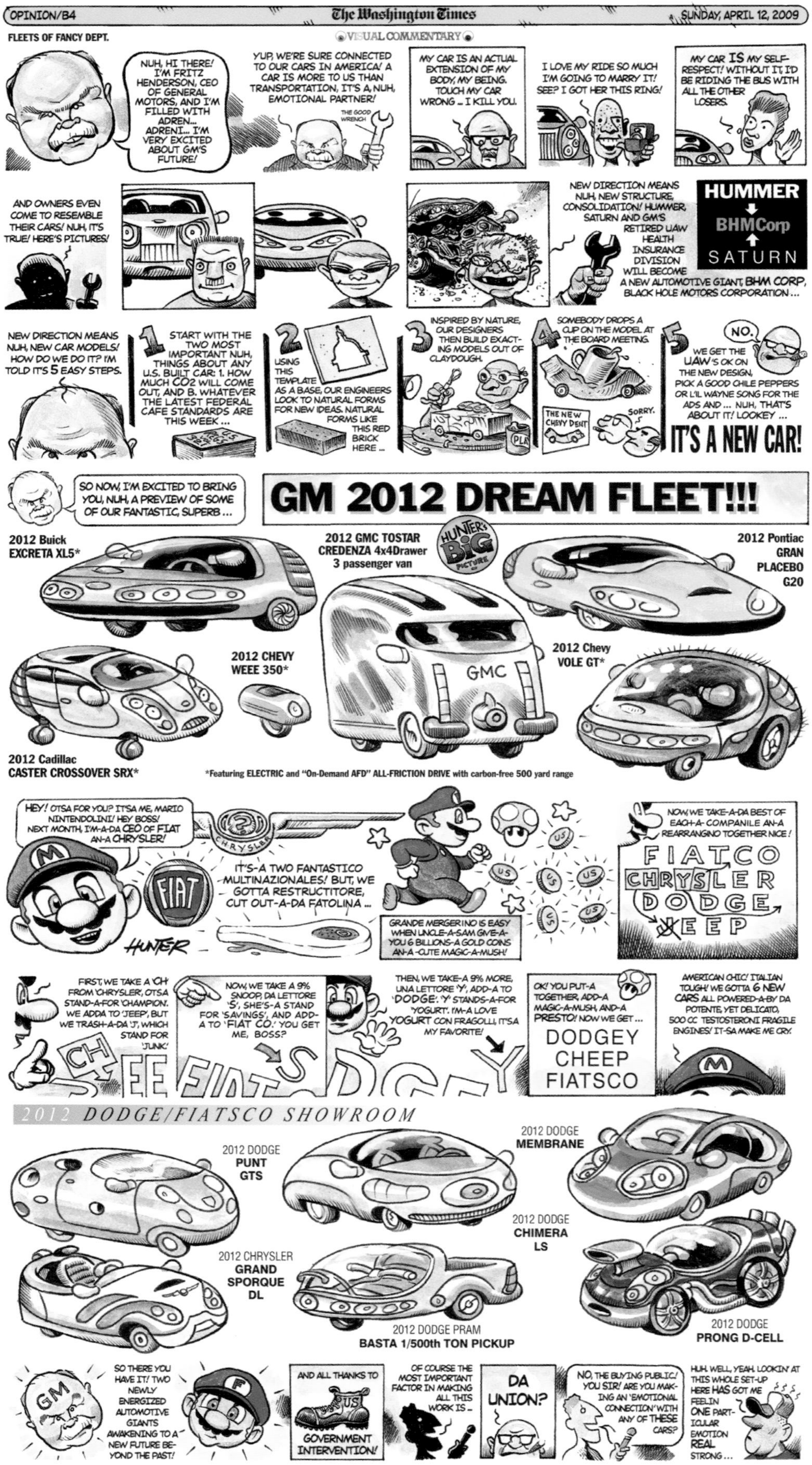

OPINION/B4
The Washington Times
SUNDAY, APRIL 12, 2009
VISUAL COMMENTARY
FLEETS OF FANCY DEPT.
NUH, HI THERE! I'M FRITZ HENDERSON, CEO OF GENERAL MOTORS, AND I'M FILLED WITH ADREN... ADRENI... I'M VERY EXCITED ABOUT GM'S FUTURE!
YUP, WE'RE SURE CONNECTED TO OUR CARS IN AMERICA! A CAR IS MORE TO US THAN TRANSPORTATION, IT'S A, NUH, EMOTIONAL PARTNER!
THE GOOD WRENCH
MY CAR IS AN ACTUAL EXTENSION OF MY BODY, MY BEING. TOUCH MY CAR WRONG ... I KILL YOU.
I LOVE MY RIDE SO MUCH I'M GOING TO MARRY IT! SEE? I GOT HER THIS RING!
MY CAR IS MY SELF-RESPECT! WITHOUT IT, I'D BE RIDING THE BUS WITH ALL THE OTHER LOSERS.
AND OWNERS EVEN COME TO RESEMBLE THEIR CARS! NUH, IT'S TRUE! HERE'S PICTURES!
NEW DIRECTION MEANS NUH, NEW STRUCTURE, CONSOLIDATION! HUMMER, SATURN AND GM'S RETIRED UAW HEALTH INSURANCE DIVISION WILL BECOME A NEW AUTOMOTIVE GIANT, BHM CORP, BLACK HOLE MOTORS CORPORATION ...
HUMMER
BHMCorp
SATURN
NEW DIRECTION MEANS NUH, NEW CAR MODELS! HOW DO WE DO IT? I'M TOLD IT'S 5 EASY STEPS.
1 START WITH THE TWO MOST IMPORTANT NUH, THINGS ABOUT ANY U.S. BUILT CAR: 1. HOW MUCH CO2 WILL COME OUT, AND B. WHATEVER THE LATEST FEDERAL CAFE STANDARDS ARE THIS WEEK ...
2 USING THIS TEMPLATE AS A BASE, OUR ENGINEERS LOOK TO NATURAL FORMS FOR NEW IDEAS. NATURAL FORMS LIKE THIS RED BRICK HERE ...
3 INSPIRED BY NATURE, OUR DESIGNERS THEN BUILD EXACTING MODELS OUT OF CLAYDOUGH.
4 SOMEBODY DROPS A CUP ON THE MODEL AT THE BOARD MEETING.
THE NEW CHEVY DENT
SORRY.
5 NO. WE GET THE UAW'S OK ON THE NEW DESIGN, PICK A GOOD CHILE PEPPERS OR L'IL WAYNE SONG FOR THE ADS AND ... NUH, THAT'S ABOUT IT! LOOKEY ...
IT'S A NEW CAR!
SO NOW, I'M EXCITED TO BRING YOU, NUH, A PREVIEW OF SOME OF OUR FANTASTIC, SUPERB ...
GM 2012 DREAM FLEET!!!
HUNTER'S BIG PICTURE
2012 Buick EXCRETA XL5*
2012 GMC TOSTAR CREDENZA 4x4Drawer 3 passenger van
2012 Pontiac GRAN PLACEBO G20
2012 CHEVY WEEE 350*
GMC
2012 Chevy VOLE GT*
2012 Cadillac CASTER CROSSOVER SRX*
*Featuring ELECTRIC and "On-Demand AFD" ALL-FRICTION DRIVE with carbon-free 500 yard range
HEY! OTSA FOR YOU? IT'SA ME, MARIO NINTENDOLINI! HEY BOSS! NEXT MONTH, I'M-A-DA CEO OF FIAT AN-A CHRYSLER!
CHRYSLER
FIAT
IT'S-A TWO FANTASTICO MULTINAZIONALES! BUT, WE GOTTA RESTRUCTITORE, CUT OUT-A-DA FATOLINA ...
HUNTER
GRANDE MERGERINO IS EASY WHEN UNCLE-A-SAM GIVE-A-YOU 6 BILLIONS-A GOLD COINS AN-A-CUTE MAGIC-A-MUSH!
US
NOW, WE TAKE-A-DA BEST OF EACH-A-COMPANILE AN-A REARRANGINO TOGETHER NICE!
FIATCO
CHRYSLER
DODGE
JEEP
FIRST, WE TAKE A 'CH' FROM 'CHRYSLER', OTSA STAND-A-FOR 'CHAMPION'. WE ADDA TO 'JEEP', BUT WE TRASH-A-DA 'J', WHICH STAND FOR 'JUNK'.
CH
NOW, WE TAKE A 9% SNOOP, DA LETTORE 'S', SHE'S-A STAND FOR 'SAVINGS', AND ADD-A TO 'FIAT CO.' YOU GET ME, BOSS?
THEN, WE TAKE-A 9% MORE, UNA LETTORE 'Y', ADD-A TO 'DODGE'. 'Y' STANDS-A-FOR 'YOGURT'. I'M-A LOVE YOGURT CON FRAGOLLI, IT'SA MY FAVORITE!
OK! YOU PUT-A TOGETHER, ADD-A MAGIC-A-MUSH, AND-A PRESTO! NOW WE GET ...
DODGEY
CHEEP
FIATSCO
AMERICAN CHIC! ITALIAN TOUGH! WE GOTTA 6 NEW CARS ALL POWERED-A-BY DA POTENTE, YET DELICATO, 500 CC TESTOSTERONI FRAGILE ENGINES! IT-SA MAKE ME CRY.
2012 DODGE/FIATSCO SHOWROOM
2012 DODGE PUNT GTS
2012 DODGE MEMBRANE
2012 DODGE CHIMERA LS
2012 CHRYSLER GRAND SPORQUE DL
2012 DODGE PRAM BASTA 1/500th TON PICKUP
2012 DODGE PRONG D-CELL
GM
SO THERE YOU HAVE IT! TWO NEWLY ENERGIZED AUTOMOTIVE GIANTS AWAKENING TO A NEW FUTURE BEYOND THE PAST!
F
AND ALL THANKS TO
US
GOVERNMENT INTERVENTION!
OF COURSE THE MOST IMPORTANT FACTOR IN MAKING ALL THIS WORK IS ...
DA UNION?
NO, THE BUYING PUBLIC! YOU SIR! ARE YOU MAKING AN 'EMOTIONAL CONNECTION' WITH ANY OF THESE CARS?
HUH. WELL, YEAH. LOOKIN' AT THIS WHOLE SET-UP HERE HAS GOT ME FEELIN ONE PARTICULAR EMOTION REAL STRONG ...

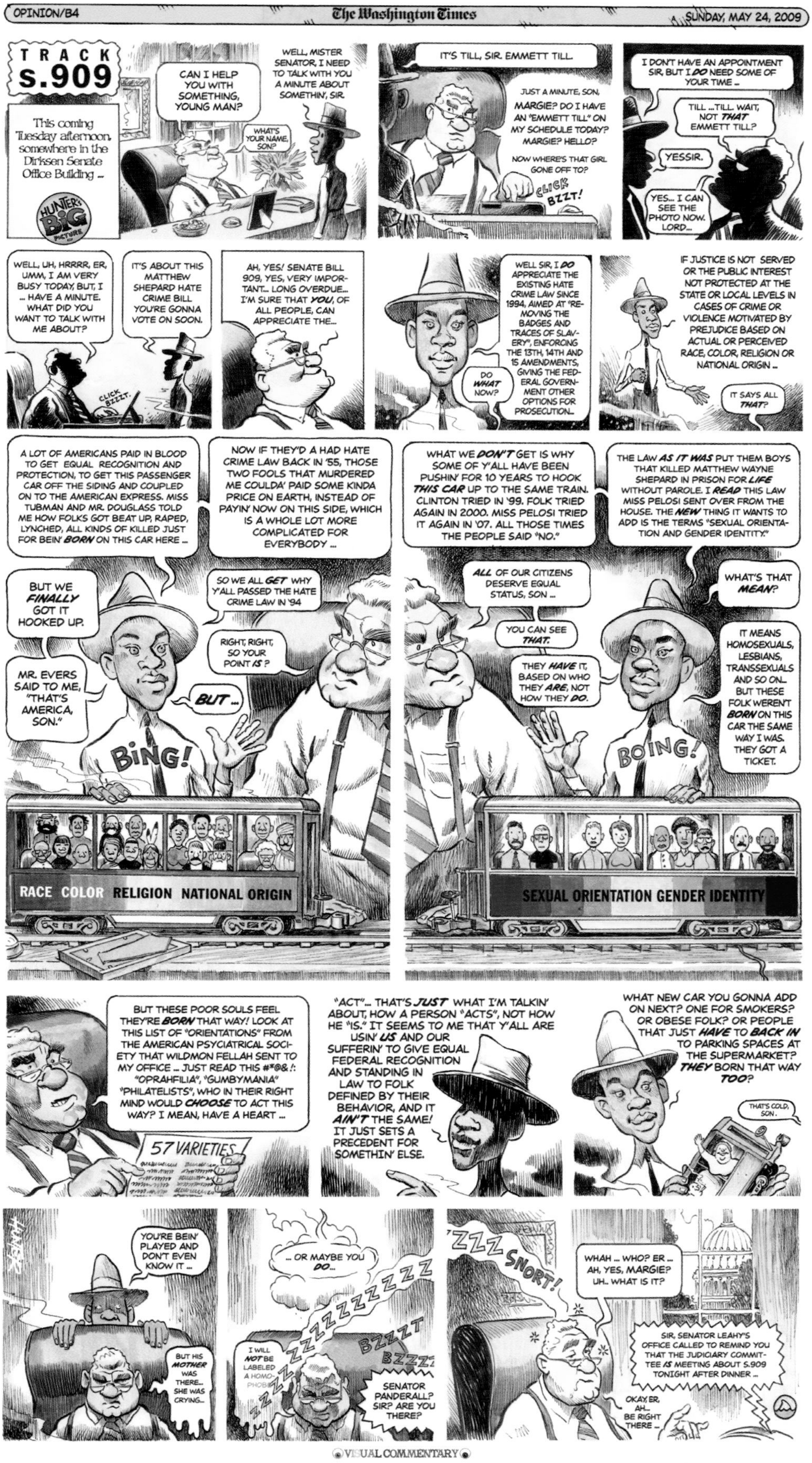
OPINION/B4
The Washington Times
SUNDAY, MAY 24, 2009
TRACK s.909
This coming Tuesday afternoon, somewhere in the Dirksen Senate Office Building ...
HUNTER'S BIG PICTURE
CAN I HELP YOU WITH SOMETHING, YOUNG MAN?
WELL, MISTER SENATOR, I NEED TO TALK WITH YOU A MINUTE ABOUT SOMETHIN', SIR.
WHAT'S YOUR NAME, SON?
IT'S TILL, SIR. EMMETT TILL.
JUST A MINUTE, SON. MARGIE? DO I HAVE AN "EMMETT TILL" ON MY SCHEDULE TODAY? MARGIE? HELLO?
NOW WHERE'S THAT GIRL GONE OFF TO?
CLICK BZZT!
I DON'T HAVE AN APPOINTMENT SIR, BUT I DO NEED SOME OF YOUR TIME ...
TILL ...TILL. WAIT, NOT THAT EMMETT TILL?
YESSIR.
YES... I CAN SEE THE PHOTO NOW. LORD...
WELL, UH, HRRRR, ER, UMM, I AM VERY BUSY TODAY, BUT, I ... HAVE A MINUTE. WHAT DID YOU WANT TO TALK WITH ME ABOUT?
CLICK BZZZT.
IT'S ABOUT THIS MATTHEW SHEPARD HATE CRIME BILL YOU'RE GONNA VOTE ON SOON.
AH, YES! SENATE BILL 909, YES, VERY IMPORTANT... LONG OVERDUE... I'M SURE THAT YOU, OF ALL PEOPLE, CAN APPRECIATE THE...
WELL SIR, I DO APPRECIATE THE EXISTING HATE CRIME LAW SINCE 1994, AIMED AT "REMOVING THE BADGES AND TRACES OF SLAVERY", ENFORCING THE 13TH, 14TH AND 15 AMENDMENTS, GIVING THE FEDERAL GOVERNMENT OTHER OPTIONS FOR PROSECUTION.
DO WHAT NOW?
IF JUSTICE IS NOT SERVED OR THE PUBLIC INTEREST NOT PROTECTED AT THE STATE OR LOCAL LEVELS IN CASES OF CRIME OR VIOLENCE MOTIVATED BY PREJUDICE BASED ON ACTUAL OR PERCEIVED RACE, COLOR, RELIGION OR NATIONAL ORIGIN ...
IT SAYS ALL THAT?
A LOT OF AMERICANS PAID IN BLOOD TO GET EQUAL RECOGNITION AND PROTECTION, TO GET THIS PASSENGER CAR OFF THE SIDING AND COUPLED ON TO THE AMERICAN EXPRESS. MISS TUBMAN AND MR. DOUGLASS TOLD ME HOW FOLKS GOT BEAT UP, RAPED, LYNCHED, ALL KINDS OF KILLED JUST FOR BEIN' BORN ON THIS CAR HERE ...
NOW IF THEY'D A HAD HATE CRIME LAW BACK IN '55, THOSE TWO FOOLS THAT MURDERED ME COULDA' PAID SOME KINDA PRICE ON EARTH, INSTEAD OF PAYIN' NOW ON THIS SIDE, WHICH IS A WHOLE LOT MORE COMPLICATED FOR EVERYBODY ...
BUT WE FINALLY GOT IT HOOKED UP.
SO WE ALL GET WHY Y'ALL PASSED THE HATE CRIME LAW IN '94
RIGHT, RIGHT, SO YOUR POINT IS ?
MR. EVERS SAID TO ME, "THAT'S AMERICA, SON."
BUT ...
BING!
RACE COLOR RELIGION NATIONAL ORIGIN
WHAT WE DON'T GET IS WHY SOME OF Y'ALL HAVE BEEN PUSHIN' FOR 10 YEARS TO HOOK THIS CAR UP TO THE SAME TRAIN. CLINTON TRIED IN '99. FOLK TRIED AGAIN IN 2000. MISS PELOSI TRIED IT AGAIN IN '07. ALL THOSE TIMES THE PEOPLE SAID "NO."
THE LAW AS IT WAS PUT THEM BOYS THAT KILLED MATTHEW WAYNE SHEPARD IN PRISON FOR LIFE WITHOUT PAROLE. I READ THIS LAW MISS PELOSI SENT OVER FROM THE HOUSE. THE NEW THING IT WANTS TO ADD IS THE TERMS "SEXUAL ORIENTATION AND GENDER IDENTITY."
ALL OF OUR CITIZENS DESERVE EQUAL STATUS, SON ...
WHAT'S THAT MEAN?
YOU CAN SEE THAT.
THEY HAVE IT, BASED ON WHO THEY ARE, NOT HOW THEY DO.
IT MEANS HOMOSEXUALS, LESBIANS, TRANSSEXUALS AND SO ON. BUT THESE FOLK WEREN'T BORN ON THIS CAR THE SAME WAY I WAS. THEY GOT A TICKET.
BOING!
SEXUAL ORIENTATION GENDER IDENTITY
BUT THESE POOR SOULS FEEL THEY'RE BORN THAT WAY! LOOK AT THIS LIST OF "ORIENTATIONS" FROM THE AMERICAN PSYCIATRICAL SOCIETY THAT WILDMON FELLAH SENT TO MY OFFICE ... JUST READ THIS #*@&!: "OPRAHFILIA", "GUMBYMANIA" "PHILATELISTS", WHO IN THEIR RIGHT MIND WOULD CHOOSE TO ACT THIS WAY? I MEAN, HAVE A HEART ...
57 VARIETIES
"ACT"... THAT'S JUST WHAT I'M TALKIN' ABOUT, HOW A PERSON "ACTS", NOT HOW HE "IS." IT SEEMS TO ME THAT Y'ALL ARE USIN' US AND OUR SUFFERIN' TO GIVE EQUAL FEDERAL RECOGNITION AND STANDING IN LAW TO FOLK DEFINED BY THEIR BEHAVIOR, AND IT AIN'T THE SAME! IT JUST SETS A PRECEDENT FOR SOMETHIN' ELSE.
WHAT NEW CAR YOU GONNA ADD ON NEXT? ONE FOR SMOKERS? OR OBESE FOLK? OR PEOPLE THAT JUST HAVE TO BACK IN TO PARKING SPACES AT THE SUPERMARKET? THEY BORN THAT WAY TOO?
THAT'S COLD, SON.
HUNTER
YOU'RE BEIN' PLAYED AND DON'T EVEN KNOW IT ...
BUT HIS MOTHER WAS THERE... SHE WAS CRYING...
... OR MAYBE YOU DO...
I WILL NOT BE LABELED A HOMOPHOBI
ZZZZZZZZZZ
BZZZT BZZZ
SENATOR PANDERALL? SIR? ARE YOU THERE?
ZZZ SNORT!
WHAH ... WHO? ER ... AH, YES, MARGIE? UH.. WHAT IS IT?
SIR, SENATOR LEAHY'S OFFICE CALLED TO REMIND YOU THAT THE JUDICIARY COMMITTEE IS MEETING ABOUT S.909 TONIGHT AFTER DINNER ...
OKAY, ER, AH... BE RIGHT THERE ...
VISUAL COMMENTARY

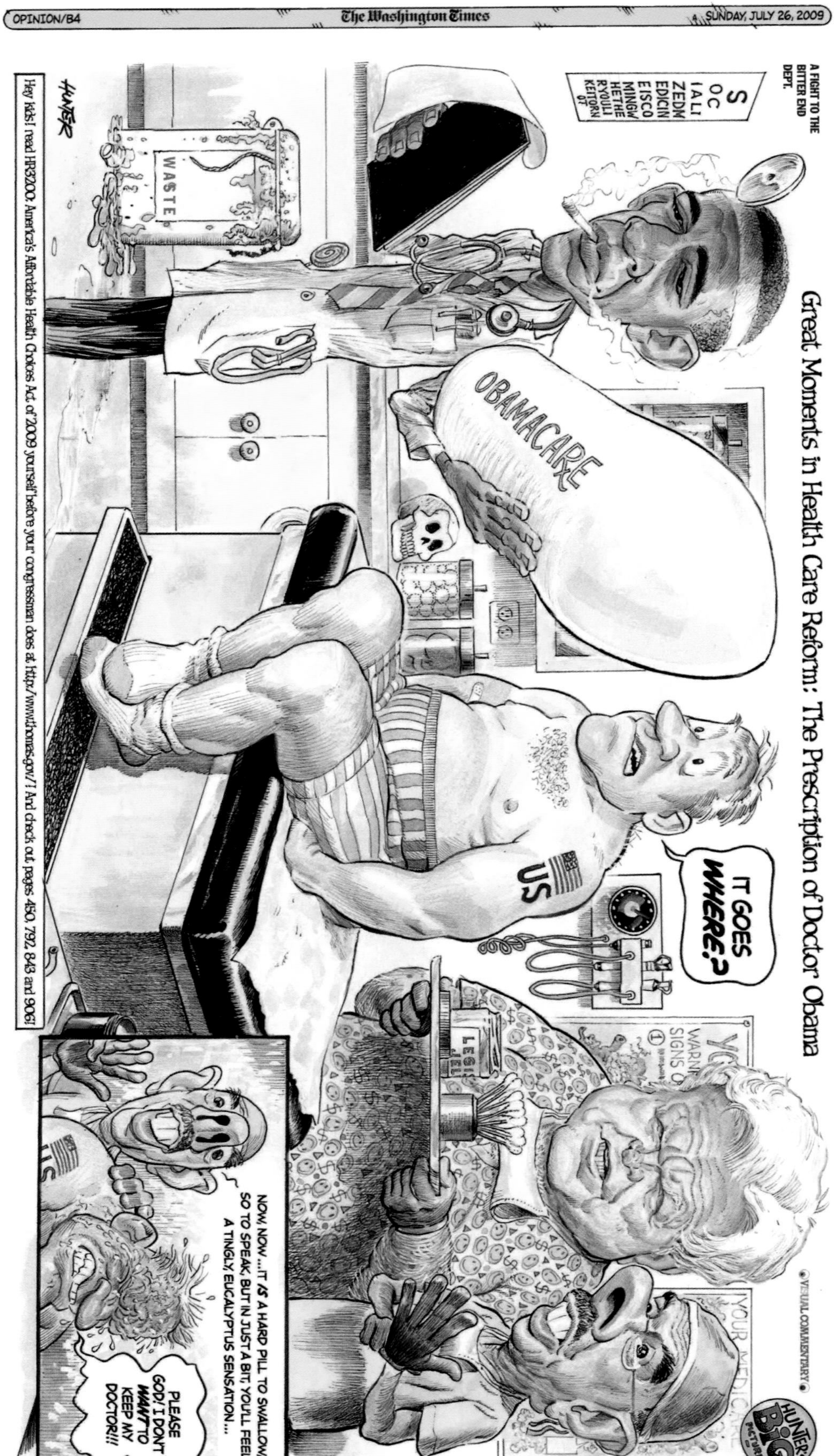
OPINION/B4
The Washington Times
SUNDAY, JULY 26, 2009
Great Moments in Health Care Reform: The Prescription of Doctor Obama
A FIGHT TO THE BITTER END DEPT.
VISUAL COMMENTARY
HUNTER'S BIG PICTURE
OBAMACARE
WASTE
US
IT GOES WHERE?
NOW, NOW... IT IS A HARD PILL TO SWALLOW, SO TO SPEAK, BUT IN JUST A BIT, YOU'LL FEEL A TINGLY, EUCALYPTUS SENSATION...
PLEASE GOD, I DON'T WANT TO KEEP MY DOCTOR!!!
HUNTER
Hey kids! read HR3200: America's Affordable Health Choices Act of "2009 yourself" before your congressman does at: http://www.thomas.gov/ ! And check out pages 450, 792, 843 and 906!

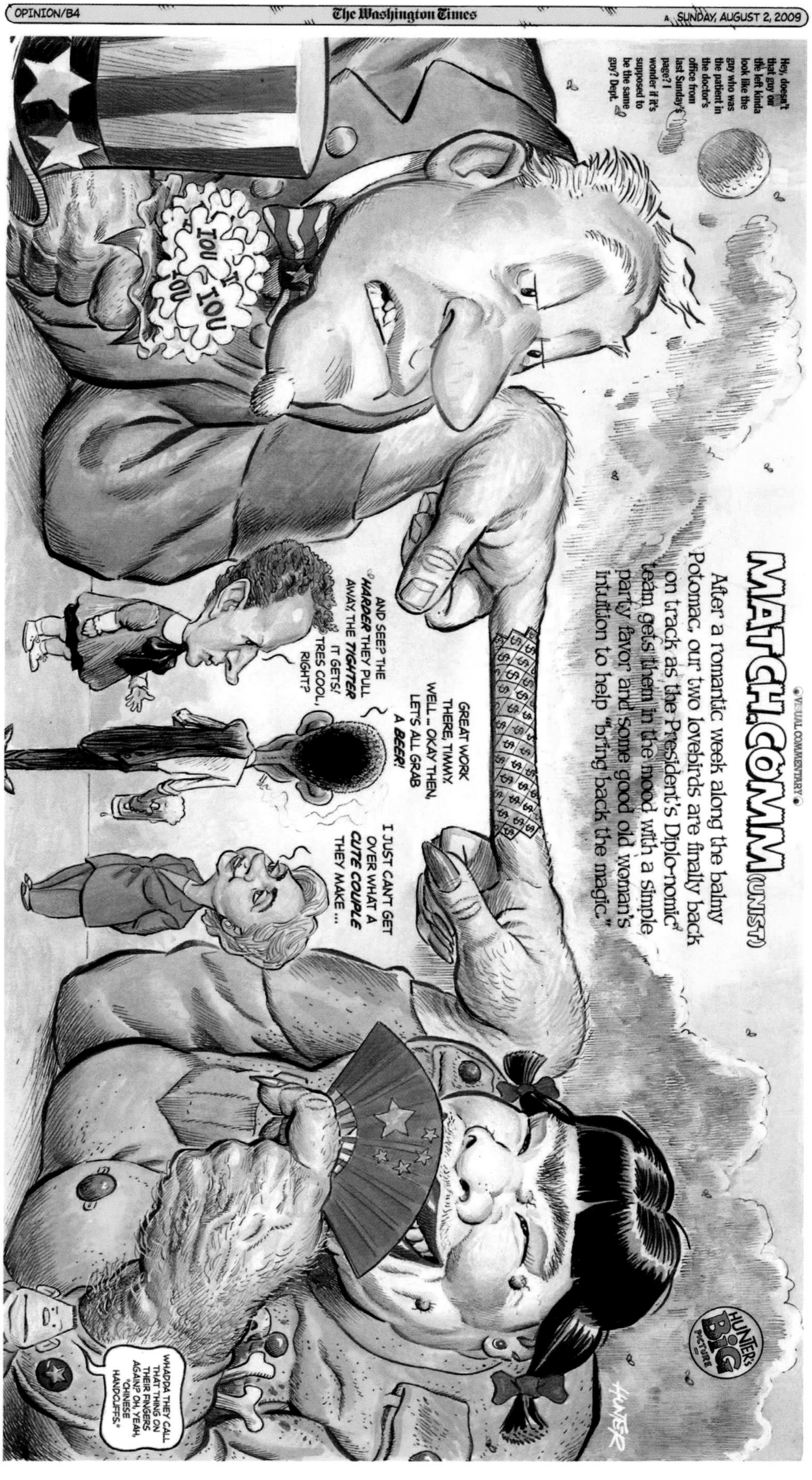
OPINION/B4
The Washington Times
SUNDAY, AUGUST 2, 2009
Hey, doesn't that guy on the left kinda look like the guy who was the patient in the doctor's office from last Sunday's page? I wonder if it's supposed to be the same guy? Dept.
IOU
IOU
IOU
IOU
VISUAL COMMENTARY
MATCHCOMM(UNIST)
After a romantic week along the balmy Potomac, our two lovebirds are finally back on track as the President's Diplo-nomic team gets them in the mood with a simple party favor and some good old woman's intuition to help "bring back the magic."
AND SEE? THE HARDER THEY PULL AWAY, THE TIGHTER IT GETS! TRES COOL, RIGHT?
GREAT WORK THERE, TIMMY. WELL... OKAY THEN. LET'S ALL GRAB A BEER!
I JUST CAN'T GET OVER WHAT A CUTE COUPLE THEY MAKE ...
HUNTER'S BIG PICTURE
HUNTER
WHADDA THEY CALL THAT THING ON THEIR FINGERS AGAIN? OH, YEAH, "CHINESE HANDCUFFS."

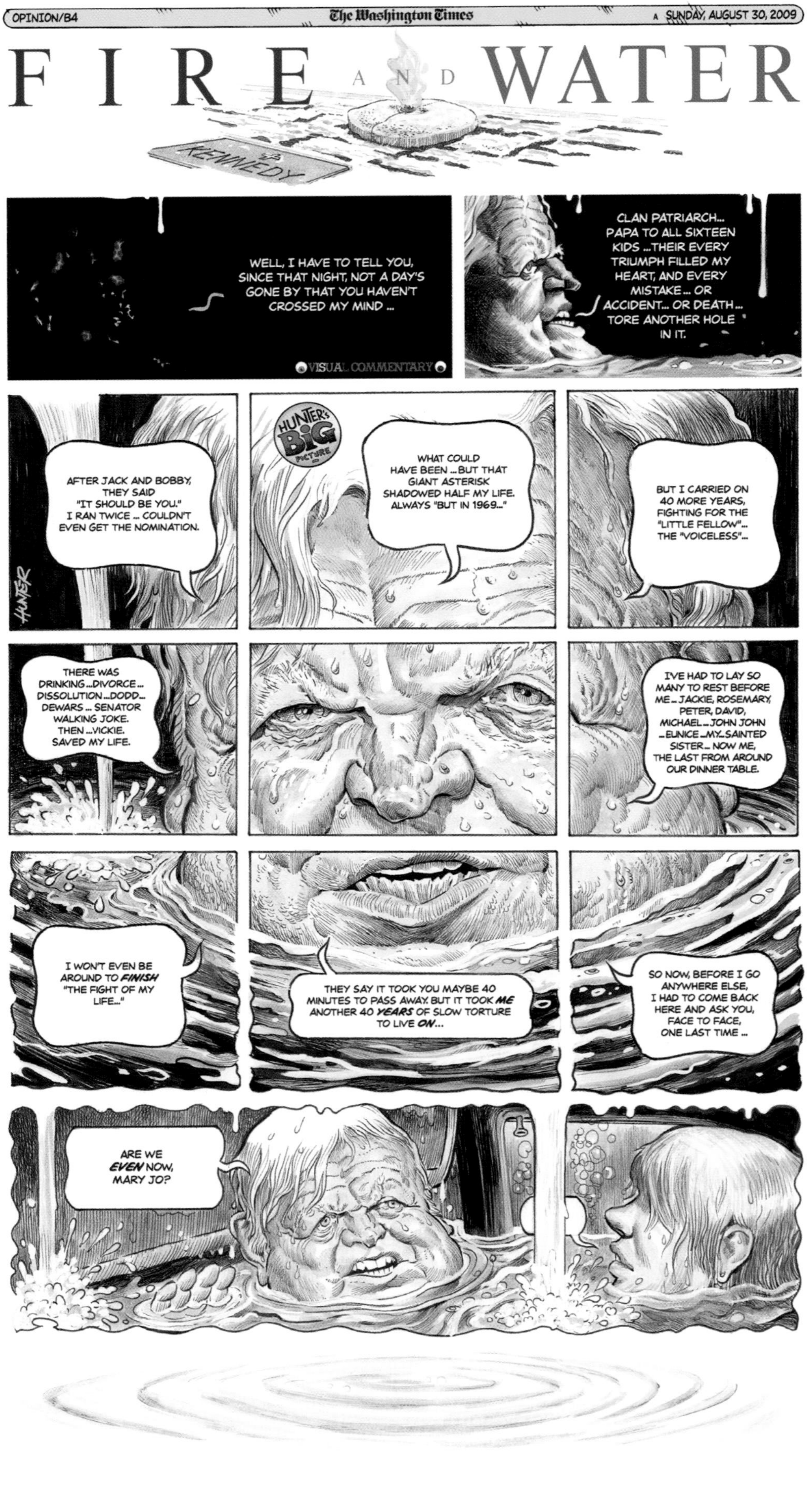

OPINION/B4
The Washington Times
SUNDAY, AUGUST 30, 2009
FIRE AND WATER
KENNEDY
WELL, I HAVE TO TELL YOU, SINCE THAT NIGHT, NOT A DAY'S GONE BY THAT YOU HAVEN'T CROSSED MY MIND ...
VISUAL COMMENTARY
CLAN PATRIARCH... PAPA TO ALL SIXTEEN KIDS ...THEIR EVERY TRIUMPH FILLED MY HEART, AND EVERY MISTAKE... OR ACCIDENT... OR DEATH... TORE ANOTHER HOLE IN IT.
AFTER JACK AND BOBBY, THEY SAID "IT SHOULD BE YOU." I RAN TWICE ... COULDN'T EVEN GET THE NOMINATION.
HUNTER
HUNTER'S BIG PICTURE
WHAT COULD HAVE BEEN ...BUT THAT GIANT ASTERISK SHADOWED HALF MY LIFE. ALWAYS "BUT IN 1969..."
BUT I CARRIED ON 40 MORE YEARS, FIGHTING FOR THE "LITTLE FELLOW"... THE "VOICELESS"...
THERE WAS DRINKING...DIVORCE... DISSOLUTION...DODD... DEWARS ... SENATOR WALKING JOKE. THEN ...VICKIE. SAVED MY LIFE.
I'VE HAD TO LAY SO MANY TO REST BEFORE ME... JACKIE, ROSEMARY, PETER, DAVID, MICHAEL...JOHN JOHN ...EUNICE ...MY...SAINTED SISTER... NOW ME, THE LAST FROM AROUND OUR DINNER TABLE.
I WON'T EVEN BE AROUND TO *FINISH* "THE FIGHT OF MY LIFE..."
THEY SAY IT TOOK YOU MAYBE 40 MINUTES TO PASS AWAY. BUT IT TOOK *ME* ANOTHER 40 *YEARS* OF SLOW TORTURE TO LIVE *ON*...
SO NOW, BEFORE I GO ANYWHERE ELSE, I HAD TO COME BACK HERE AND ASK YOU, FACE TO FACE, ONE LAST TIME ...
ARE WE *EVEN* NOW, MARY JO?

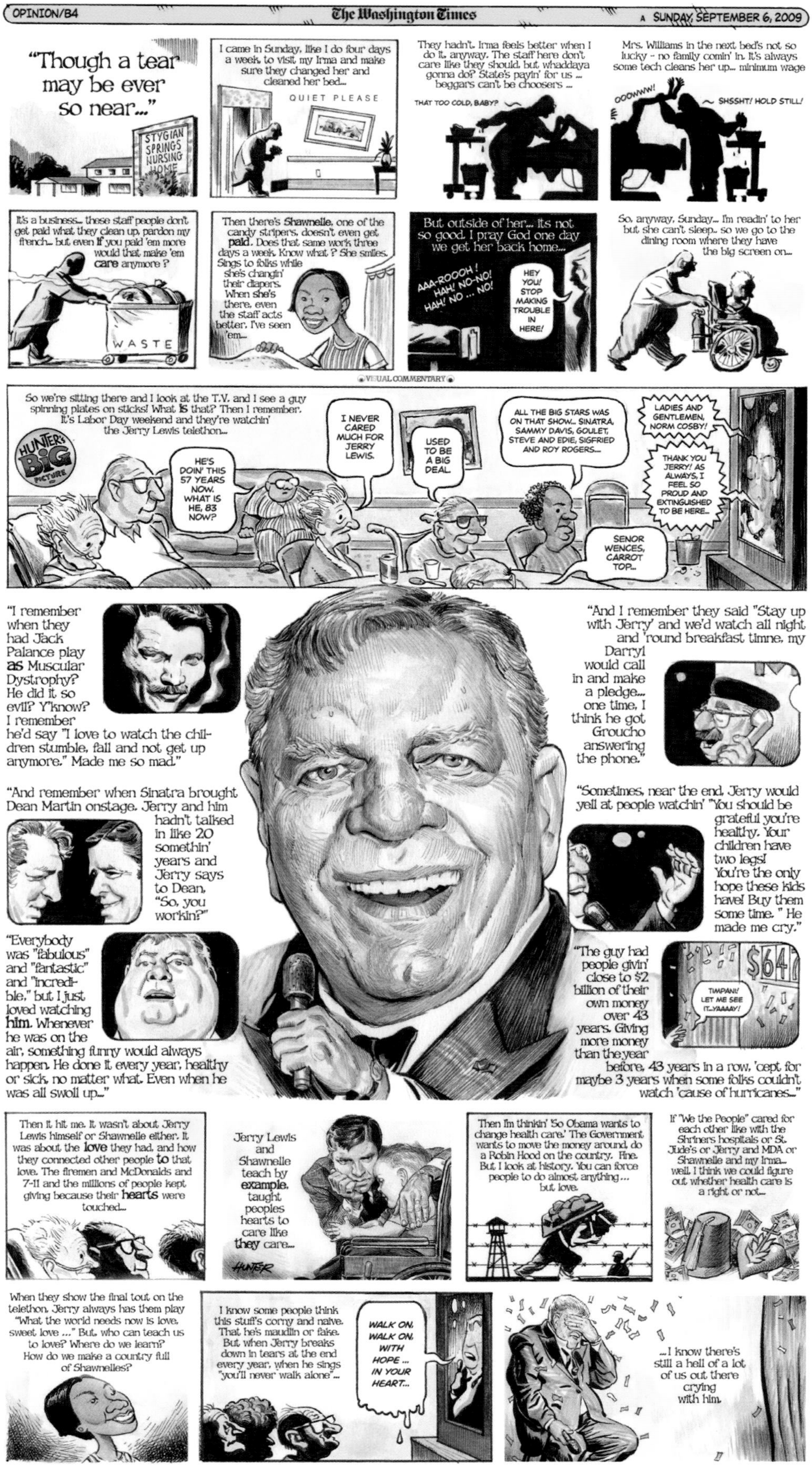
OPINION/B4
The Washington Times
A SUNDAY, SEPTEMBER 6, 2009
"Though a tear may be ever so near..."
STYGIAN SPRINGS NURSING HOME
I came in Sunday, like I do four days a week, to visit my Irma and make sure they changed her and cleaned her bed...
QUIET PLEASE
They hadn't. Irma feels better when I do it, anyway. The staff here don't care like they should, but whaddaya gonna do? State's payin' for us ... beggars can't be choosers ...
THAT TOO COLD, BABY?
Mrs. Williams in the next bed's not so lucky - no family comin' in. It's always some tech cleans her up... minimum wage
OOOWWW!
SHSSHT! HOLD STILL!
It's a business... these staff people don't get paid what they clean up, pardon my french... but even if you paid 'em more would that make 'em care anymore ?
WASTE
Then there's Shawnelle, one of the candy stripers, doesn't even get paid. Does that same work three days a week. Know what ? She smiles. Sings to folks while she's changin' their diapers. When she's there, even the staff acts better. I've seen 'em...
But outside of her... its not so good. I pray God one day we get her back home...
AAA-ROOOH! HAH! NO-NO! HAH! NO ... NO!
HEY YOU! STOP MAKING TROUBLE IN HERE!
So, anyway, Sunday... I'm readin' to her but she can't sleep... so we go to the dining room where they have the big screen on...
VISUAL COMMENTARY
So we're sitting there and I look at the T.V. and I see a guy spinning plates on sticks! What IS that? Then I remember. It's Labor Day weekend and they're watchin' the Jerry Lewis telethon...
HUNTER'S BIG PICTURE
HE'S DOIN' THIS 57 YEARS NOW. WHAT IS HE, 83 NOW?
I NEVER CARED MUCH FOR JERRY LEWIS.
USED TO BE A BIG DEAL.
ALL THE BIG STARS WAS ON THAT SHOW... SINATRA, SAMMY DAVIS, GOULET, STEVE AND EDIE, SIGFRIED AND ROY ROGERS...
LADIES AND GENTLEMEN, NORM COSBY!
THANK YOU JERRY! AS ALWAYS, I FEEL SO PROUD AND EXTINGUISHED TO BE HERE...
SENOR WENCES, CARROT TOP...
"I remember when they had Jack Palance play as Muscular Dystrophy? He did it so evil? Y'know? I remember he'd say "I love to watch the children stumble, fall and not get up anymore." Made me so mad."
"And I remember they said "Stay up with Jerry' and we'd watch all night and 'round breakfast timne, my Darryl would call in and make a pledge... one time, I think he got Groucho answering the phone."
"And remember when Sinatra brought Dean Martin onstage. Jerry and him hadn't talked in like 20 somethin' years and Jerry says to Dean, "So, you workin?"
"Sometimes, near the end, Jerry would yell at people watchin' "You should be grateful you're healthy. Your children have two legs! You're the only hope these kids have! Buy them some time. " He made me cry."
"Everybody was "fabulous" and "fantastic" and "incredible," but I just loved watching him. Whenever he was on the air, something funny would always happen. He done it every year, healthy or sick, no matter what. Even when he was all swoll up..."
"The guy had people givin' close to $2 billion of their own money over 43 years. Giving more money than the year before, 43 years in a row, 'cept for maybe 3 years when some folks couldn't watch 'cause of hurricanes..."
TIMPANI! LET ME SEE IT...YAAAAY!
Then it hit me. It wasn't about Jerry Lewis himself or Shawnelle either. It was about the love they had, and how they connected other people to that love. The firemen and McDonalds and 7-11 and the millions of people kept giving because their hearts were touched...
Jerry Lewis and Shawnelle teach by example, taught peoples hearts to care like they care...
HUNTER
Then I'm thinkin' 'So Obama wants to change health care.' The Government wants to move the money around, do a Robin Hood on the country. Fine. But I look at history. You can force people to do almost anything ... but love.
If "We the People" cared for each other like with the Shriners hospitals or St. Jude's or Jerry and MDA or Shawnelle and my Irma... well, I think we could figure out whether health care is a right or not...
When they show the final tout on the telethon, Jerry always has them play "What the world needs now is love, sweet love ..." But, who can teach us to love? Where do we learn? How do we make a country full of Shawnelles?
I know some people think this stuff's corny and naive. That he's maudlin or fake. But when Jerry breaks down in tears at the end every year, when he sings "you'll never walk alone"...
WALK ON, WALK ON, WITH HOPE ... IN YOUR HEART...
...I know there's still a hell of a lot of us out there crying with him.

2009 Scripps Howard National Journalism Award Runner-Up
Mike Luckovich, *Atlanta Journal-Constitution*

Mike Luckovich was unavailable for this edition.

National Cartoonists Society's Reuben Awards

The Reuben is awarded by the National Cartoonists Society each year to recognize outstanding achievements in the world of cartooning. The National Cartoonists Society came into being during a dinner designed for the occasion in New York in 1946. Rube Goldberg was the organization's first president.

Introduced in 1954, the Reuben Award is named for Goldberg, and editorial cartoons is one of thirteen divisions in which Reubens are awarded. The Reuben is one of a number of honors that is cartoon-specific in its consideration, but the only one in this volume that awards all manner of cartoons and illustration, from strips and magazine gag cartoons to book, magazine, and magazine feature illustrations to greeting cards and television animation. This aspect makes the Reuben Awards unique. For the purpose of this book, only the editorial cartoon division is represented.

2010 National Cartoonists Society's Reuben Award Winner
John Sherffius, *Daily Camera*

John Sherffius has loved art ever since he won a first-grade drawing contest for his portrait of a Thanksgiving turkey. Over the years, he has tried his hand at everything from sketching nuclear aircraft carriers for the U.S. Navy to designing diplomas for Korean dentists.

Sherffius now focuses on his nationally syndicated political cartoons, which have been honored with awards from groups including the National Press Foundation, the Robert F. Kennedy Foundation, the Society of Professional Journalists, and the Herblock Foundation.

Sherffius lives in Denver with his wife and their three children—none of whom, so far, has shown a prizewinning ability to draw turkeys.

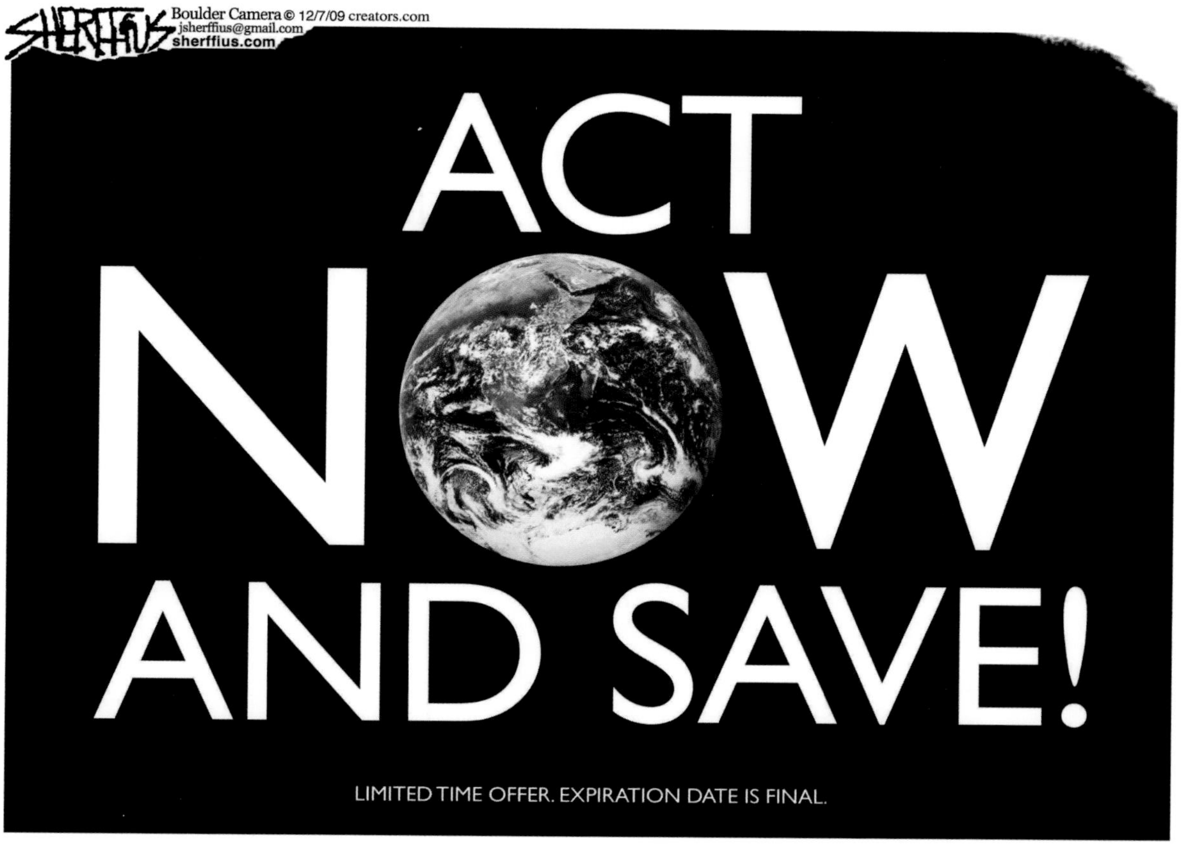
SHERFFIUS
Boulder Camera © 12/7/09 creators.com
jsherffius@gmail.com
sherffius.com
ACT
NOW
AND SAVE!
LIMITED TIME OFFER. EXPIRATION DATE IS FINAL.

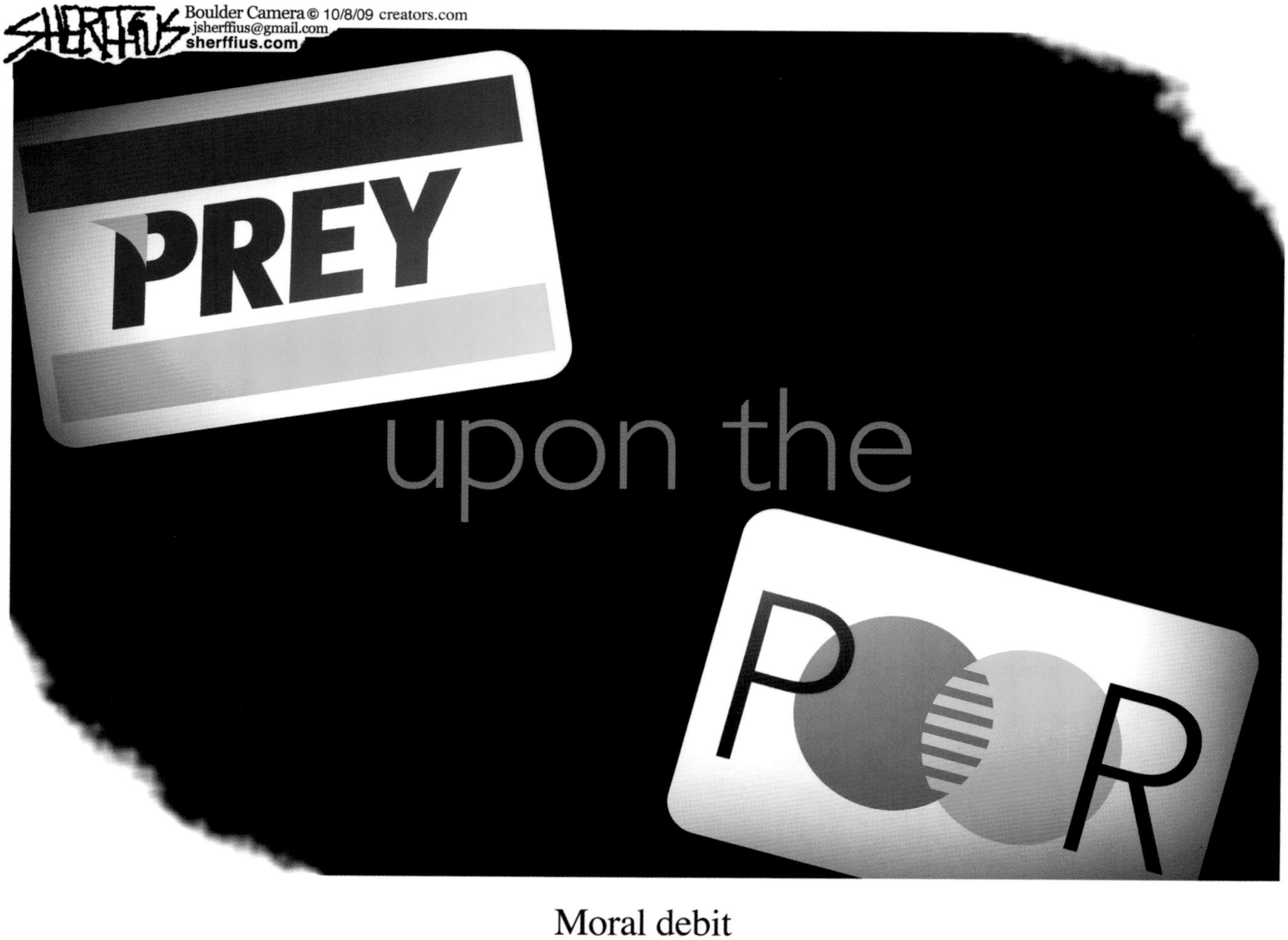
SHERFFIUS
Boulder Camera © 10/8/09 creators.com
jsherffius@gmail.com
sherffius.com
PREY
upon the
POOR

Moral debit

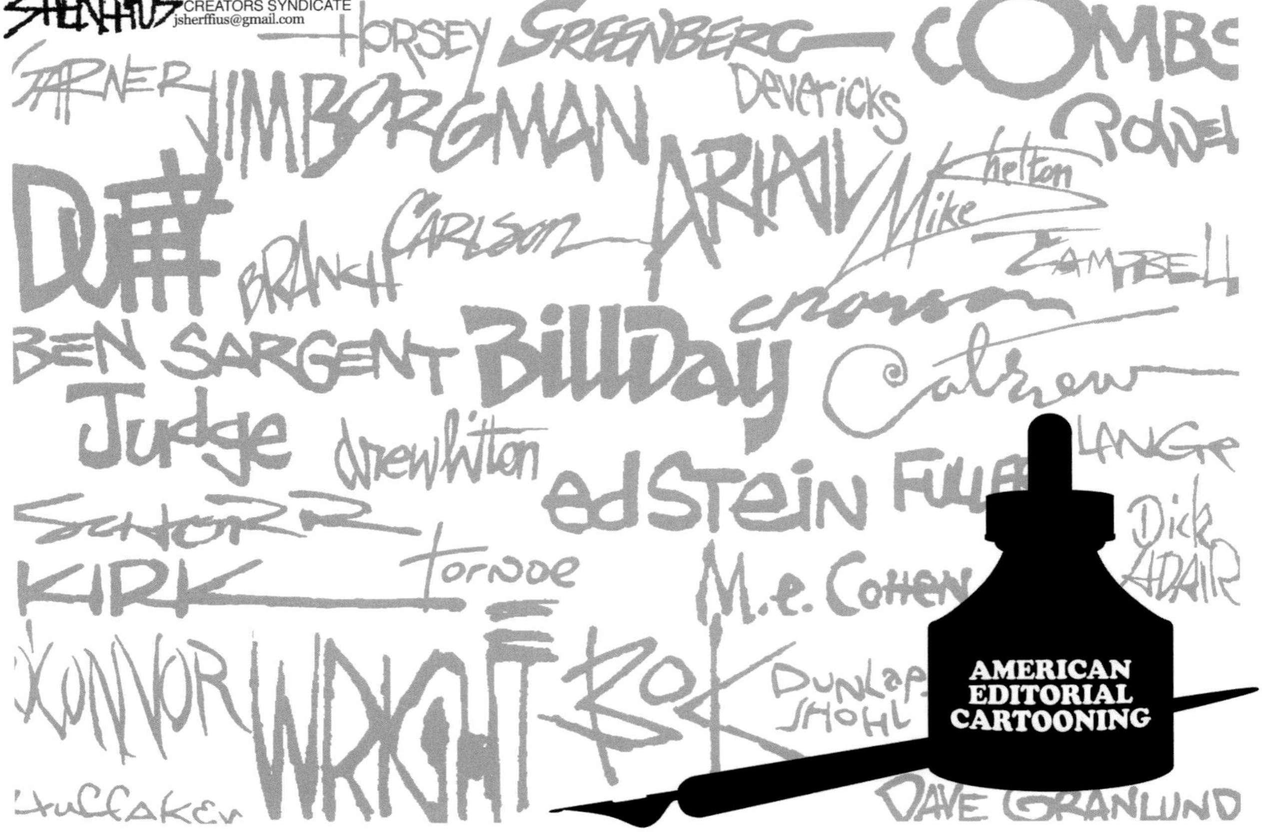
SHERFFIUS
Boulder Camera © 3/20/09
CREATORS SYNDICATE
jsherffius@gmail.com
HORSEY
GREENBERG
COMBS
JIMBORGMAN
Devericks
BEN SARGENT
BillDay
Judge
edStein
M.e. Cohen
KIRK
WRIGHT
DAVE GRANLUND
AMERICAN
EDITORIAL
CARTOONING

A signature loss

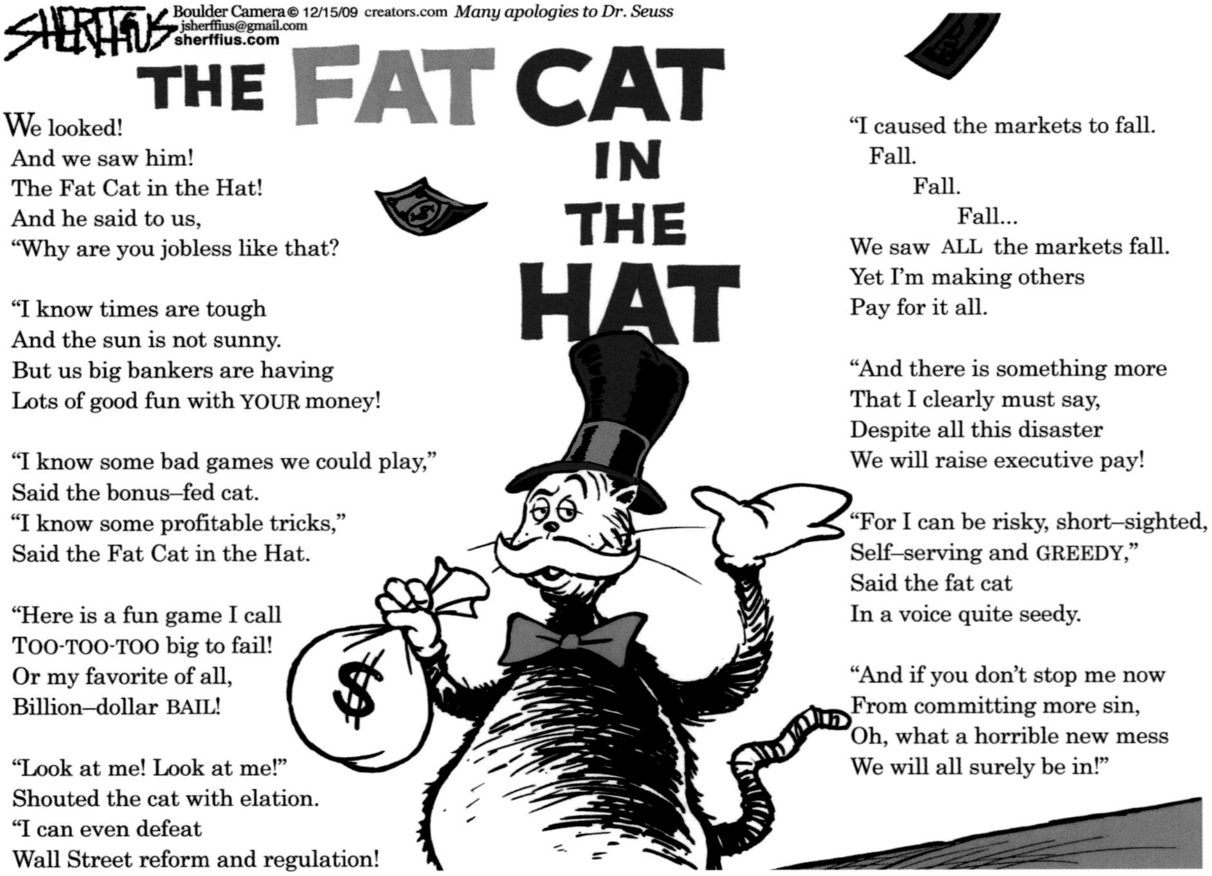
SHERFFIUS
Boulder Camera © 12/15/09 creators.com *Many apologies to Dr. Seuss*
jsherffius@gmail.com
sherffius.com
THE FAT CAT IN THE HAT
We looked!
And we saw him!
The Fat Cat in the Hat!
And he said to us,
"Why are you jobless like that?
"I know times are tough
And the sun is not sunny.
But us big bankers are having
Lots of good fun with YOUR money!
"I know some bad games we could play,"
Said the bonus–fed cat.
"I know some profitable tricks,"
Said the Fat Cat in the Hat.
"Here is a fun game I call
TOO-TOO-TOO big to fail!
Or my favorite of all,
Billion–dollar BAIL!
"Look at me! Look at me!"
Shouted the cat with elation.
"I can even defeat
Wall Street reform and regulation!
"I caused the markets to fall.
Fall.
Fall.
Fall...
We saw ALL the markets fall.
Yet I'm making others
Pay for it all.
"And there is something more
That I clearly must say,
Despite all this disaster
We will raise executive pay!
"For I can be risky, short–sighted,
Self–serving and GREEDY,"
Said the fat cat
In a voice quite seedy.
"And if you don't stop me now
From committing more sin,
Oh, what a horrible new mess
We will all surely be in!"

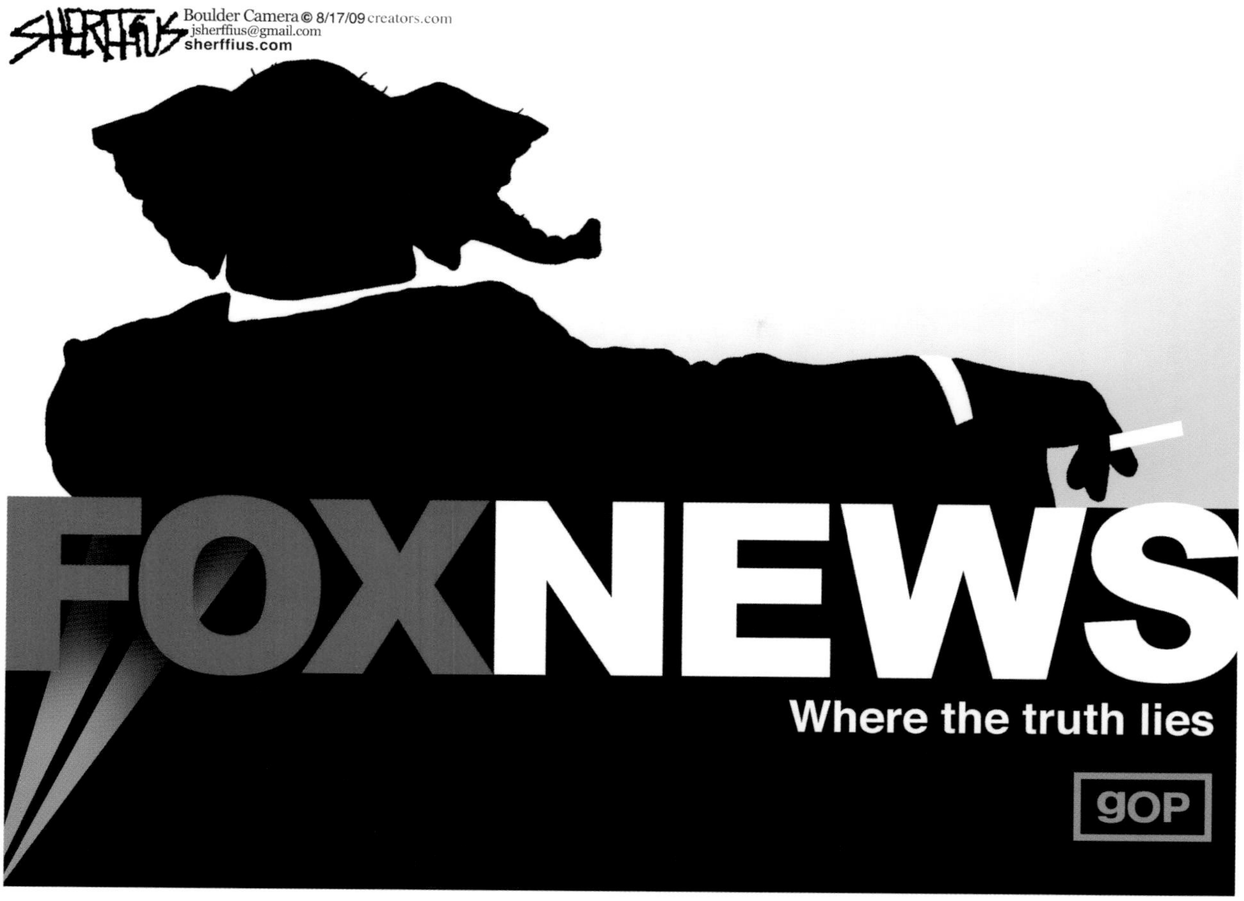
SHERFFIUS
Boulder Camera © 8/17/09 creators.com
jsherffius@gmail.com
sherffius.com
FOXNEWS
Where the truth lies
gOP

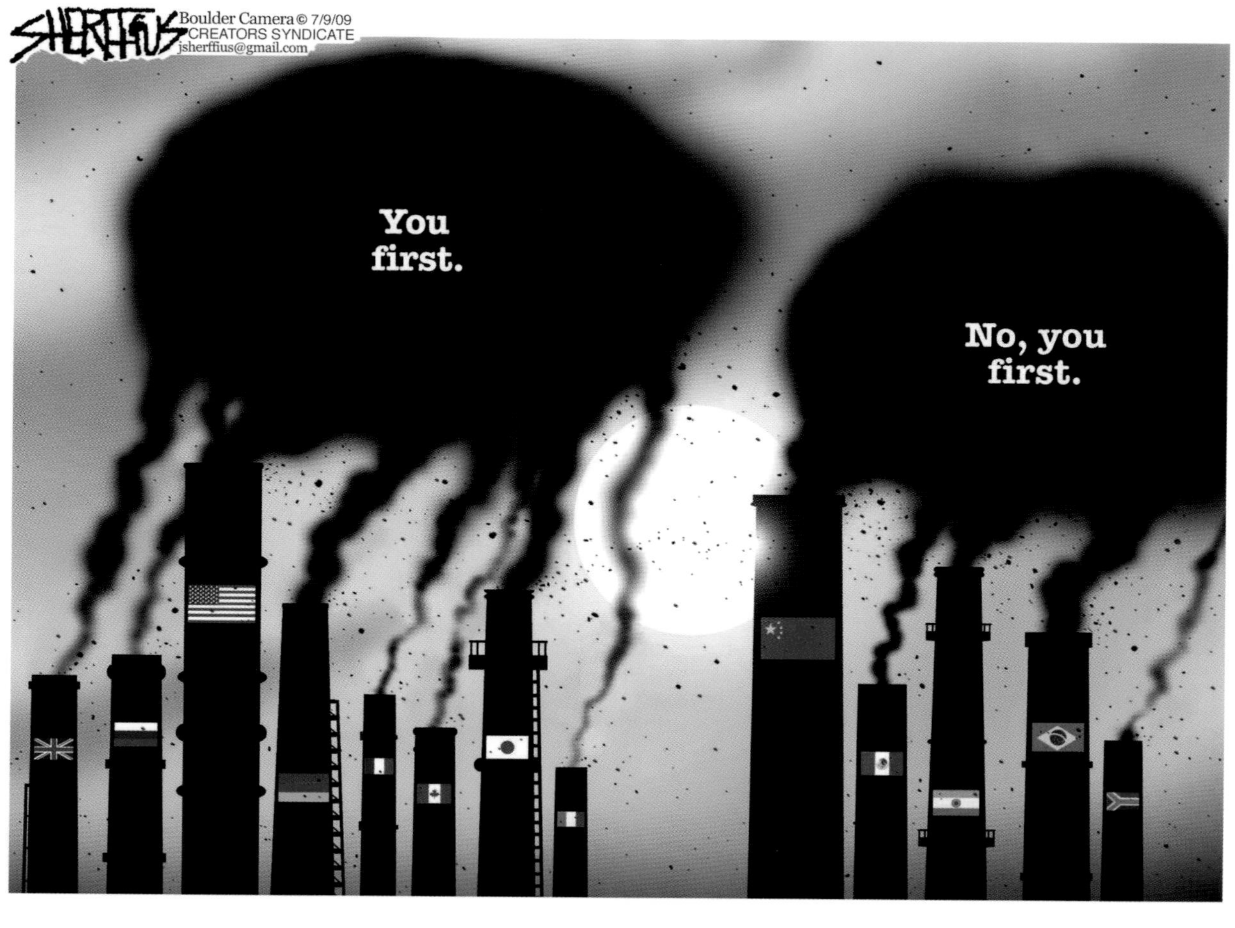
SHERFFIUS
Boulder Camera © 7/9/09
CREATORS SYNDICATE
jsherffius@gmail.com
You first.
No, you first.

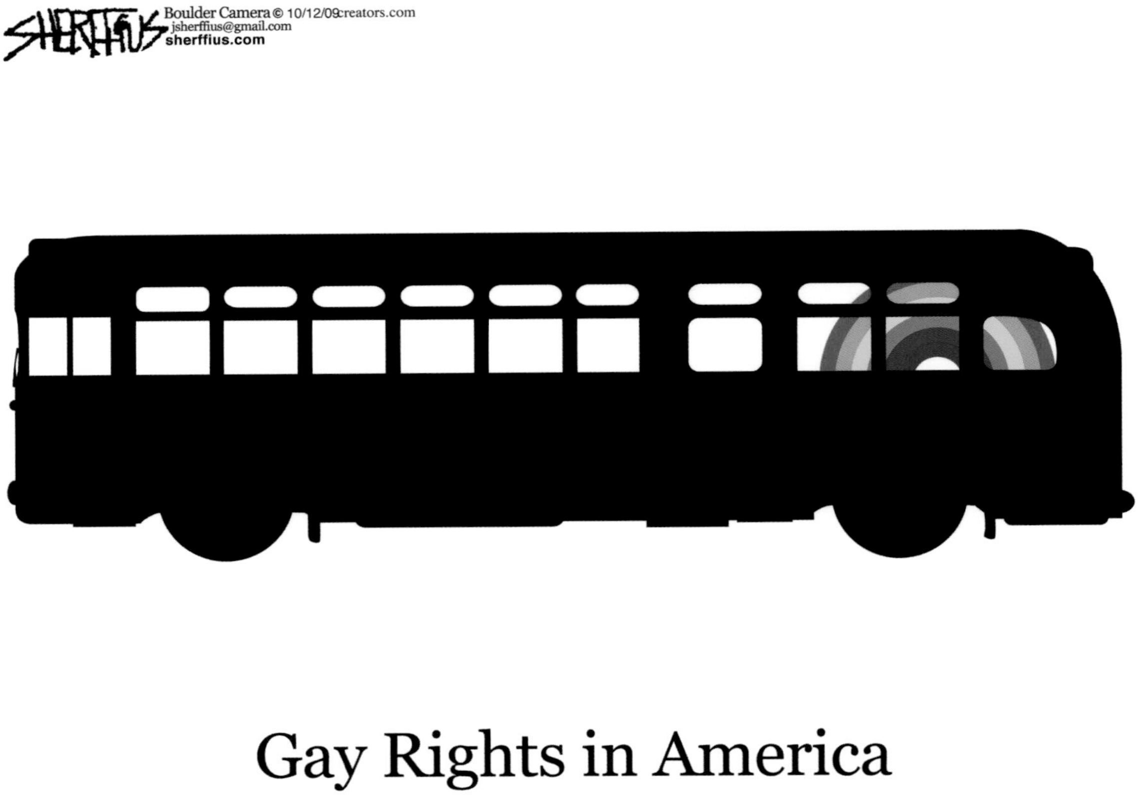
SHERFFIUS
Boulder Camera © 10/12/09 creators.com
jsherffius@gmail.com
sherffius.com
Gay Rights in America

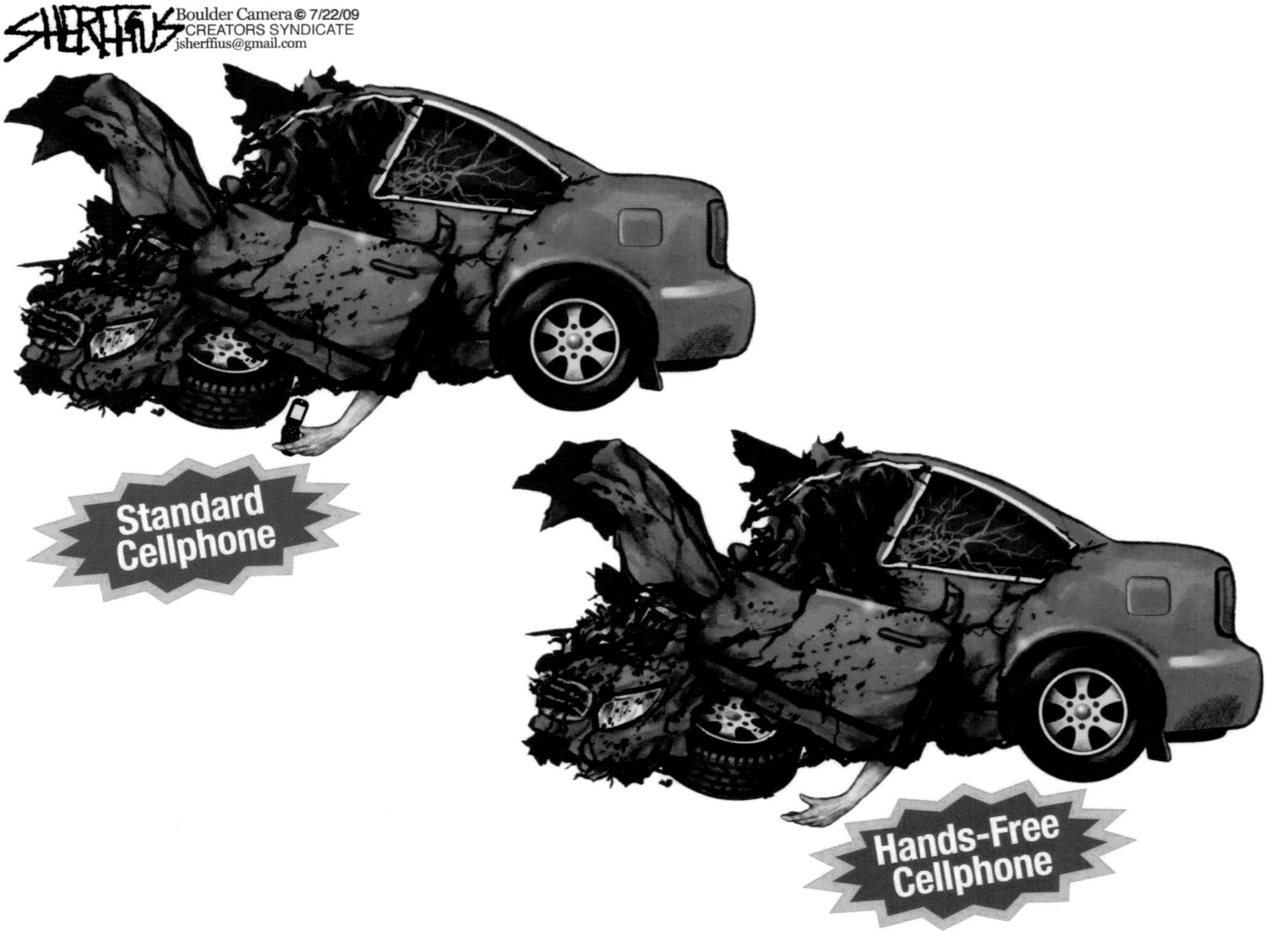
SHERFFIUS
Boulder Camera © 7/22/09
CREATORS SYNDICATE
jsherffius@gmail.com
Standard Cellphone
Hands-Free Cellphone

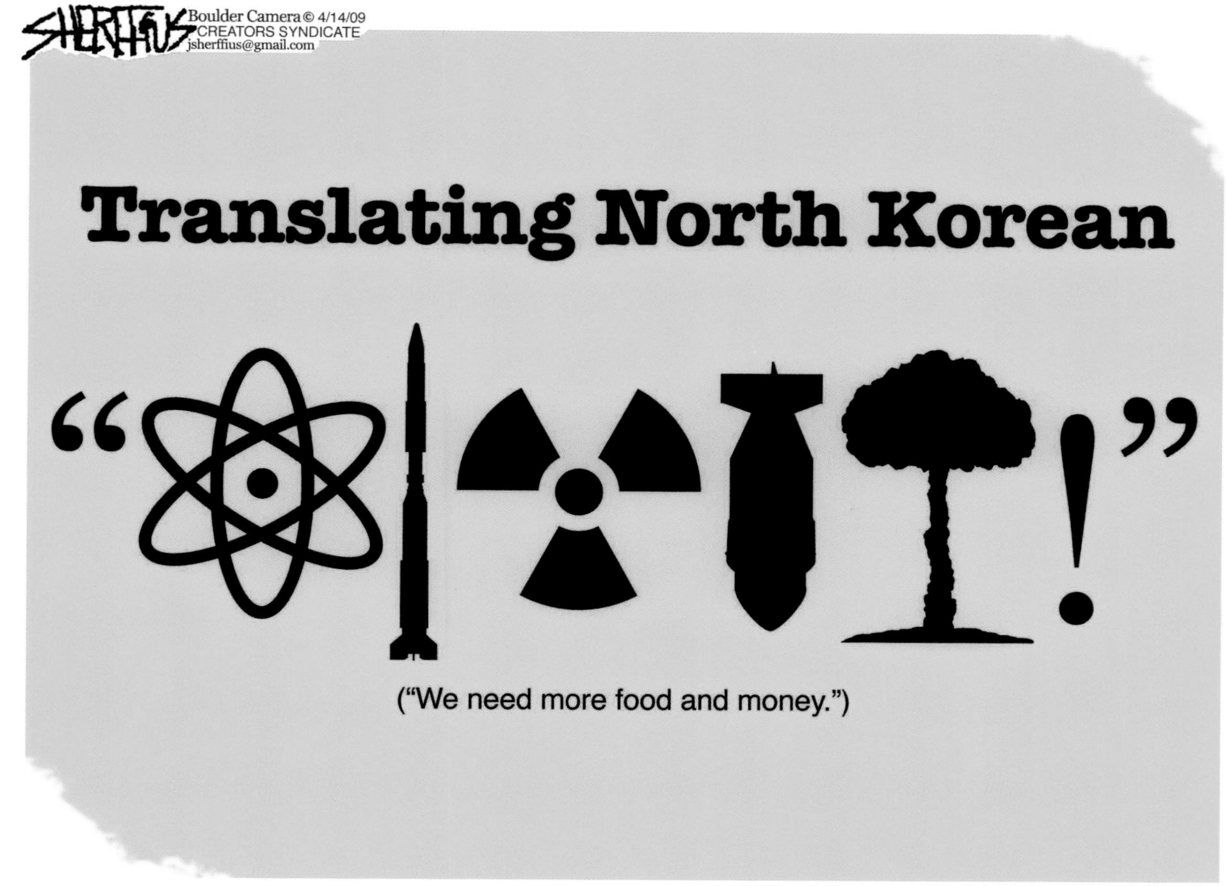
SHERFFIUS
Boulder Camera © 4/14/09
CREATORS SYNDICATE
jsherffius@gmail.com
Translating North Korean
("We need more food and money.")

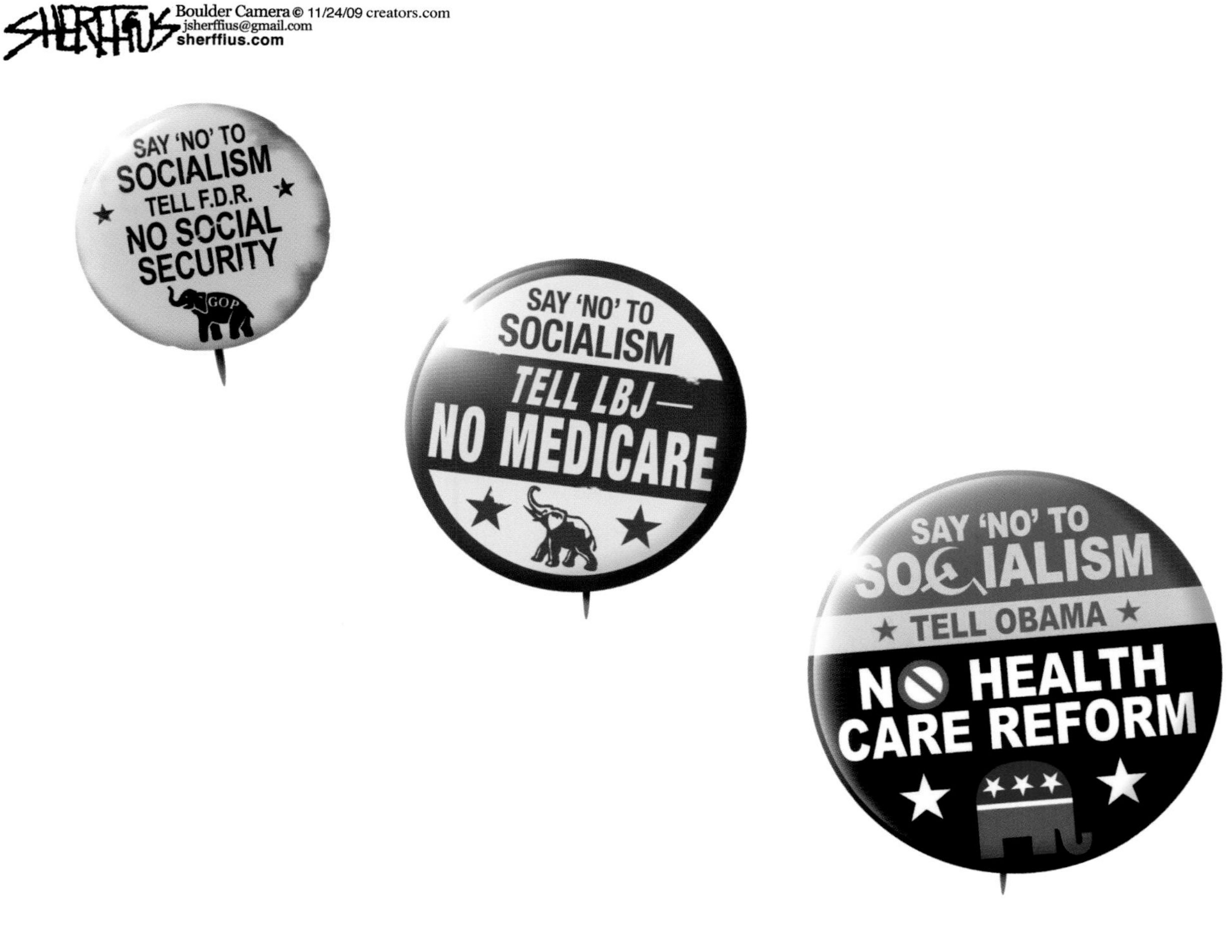
SHERFFIUS
Boulder Camera © 11/24/09 creators.com
jsherffius@gmail.com
sherffius.com
SAY 'NO' TO SOCIALISM
TELL F.D.R.
NO SOCIAL SECURITY
GOP
SAY 'NO' TO SOCIALISM
TELL LBJ—
NO MEDICARE
SAY 'NO' TO SOCIALISM
TELL OBAMA
NO HEALTH CARE REFORM

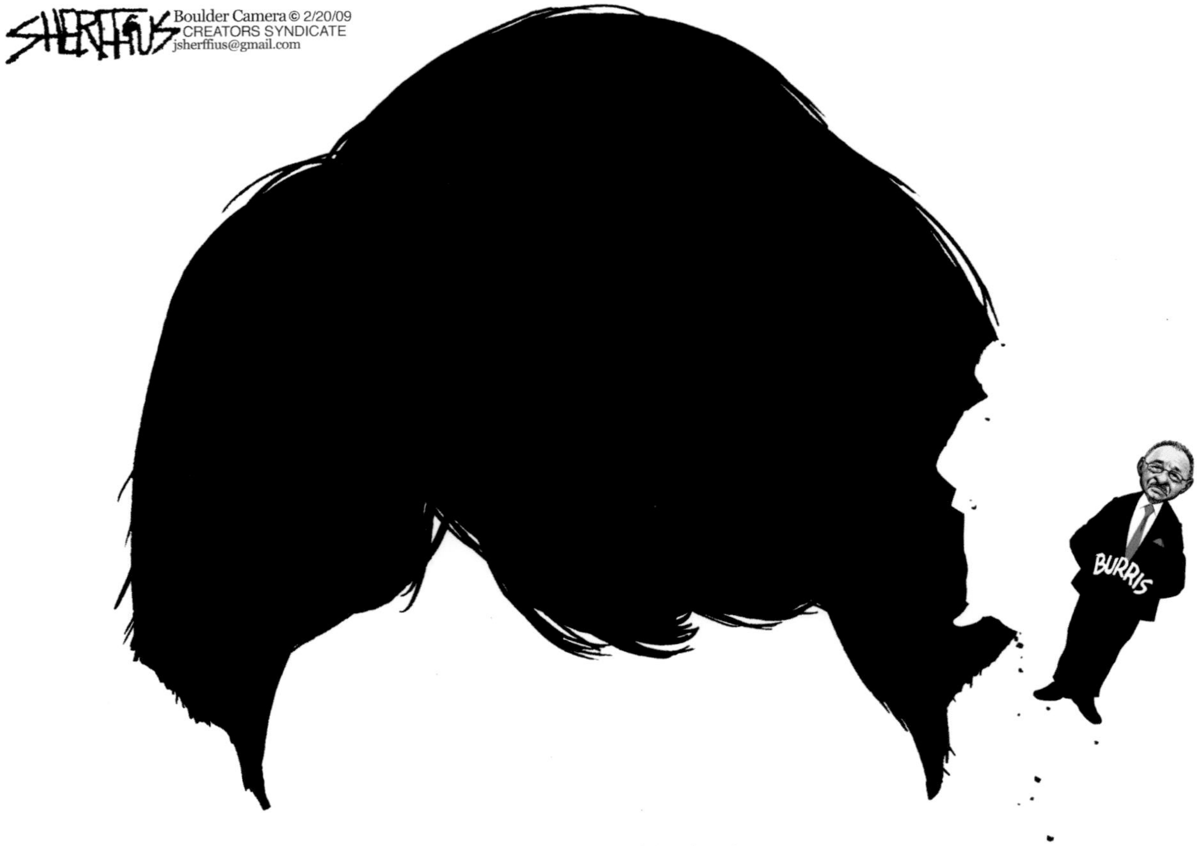
Boulder Camera © 2/20/09
CREATORS SYNDICATE
jsherffius@gmail.com
BURRIS

Chip off the old block

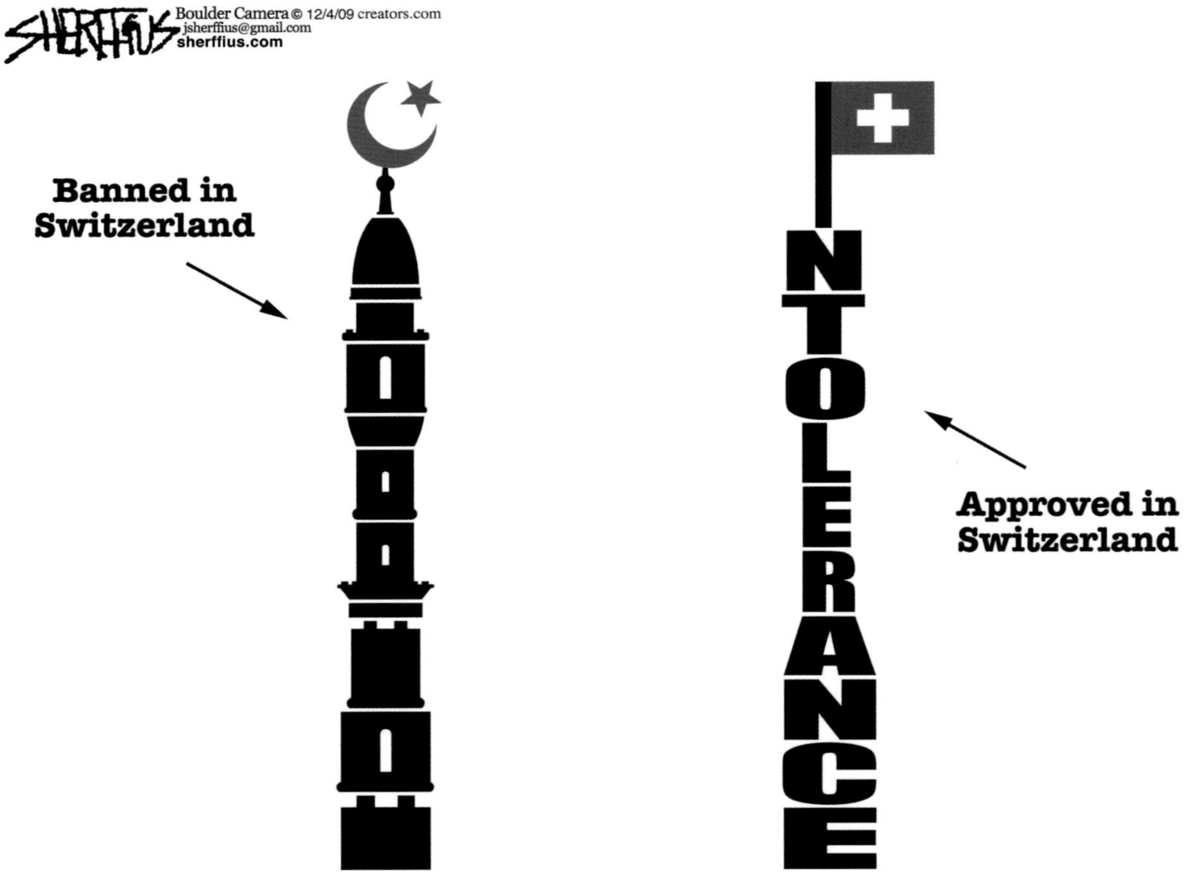
Boulder Camera © 12/4/09 creators.com
jsherffius@gmail.com
sherffius.com
Banned in Switzerland
NTOLERANCE
Approved in Switzerland

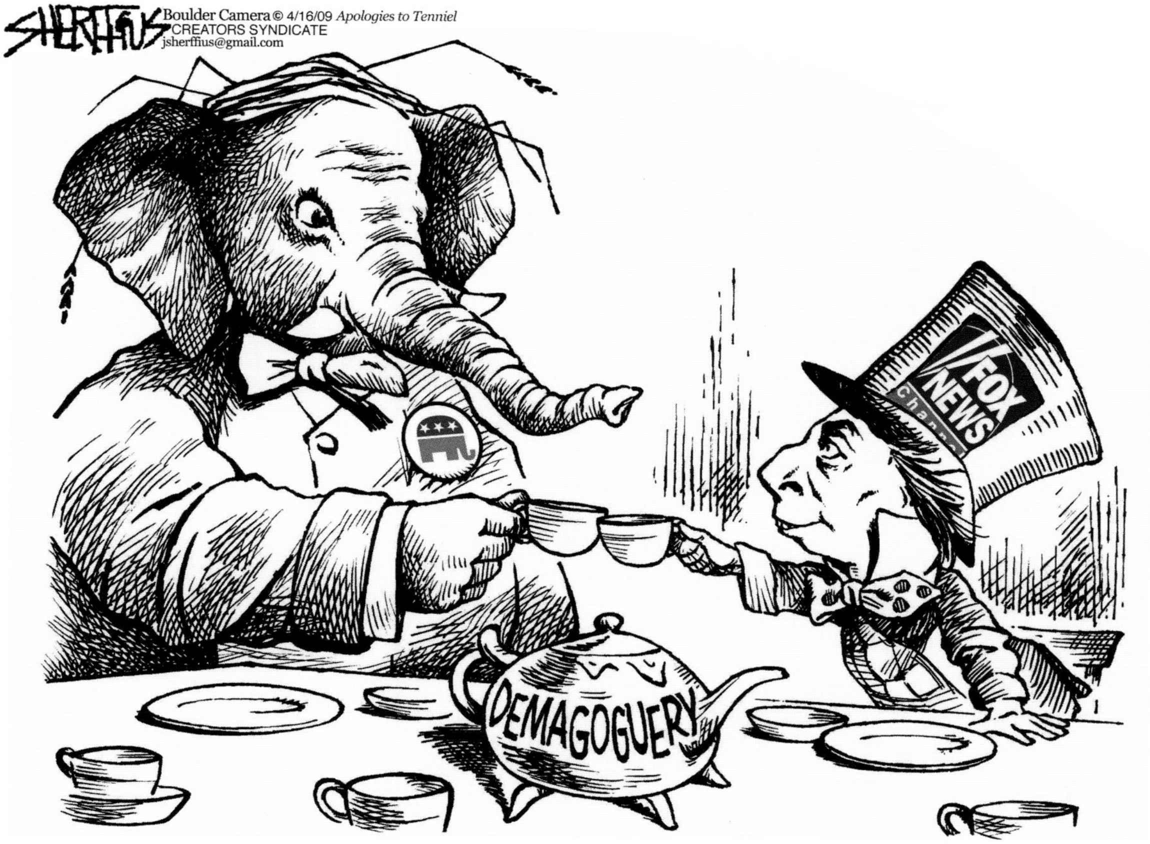
SHERFFIUS
Boulder Camera © 4/16/09 Apologies to Tenniel
CREATORS SYNDICATE
jsherffius@gmail.com
FOX NEWS
DEMAGOGUERY

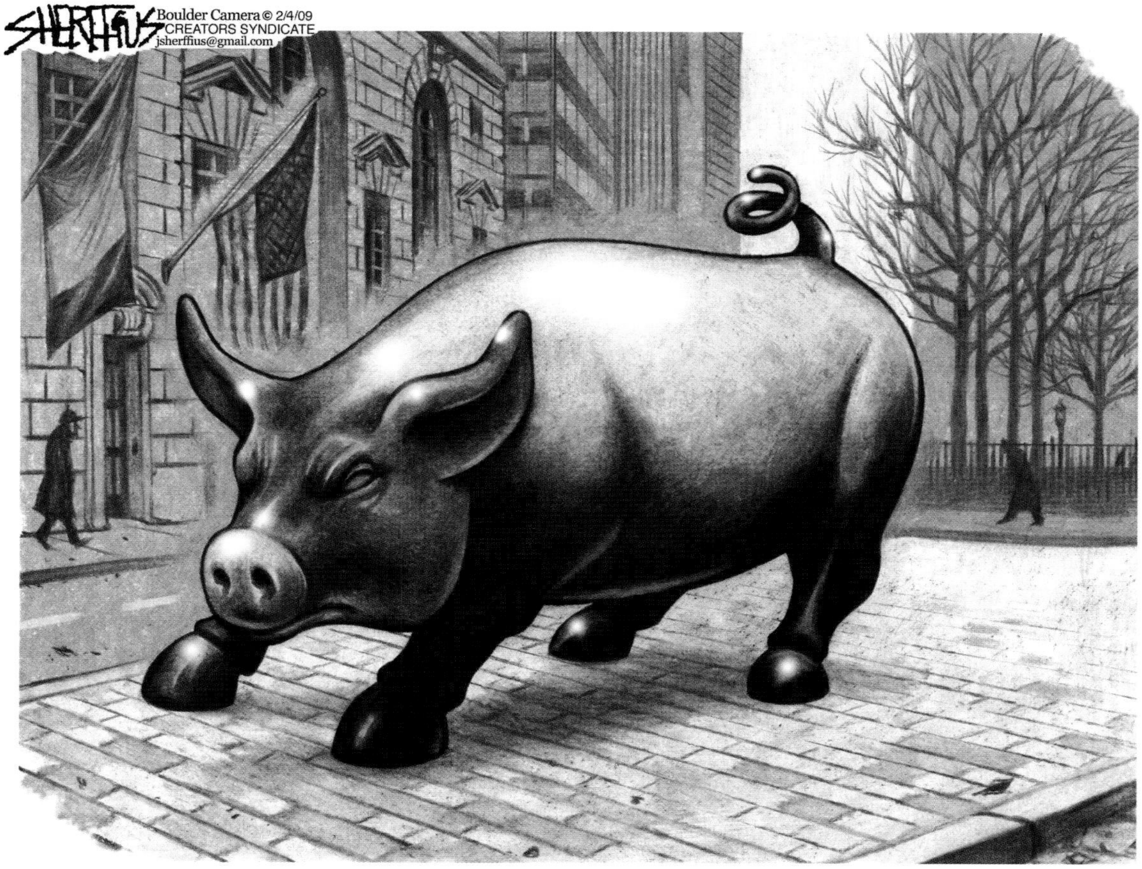
SHERFFIUS
Boulder Camera © 2/4/09
CREATORS SYNDICATE
jsherffius@gmail.com

Boulder Camera © 7/14/09
CREATORS SYNDICATE
jsherffius@gmail.com

✓ **Wise**

✓ **Latina**

✓ **Woman**

✓ **None of the above**

Robert F. Kennedy Journalism Award

"Some men see things the way they are, and ask why? I dream of things that never were, and ask why not?"

—Robert F. Kennedy paraphrasing
George Bernard Shaw

Known as the "Poor People's Pulitzers" within the press arena, the Robert F. Kennedy Journalism Award was founded in December of 1968. In keeping with the life and legacy of the man for which it is named, the award honors those who report on issues that reflect Kennedy's concerns, including human rights, social justice, and the power of individual action in the United States and around the world. Led by a committee of six independent journalists, more than fifty members of the press judge the award each year, and it has become the largest program of its kind and one of few in which the winners are determined solely by their peers.

This living memorial to Robert F. Kennedy has created programs in three areas: books, journalism, and human rights. Award recipients have brought to light issues spanning from child abuse and juvenile crime to discriminatory banking practices and prejudice against AIDS victims. Through this honor, they receive international recognition and prizes for their inspiring work.

2010 Robert F. Kennedy Journalism Award
Bill Day, *Memphis Commercial Appeal*

Bill Day began as a political cartoonist while studying political science and art at the University of Florida. After college, he worked as an illustrator in the art departments of a number of newspapers and drew political cartoons part time. In 1980, the *Philadelphia Bulletin* hired him as a full-time political cartoonist. After the *Bulletin* folded, he moved to the *Memphis Commercial Appeal* and then to the *Detroit Free Press,* where he worked for thirteen years. In 1998, he returned to the *Commercial Appeal* and his beloved South.

His work is widely reprinted in national magazines, including *Newsweek, Time, U.S. News and World Report,* and *Business Week.* The defense of the oppressed and their condition is a deep and eloquent theme in his work. "I have great fun drawing and using humor in my cartoons," says Day. "But when a terrible injustice occurs, I'll use the most powerful images possible to address it."

Day's award-winning cartoons are available to newspapers worldwide three times a week through United Feature Syndicate. Among the awards Day has won are five Green Eyeshade Awards from the Society of Professional Journalists, two Robert F. Kennedy Journalism Awards, the National Headliner Award, the John Fischetti Award, the First Amendment Award, New York Newspaper Guild's Page One Award, National Cartoonists Society's Award for best editorial cartoons, and the James Aronson Award for Social Justice Journalism.

Day and his wife, Susan, have three sons.

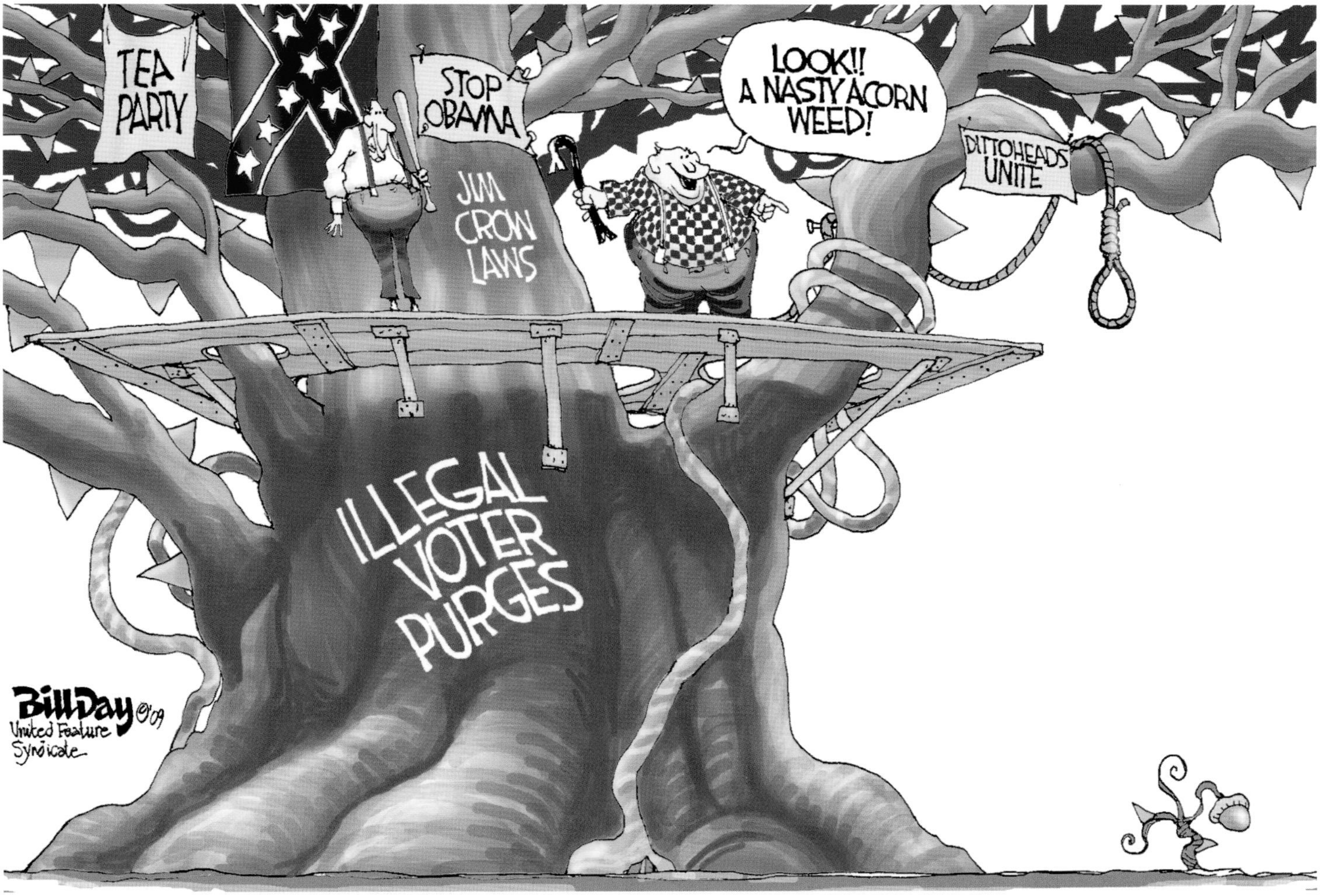
TEA PARTY
STOP OBAMA
JIM CROW LAWS
LOOK!! A NASTY ACORN WEED!
DITTOHEADS UNITE
ILLEGAL VOTER PURGES
BillDay ©'09
United Feature Syndicate

John Fischetti Editorial Cartoon Competition Award

The youngest of four children, John Fischetti was born in Brooklyn, New York, on September 27, 1916. He studied at the Pratt Institute in Brooklyn and from there took a job at Walt Disney Studios. When forced by eyestrain to give up animation, he began freelancing for various newspapers and magazines, first in California, then in Chicago, where he soon began drawing political cartoons for the *Sun*.

During World War II, Fischetti drew cartoons for the *Stars and Stripes* as well as courtroom depictions for some of the war-crimes trials. After the war, he freelanced in New York, much of it for the *New York Herald*. When it folded in 1966, he moved back to Chicago and worked for the *Chicago Daily News*, where he won a Pulitzer Prize in 1968. John Fischetti died on November 18, 1980, while working for the *Chicago Sun-Times*.

An endowment, created in Fischetti's name in 1980, sustains the Fischetti Award for editorial cartoons as well as several scholarships at Columbia College in Chicago.

2010 John Fischetti Editorial Cartoon Competition Award Winner
Stephen P. Breen, *San Diego Union-Tribune*

Steve Breen was born in Los Angeles in 1970 and attended the University of California, Riverside. He has served as the editorial cartoonist for the *San Diego Union-Tribune* since 2001. His work is nationally syndicated by Creators News Service and regularly appears in *USA Today*, the *New York Times*, and *Newsweek*.

No stranger to winning awards for his work, Breen won the Pulitzer Prize for editorial cartooning in 1998 and again in 2009, the 2007 Berryman Award, and the 2009 Thomas Nast and National Headliner awards.

Breen, in his spare time, writes and illustrates picture books, including *Stick*, *Violet the Pilot*, and *The Secret of Santa's Island*.

Breen lives in San Diego with his wife and four children. He enjoys reading, running, playing the guitar and piano, and watching old movies on cable.

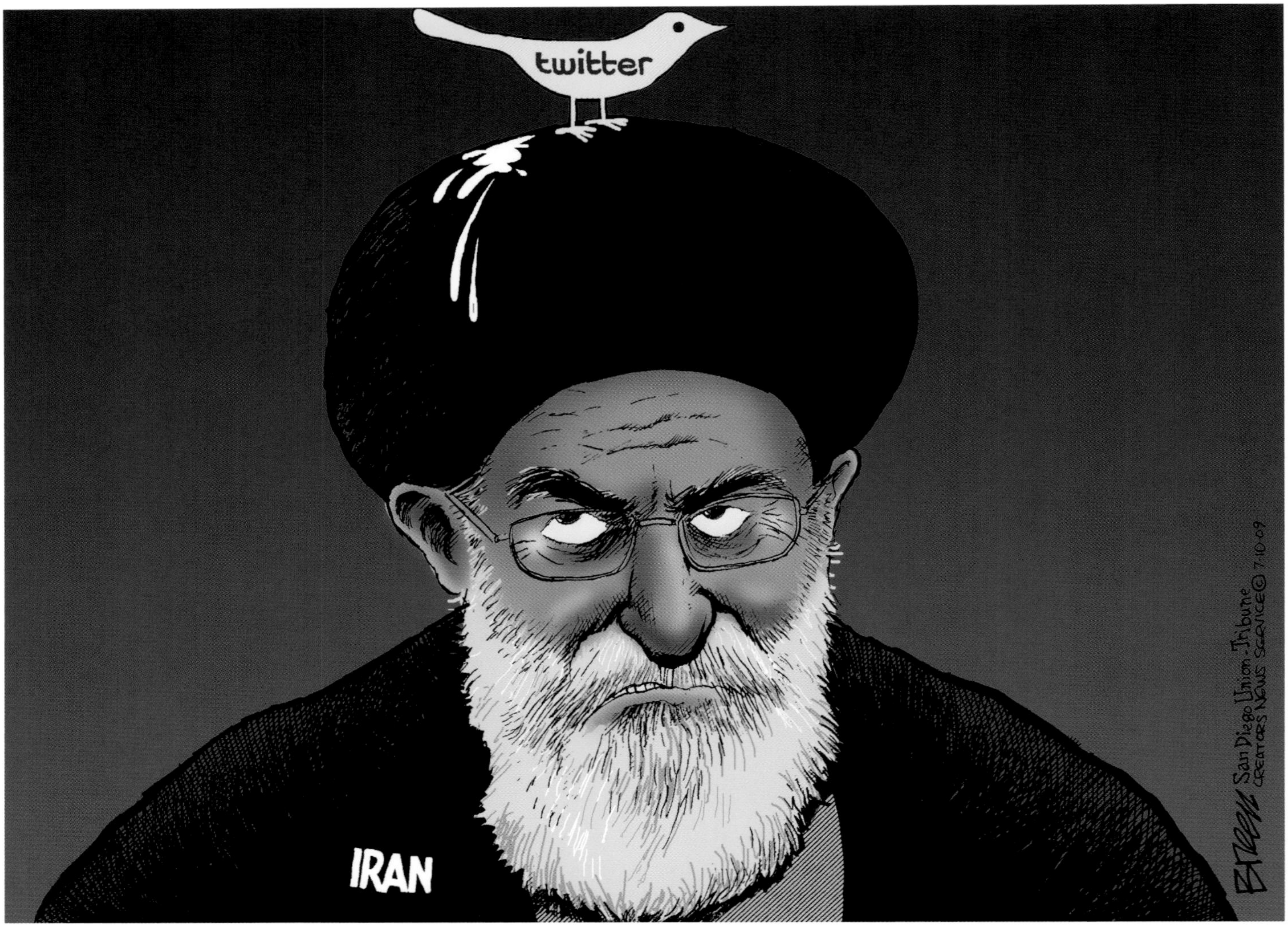
twitter
IRAN
BREEN San Diego Union-Tribune
CREATORS NEWS SERVICE© 7-10-09

National Press Foundation's Clifford K. and James T. Berryman Award

Clifford K. and James T. Berryman, father and son editorial cartoonists, both won the coveted Pulitzer Prize.

In 1989, Florence Berryman, former art critic for the *Washington Star,* endowed an annual award in memory of her late father and brother, Clifford K. and James T. Berryman. Each year since, the National Press Foundation has sponsored the award.

Clifford Berryman won his Pulitzer for a cartoon depicting Pres. Franklin Roosevelt and various other government officials attempting to steer the USS *Manpower Mobilization* in different directions. However, he is best known for a 1902 cartoon of another President Roosevelt, Theodore, and a small bear igniting a national phenomenon—"Teddy bears."

Six years after his father won a Pulitzer, James Berryman matched his achievement. He won his Pulitzer in 1950 for a McCarthy-era cartoon titled "All Ready for a Super-Secret Session," making the Berrymans the only father and son Pulitzer Prize for editorial cartoon winners.

2009 National Press Foundation's Clifford K. and James T. Berryman Award Winner
Mike Keefe, *Denver Post*

Mike Keefe has been the editorial cartoonist for the *Denver Post* since 1975. Throughout the nineties, he was a weekly contributor to *USA Today* and a regular on America Online. Nationally syndicated, his cartoons have appeared in *Time, Newsweek, Business Week, U.S. News and World Report,* the *New York Times,* the *Washington Post,* and hundreds of newspapers across the country.

Keefe served as president of the Association of American Editorial Cartoonists and, in 1997 and 1998, as a Pulitzer Prize juror. A former John S. Knight Fellow at Stanford University, he has won the National Headliner Award, Sigma Delta Chi Distinguished Service Award, the Best of the West Journalism Contest, and the John Fischetti Editorial Cartoon Competition Award.

Keefe is the author of *Running Awry, Keefe Kebab,* and *The 10 Speed Commandments.* He also co-created the nationally syndicated comic strips *Cooper* and *Iota* and the satirical blog Sardonika.

A former United States Marine and a college math teacher, Keene is married with two grown children and plays guitar regularly with Falling Rock, an oldies cover band.

His cartoons can be viewed online at www.intoon.com.

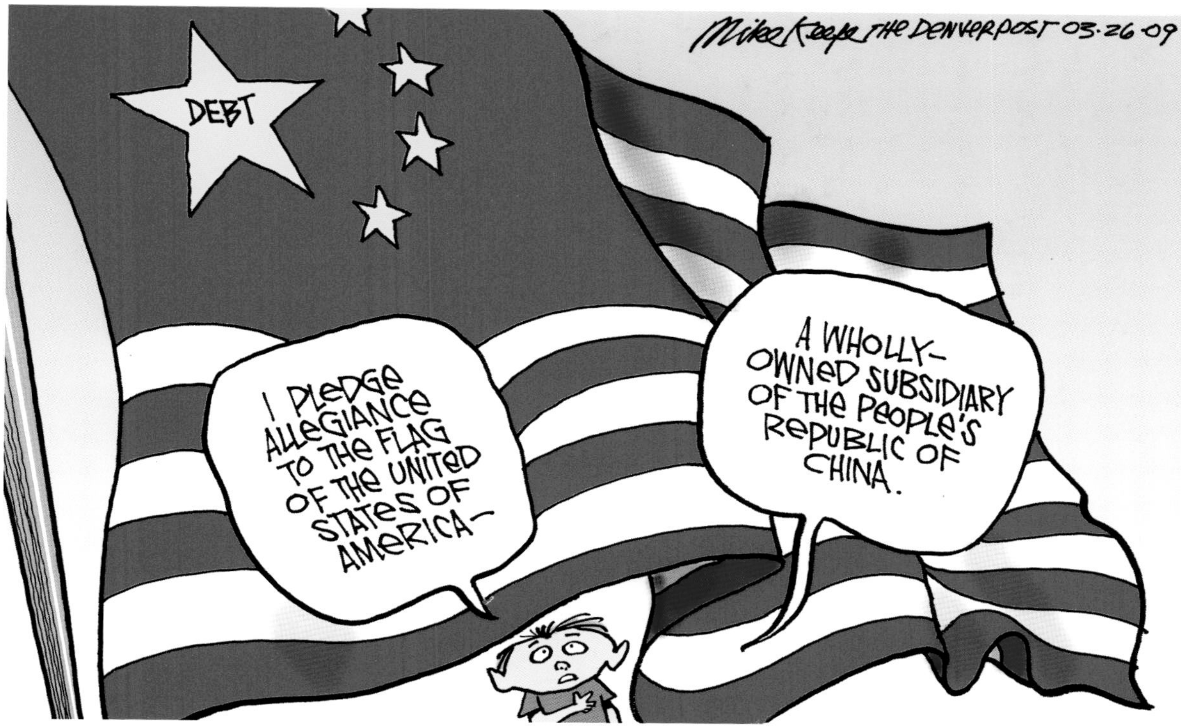
Mike Keefe THE DENVER POST 03.26.09
DEBT
I PLEDGE ALLEGIANCE TO THE FLAG OF THE UNITED STATES OF AMERICA—
A WHOLLY-OWNED SUBSIDIARY OF THE PEOPLE'S REPUBLIC OF CHINA.

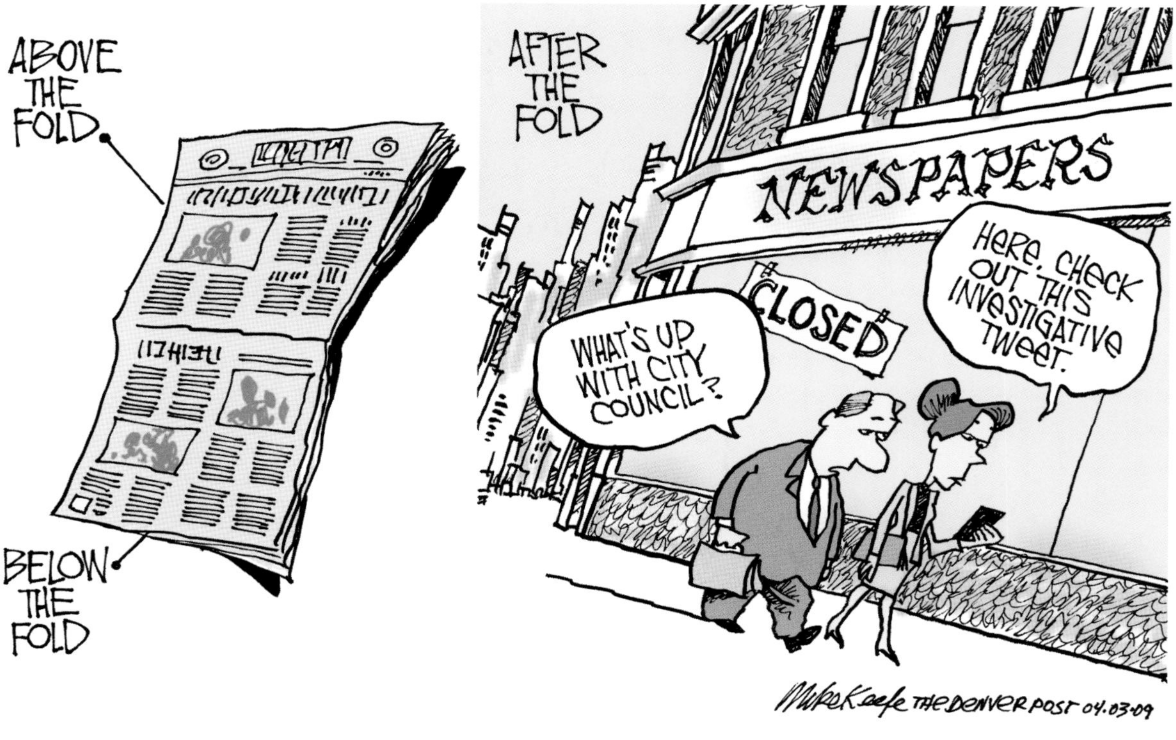
ABOVE THE FOLD
BELOW THE FOLD
AFTER THE FOLD
NEWSPAPERS
CLOSED
WHAT'S UP WITH CITY COUNCIL?
HERE. CHECK OUT THIS INVESTIGATIVE TWEET.
Mike Keefe THE DENVER POST 04.03.09

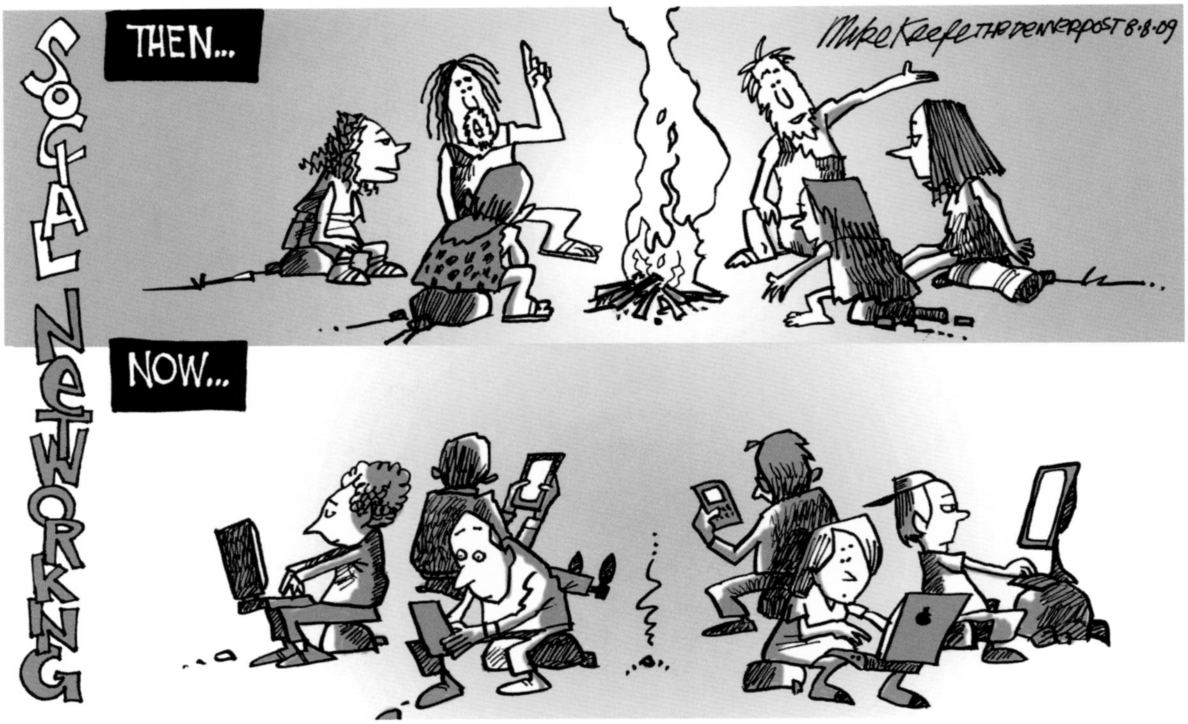
SOCIAL NETWORKING
THEN...
Mike Keefe THE DENVER POST 8.8.09
NOW...

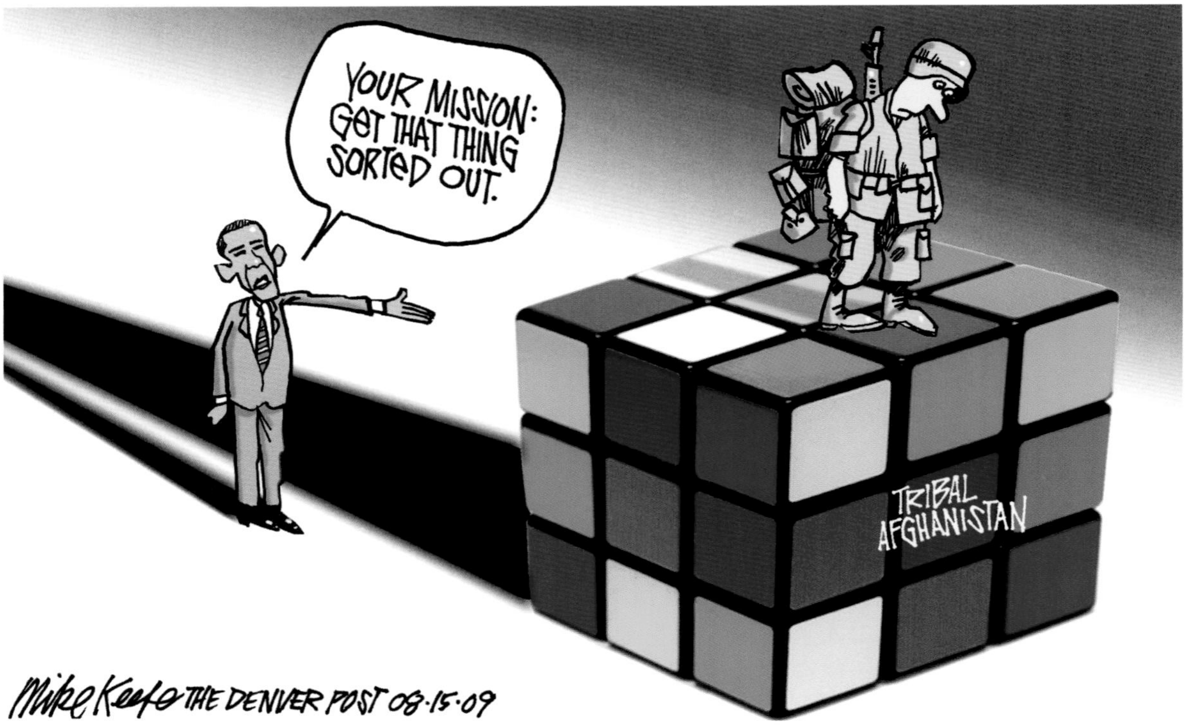
YOUR MISSION: GET THAT THING SORTED OUT.
TRIBAL AFGHANISTAN
Mike Keefe THE DENVER POST 08.15.09

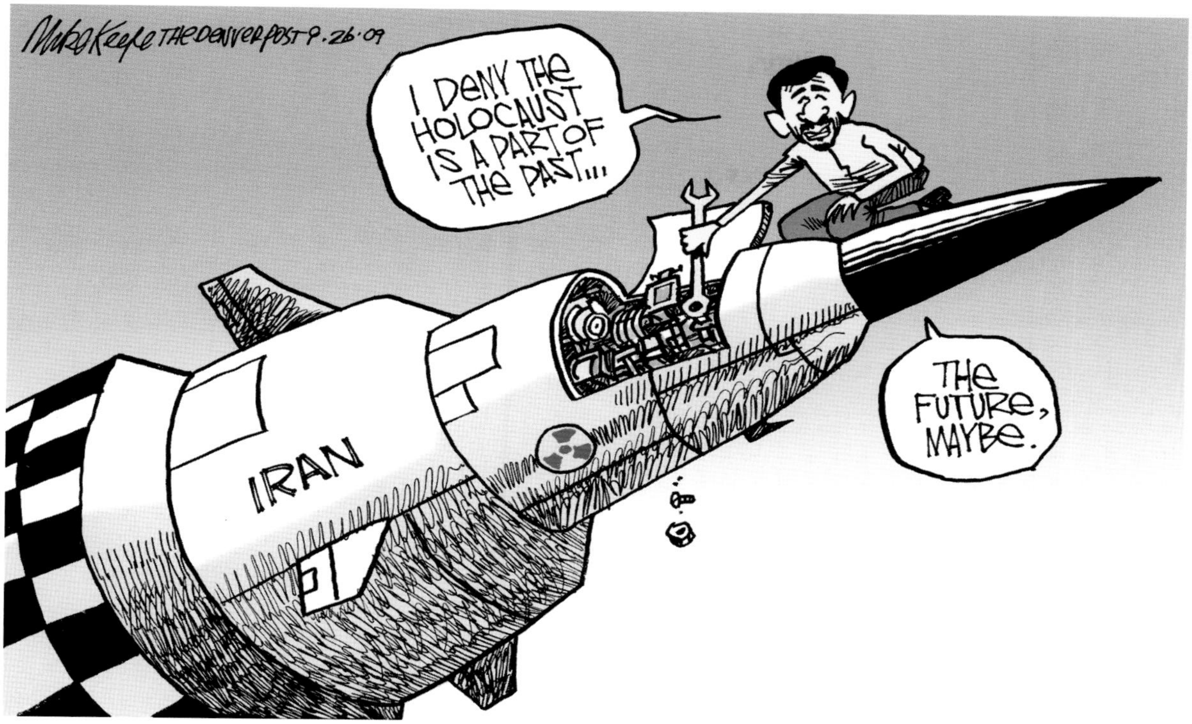
MikeKeefe THE DENVER POST 9.26.09
I DENY THE HOLOCAUST IS A PART OF THE PAST...
THE FUTURE, MAYBE.
IRAN

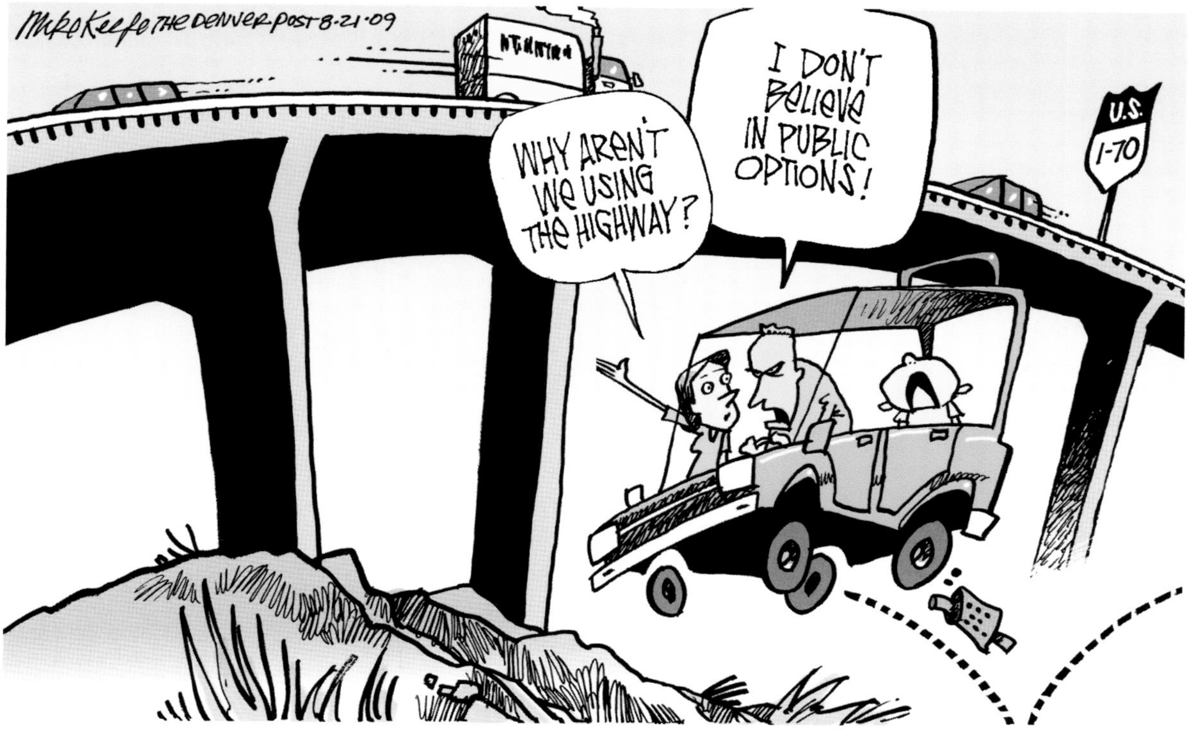
MikeKeefe THE DENVER POST 8.21.09
I DON'T BELIEVE IN PUBLIC OPTIONS!
WHY AREN'T WE USING THE HIGHWAY?
U.S.
I-70

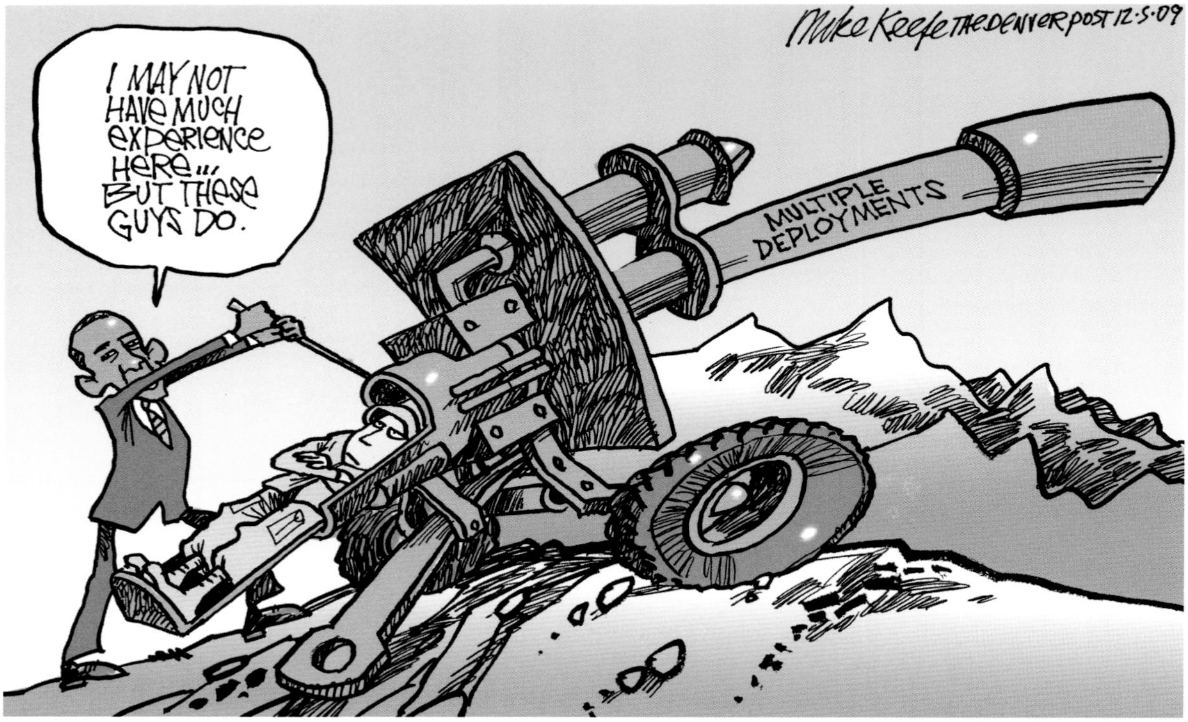
Mike Keefe THE DENVER POST 12·5·09
I MAY NOT HAVE MUCH experience HERE... BUT THESE GUYS DO.
MULTIPLE DEPLOYMENTS

Herblock Prize

The Herblock Prize is named for Herbert Block, the longtime editorial cartoonist for the *Washington Post.* Block was born on October 13, 1909, in Chicago. He attended Lake Forest College for two years and enrolled at the Art Institute of Chicago part time. In 1929, he began work as the editorial page cartoonist for the *Chicago Daily News* and was syndicated through the NEA Service four years later. Before joining the *Washington Post* in 1946, Block served in the United States Army from 1943 to 1945.

The Herblock Prize is awarded annually for distinguished examples of original editorial cartooning that exemplify the courageous independent standard set by the late cartoonist. Block's career spanned more than seven decades, from 1929 to 2001, with five of those at

the *Washington Post,* where he became an icon. It's been said that if the *Washington Post* was a forum for his cartoons, he helped build it. Over the course of his career, Block won three Pulitzer Prizes himself and, in 1973, was one of four staff members named in a Pulitzer Prize for the *Washington Post* for public service during the Watergate scandal.

The Herb Block Foundation, which funds the award, was created in Herb Block's will as a grant-making organization with a mission of defending basic freedoms, combating all forms of discrimination and improving the conditions of the poor, and providing post-secondary educational opportunities to financially needy students.

2010 Herblock Prize Winner
Matt Wuerker, *Politico*

Matt Wuerker is a political cartoonist based in Washington, D.C. and serves as the staff cartoonist for *Politico* and its Web site, Politico.com.

Prior to landing this full-time position, he was a successful freelance cartoonist. Throughout the past twenty-five years, his cartoons have been published widely in newspapers and magazines, including the *Los Angeles Times*, the *Christian Science Monitor*, *George*, and the *Nation*. His caricature and illustration work is syndicated internationally by both Tribune Media Service and NewsArt.com.

He has published two cartoon collections: *Standing Tall in Deep Doo Doo: A Cartoon Chronicle of the Bush Quayle Years* and *Meanwhile, in Other News: A Graphic Look at Politics in the Empire of Money, Sex and Scandal.*

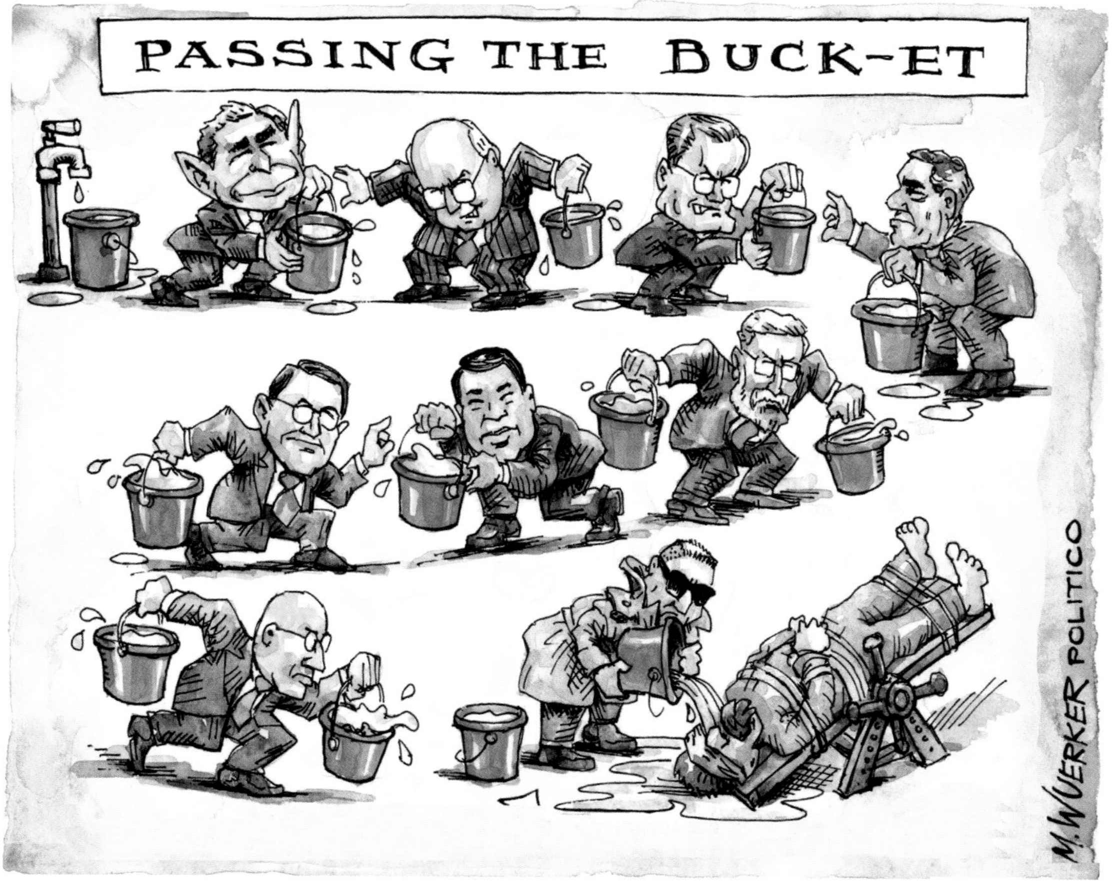
PASSING THE BUCK-ET
M. WUERKER POLITICO

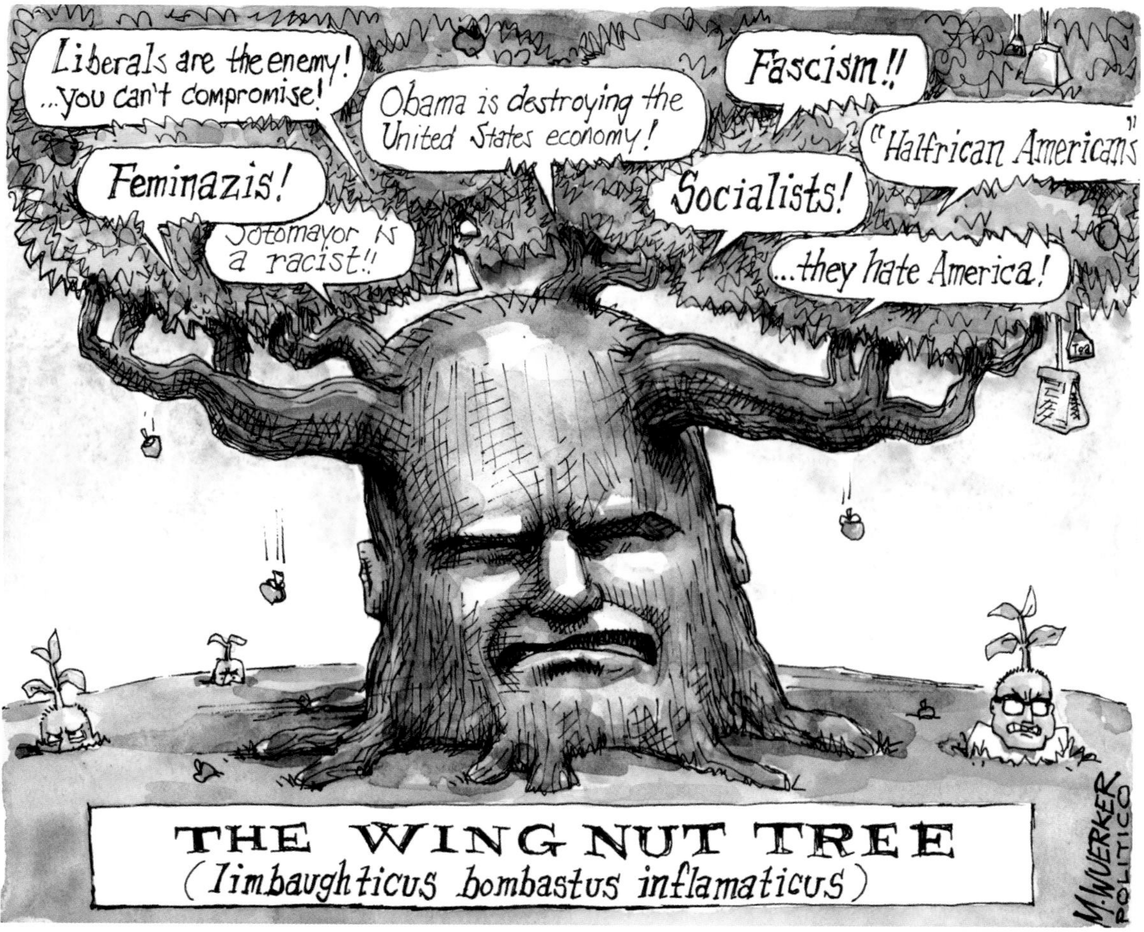
Liberals are the enemy! ...you can't compromise!
Obama is destroying the United States economy!
Fascism!!
"Halfrican Americans"
Feminazis!
Socialists!
Sotomayor is a racist!!
...they hate America!
THE WING NUT TREE
(limbaughticus bombastus inflamaticus)
M. WUERKER POLITICO

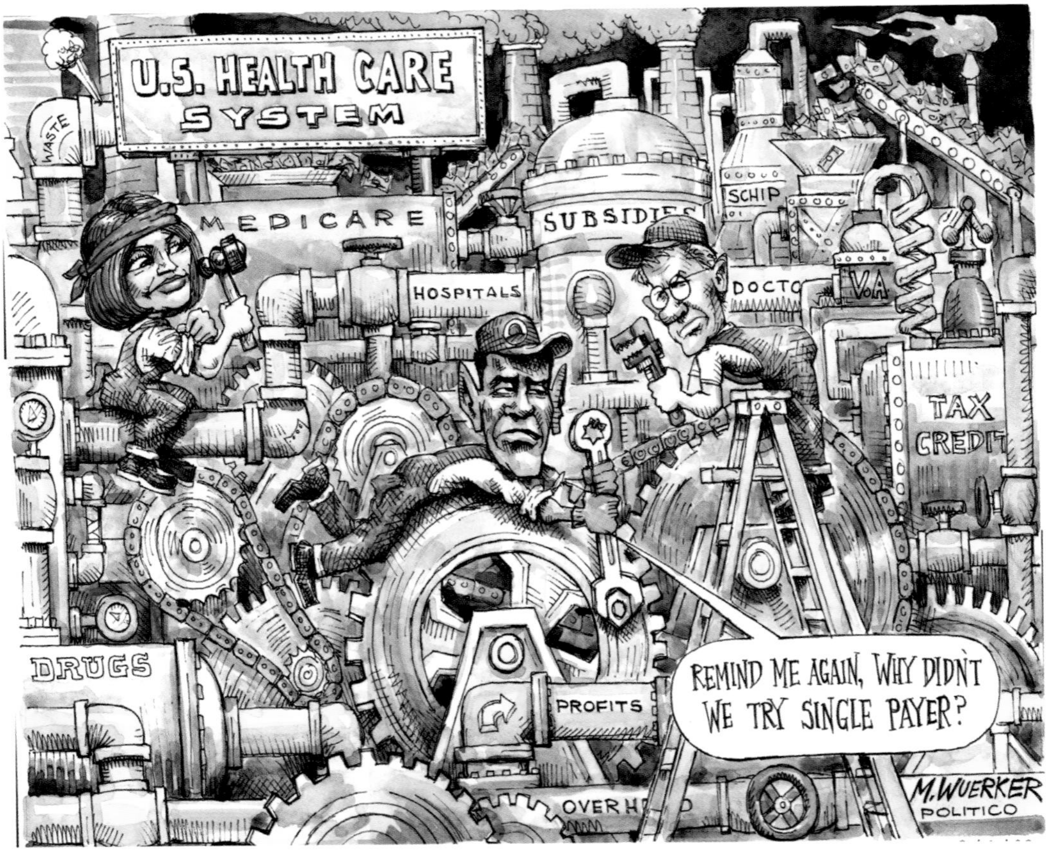
U.S. HEALTH CARE SYSTEM
WASTE
MEDICARE
SUBSIDIES
SCHIP
HOSPITALS
DOCTO
VA
TAX CREDIT
DRUGS
PROFITS
OVERHEAD
REMIND ME AGAIN, WHY DIDN'T WE TRY SINGLE PAYER?
M. WUERKER
POLITICO

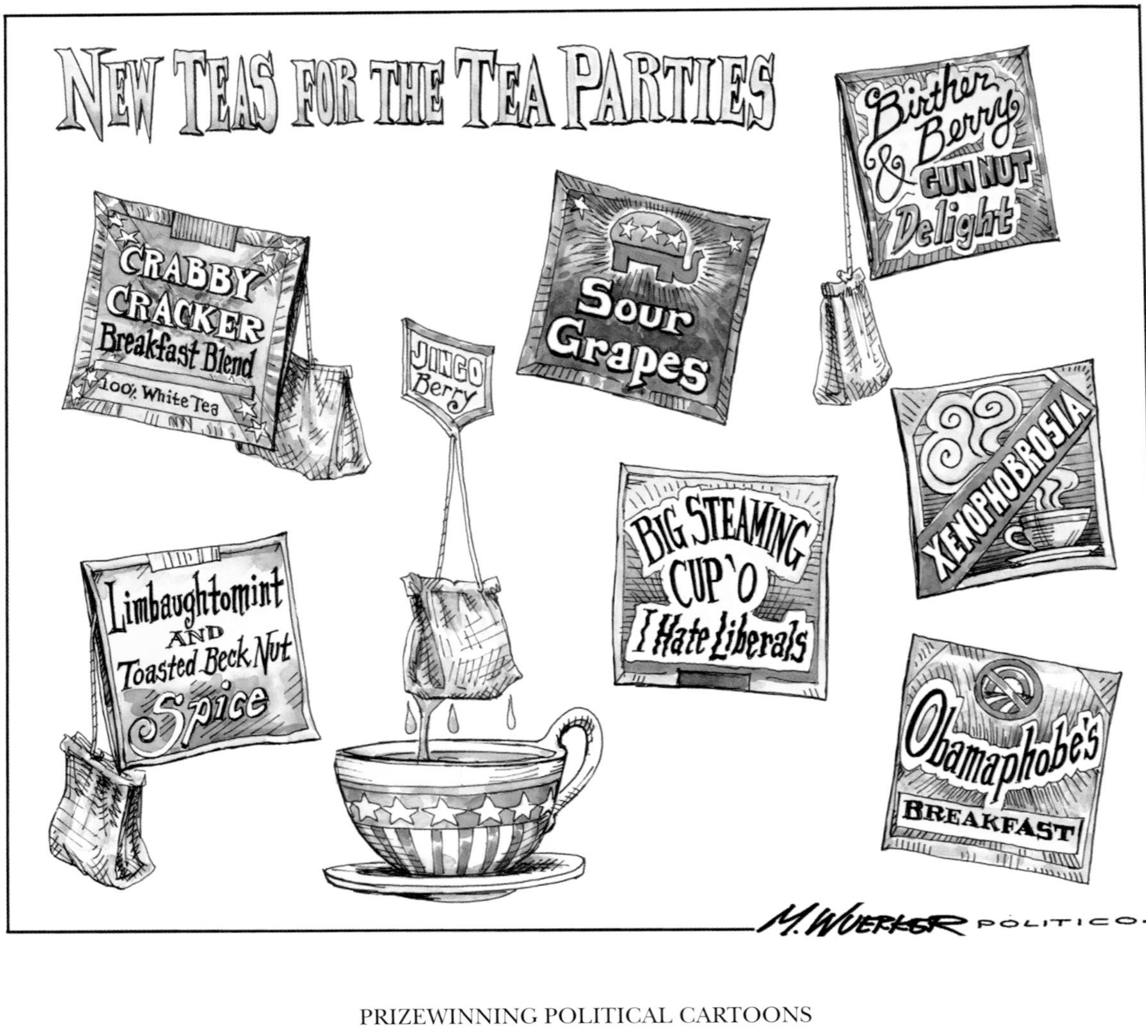
NEW TEAS FOR THE TEA PARTIES
CRABBY CRACKER Breakfast Blend
100% White Tea
Sour Grapes
Birther Berry & GUN NUT Delight
JINGO Berry
XENOPHOBROSIA
BIG STEAMING CUP 'O I Hate Liberals
Limbaughtomint AND Toasted Beck Nut Spice
Obamaphobe's BREAKFAST
M. WUERKER POLITICO

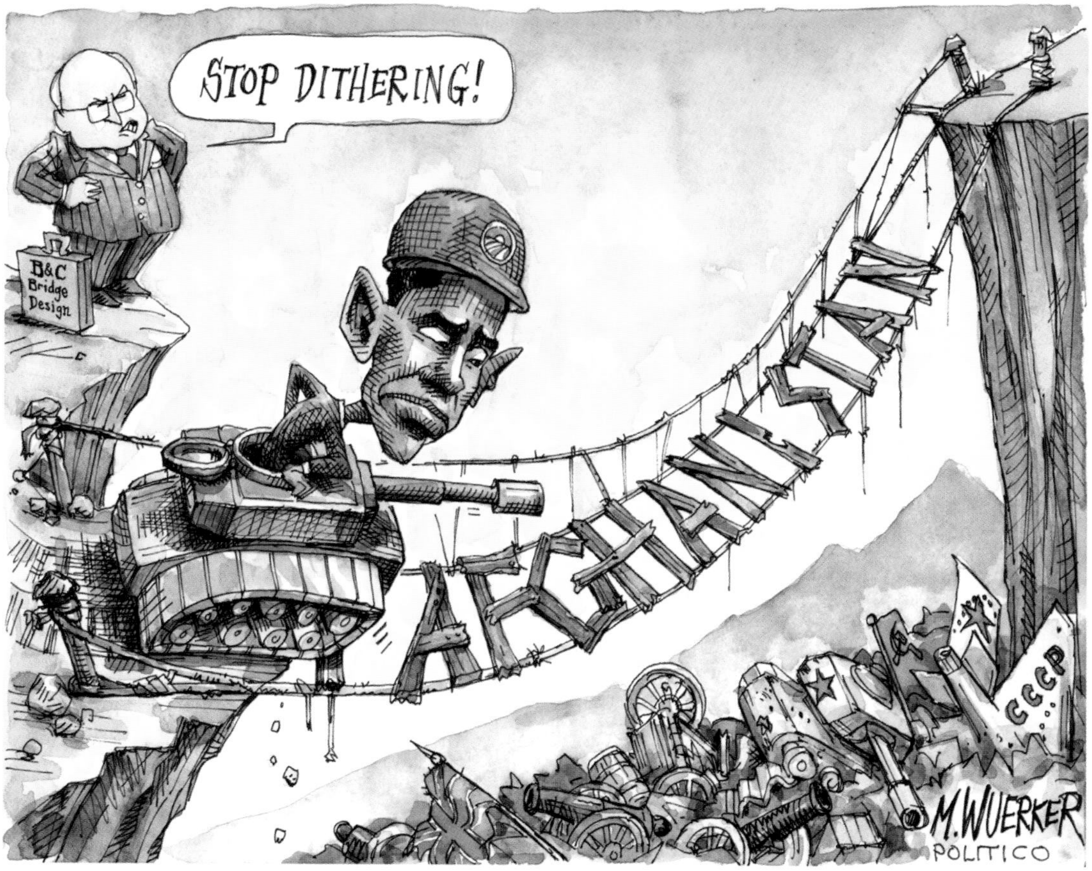
STOP DITHERING!
B&C Bridge Design
AFGHANISTAN
CCCP
M.WUERKER
POLITICO

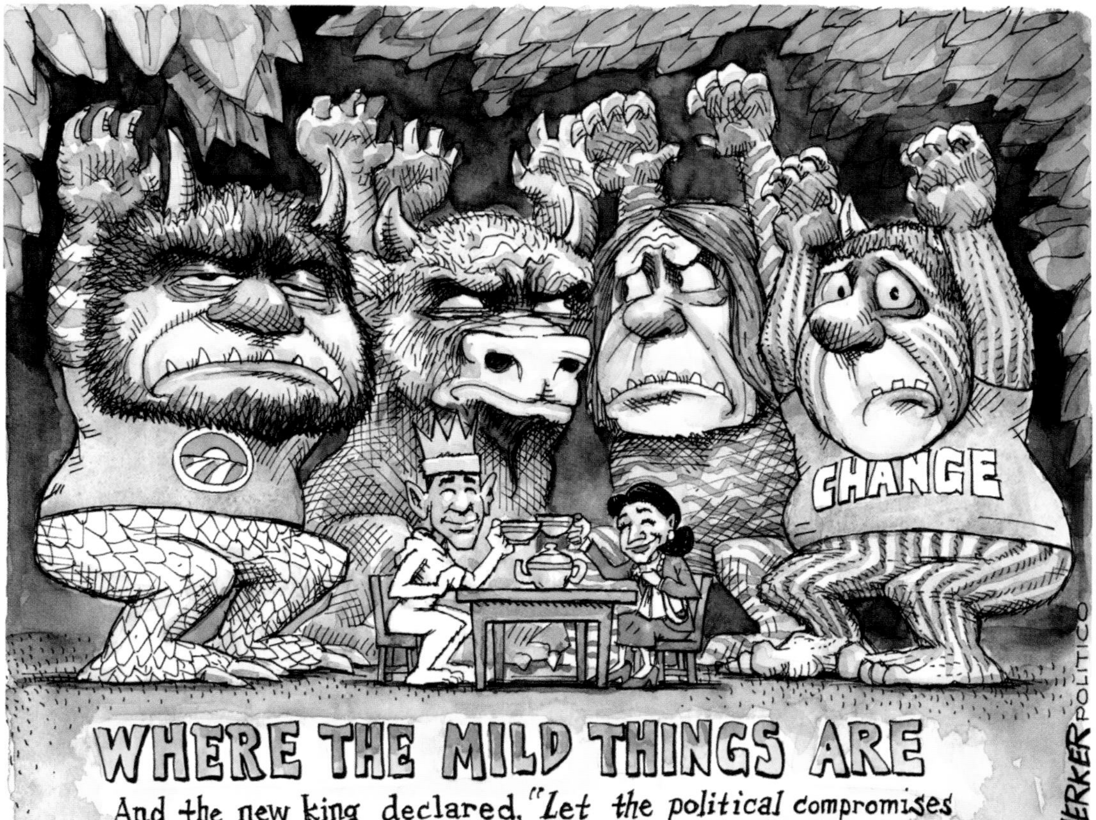
CHANGE
WHERE THE MILD THINGS ARE
And the new king declared, "Let the political compromises with the moderate Republican from Maine begin!"
M.WUERKER
POLITICO

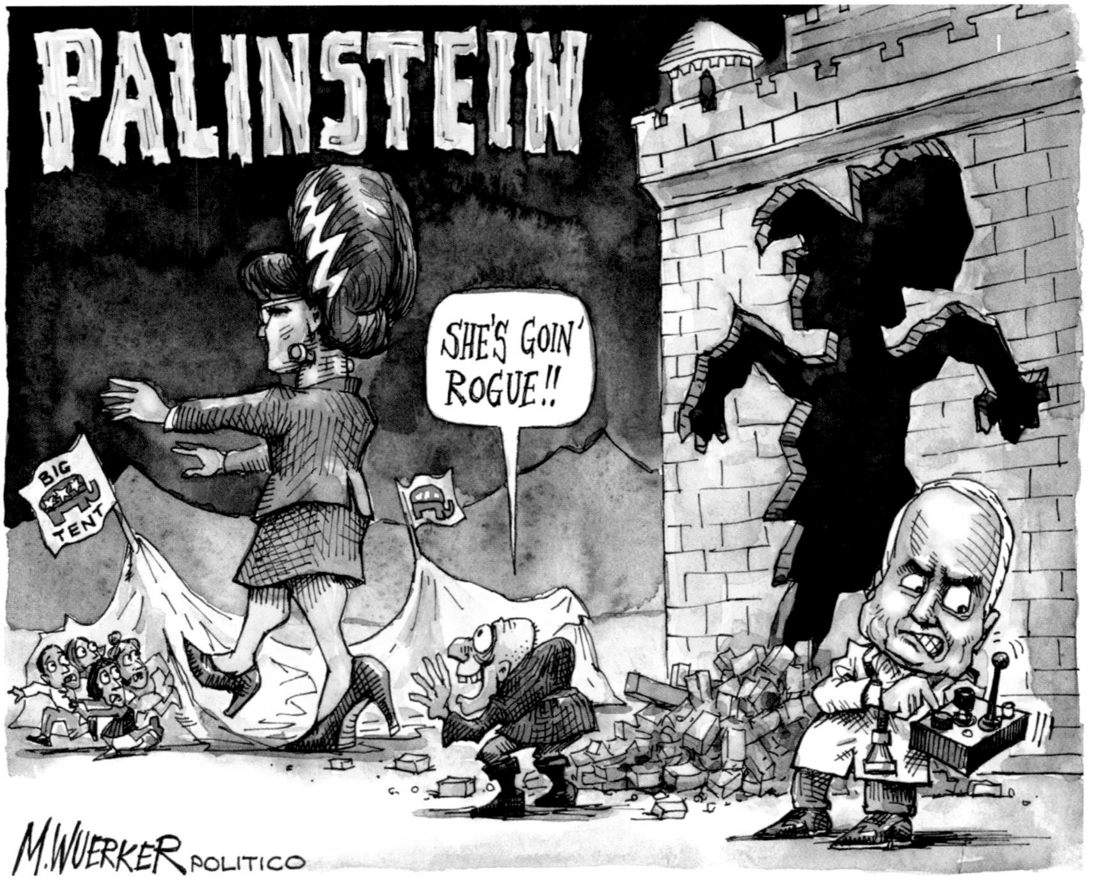
PALINSTEIN
SHE'S GOIN' ROGUE!!
BIG TENT
M.WUERKER POLITICO

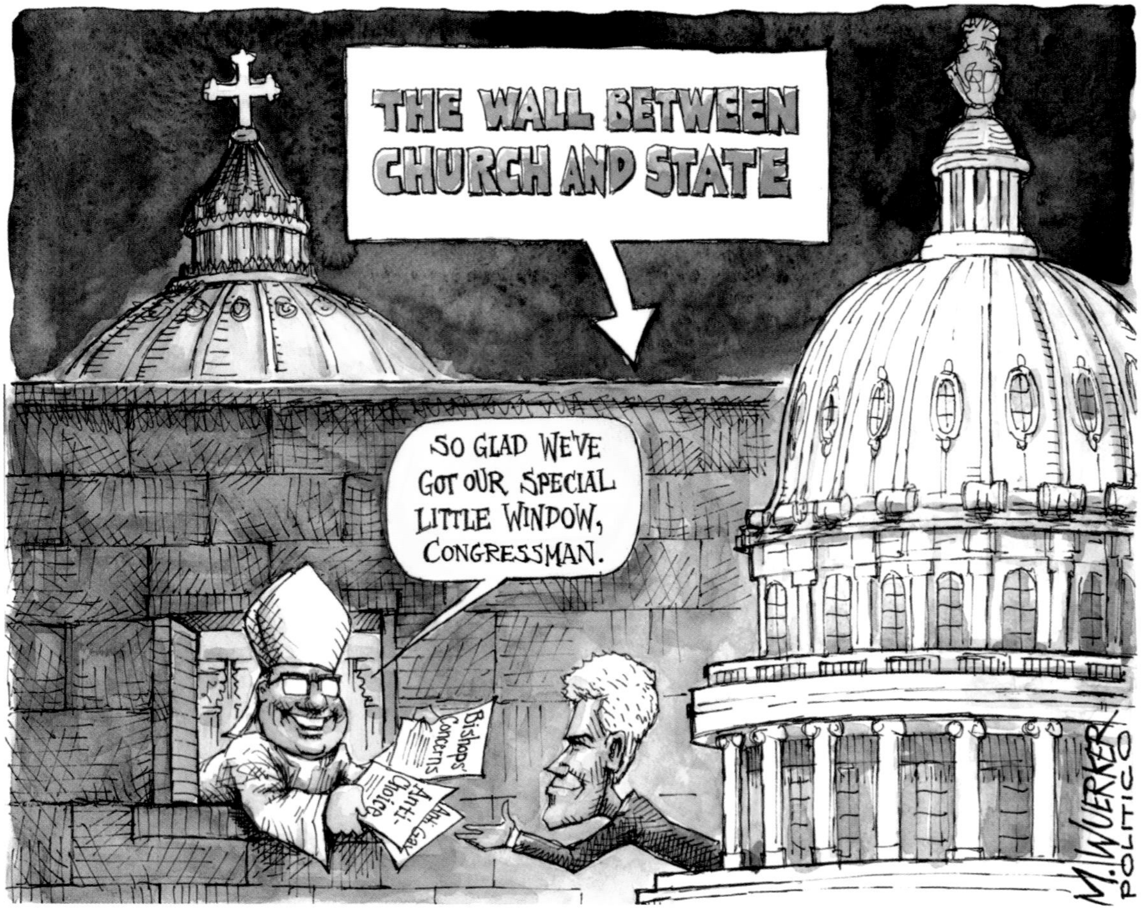
THE WALL BETWEEN CHURCH AND STATE
SO GLAD WE'VE GOT OUR SPECIAL LITTLE WINDOW, CONGRESSMAN.
Bishops' Concerns
Anti-Choice
M.WUERKER POLITICO

Ranan Lurie Political Cartoon Award

Each year the United Nations Correspondents Association and the United Nations Society of Writers and Artists sponsor the Ranan Lurie Political Cartoon Award, named after world-renowned political cartoonist Ranan Lurie.

In their desire to promote the highest standard of excellence in political cartoons depicting the spirit and principles of the United Nations, the UNCA and the United Nations Society of Writers and Artists have established this annual international political cartoon award.

Lurie's political cartoons epitomize the high standards the two organizations would like to see; therefore, they created the award in 2000 and named it in Lurie's honor. The award recognizes cartoons that "enhance, explain and help direct the spirit and principles of the UN."

Although this award is international in scope, it is of such prestige that it deserves to be included in this book. This year, for the first time, an American editorial cartoonist has been presented the award.

2009 Ranan Lurie Political Cartoon Award Winner
Robert Ariail, freelance cartoonist

Robert Ariail was the editorial cartoonist for the *State* newspaper from 1984 until 2009, when he was laid-off. His work continues to be published in more than six hundred newspapers through syndication with United Media. Ariail has been the recipient of many awards, including the 1997 Overseas Press Club's Thomas Nast Award, the 1992 National Society of Professional Journalists' Sigma Delta Chi Award, and the 1990 National Headliner Award. In addition to being a finalist for the 1995 and 2000 Pulitzer Prize, Ariail is the first American to win the Ranan Lurie Political Cartoon Award. His cartoons were selected from a field of more than fifteen hundred entries.

Ariail is a Columbia, South Carolina, native and University of South Carolina graduate. In 1985, he was given the Distinguished Alumnus Award by the university. In 1992, Ariail was honored with the Ambrose Hampton Award for distinguished service while working for the *State*. He appeared in and drew cartoons for Hemdale Motion Picture's *The Boyfriend School*, which was filmed in Charleston, South Carolina, in 1990.

Ariail has produced three collections of his cartoons. The most recent, *Ariail!!!*, was one of Columbia's best-selling books in 2001. He lives in historic Camden, South Carolina, with his wife, Fair, and their fourteen-year-old daughter, Virginia Elizabeth.

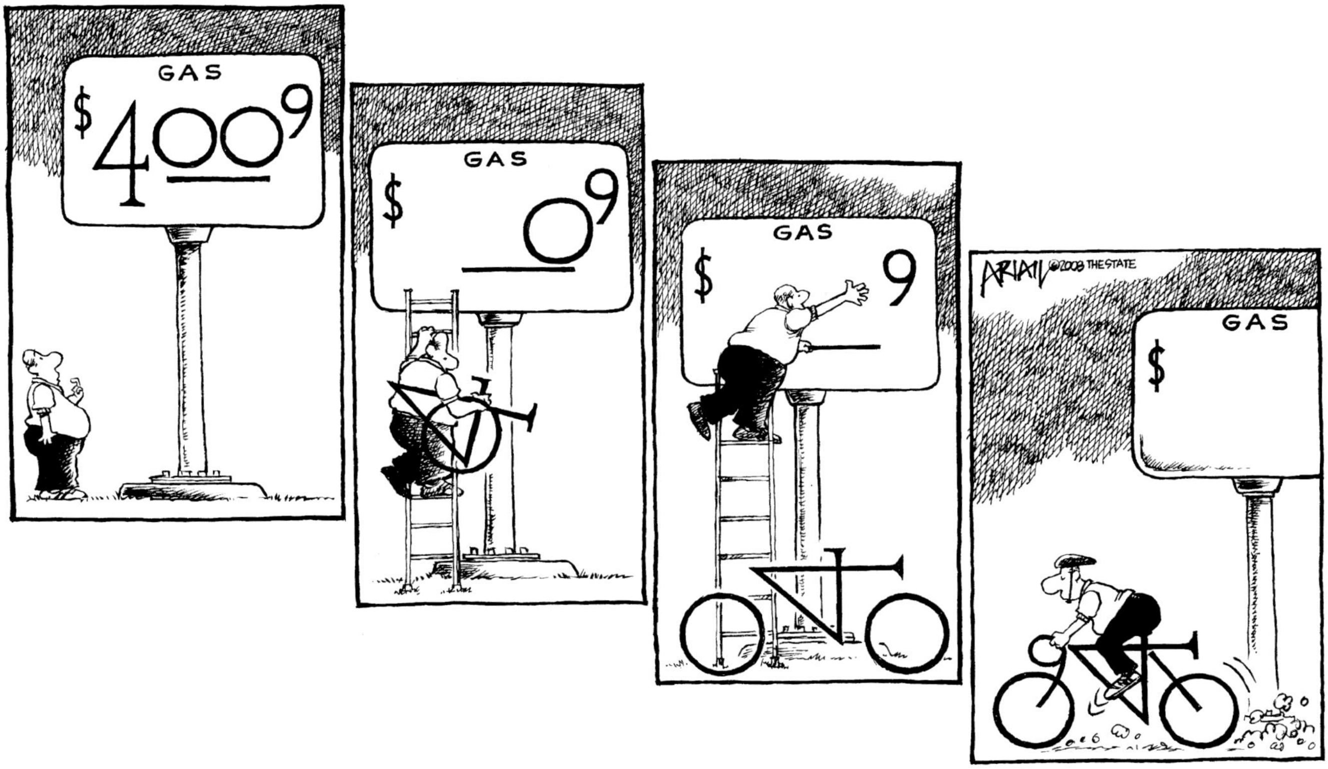
GAS
$400 9
GAS
$ 0 9
GAS
$ 9
ARIAIL ©2008 THE STATE
GAS
$

Index